Of Firebirds & Moonmen

Of Firebirds & Moonmen

A Designer's Story From The Golden Age

Norman J. James

Library of Congress Control Number: 2007902519
ISBN: Hardcover   978-1-4257-7659-6
               Softcover   978-1-4257-7653-4

To order additional copies of this book, contact:
Xlibris Corporation
1-888-795-4274
www.Xlibris.com
Orders@Xlibris.com

37096

Contents

In memory of my brother, Herb.

The author wishes to thank the General Motors Corporation, and especially the GM Media Archives, for their permission to use, and assistance in the collection of, photographic and graphic materials that appear in this book and on its covers.

Materials from the GM Defense Research Laboratories were prepared for proposal or contract deliverable purposes and are taken from Lunar Sample Return, Surveyor Lunar Roving Vehicle (SLRV), Mobile Lunar Laboratory (MOLAB), Local Site Survey Module (LSSM) and Lunar Wheel and Drive Test documentation.

Other graphics that have been created, reconstructed or otherwise prepared especially for this book may be identified by the appended /06 symbol. Unaccredited photographs or graphics that appear in this book are from the author's personal or family archives. All illustrations in this book are by the author.

Author's Note

This book began in response to a publisher's request for an article on the design of the General Motors Firebird III gas turbine concept car. The publisher requested that I, as the designer of record, address the elements that I applied in its design and that I note any formal training I may have had, as it would be relevant. I submitted the article as he requested, then waited for a response—which never came. I learned later that his magazine had ceased publication. There was a personal letdown; however, I was glad that—at last—I had collected the material in a semi-structured way. I found myself returning to the draft from time to time, filling in details as memories fell into place, and expanded the scope of the material collected in the process.

I continued looking for linkages in the material, i.e., relationships that may have existed between my training and the design as it was finally executed. This turned out to be very difficult because it appeared that almost everything seemed to have happened more by chance and circumstance than by any coherent process. I also noticed that the content did not end with the Firebird III but logically continued through my final four years with General Motors in Santa Barbara, designing lunar roving vehicles.

That was when I realized that my entire thirteen and a half years with General Motors was an extraordinary period, having had the opportunity to work on projects that one could normally only dream of. As a young man, I had the great fortune of being assigned to the best Styling and Research Staff teams in General Motors, working under Harley Earl and with many other very talented people. The real story, it appeared, was not of the Firebird III but rather of those chances and circumstances that brought it all about.

Within that context, however—as the last surviving member of the principals in its design (Harley Earl, Robert F. McLean, and Stefan Habsburg being the others)—I felt a concurrent obligation to be faithful to the original theme: that of documenting the design of the Firebird III. This occurred almost exactly half a century ago, during General Motors's golden years, and as a young man, this was truly a designer's odyssey.

—Norman J. James
San Diego, California, March 18, 2007

NormanJJames1@aol.com

Prologue

My parents were both born in Korce, Albania, near the start of the last century. Korce is located in the inland foothills of the Monrovia mountain range, east of the Adriatic Sea and across from the heel of Italy. While still considered a poorly developed country, the region was once a cultural center, some six thousand years ago, during the Copper and Bronze Ages. The earliest known settlers were the Illyrians, who may have been the same people of Homer's the *Iliad* and the *Odyssey*. The region fell under many cultural influences on up into the sixth century BC, passing through Roman and then Byzantine rule, when Christianity became the official religion.

It was subsequently overrun by Asians, Goths, and Huns (into the eighth century) with invasions continuing by the Slavs, Vikings, Serbians, and most notably the Ottoman (Turkish) empire in 1430 (lasting some five hundred years). The most profound influence of that last invasion was that two-thirds of its populace became Muslim.

There were many unsuccessful uprisings during the Ottoman rule until finally, following the Balkan Wars, in 1912 the Turks were expelled, and Albania, as a nation, became recognized by the world community. My father was born in 1892, near the end of this tumultuous period.

I know very little else of my ancestry, other than my father's father was a builder of watermills in a highland region comprised mostly of small pastures and where sheep herding was the predominant occupation. While he was still a young man, my father and his younger brother immigrated into the United States, before the outbreak of World War I. They entered through Ellis Island, and my father remained in New York City long enough to learn the tailoring trade. They then moved upstate to the small town of Jamestown, which was one of only a handful of communities in the United States with an Albanian Orthodox Church. There was also a good smattering of Greek, Italian, and Turkish families in the neighborhoods, but Jamestown, a town of forty thousand people, was predominantly Swedish, and furniture manufacture was its main industry.

My father's first name was Vasile, which was Americanized to Basil. He also changed his surname to James, obviously taken after the town. His brother took on the name of George Miller. They both found work in the downtown Brooklyn Square area, my father as a tailor and his brother as a confectioner.

My mother, Costandina, was ten years younger and did not immigrate until after the war, in the early 1920s, entering as a young lady, accompanying her aunt, uncle, and their two sons. They also settled in Jamestown. Subsequently, my parents met and were married and remained in Jamestown. Basil's brother George, still single, moved to Westfield, New York, a smaller town some twenty-seven miles northwest and just off Lake Erie, where he opened a restaurant along busy NY Route 20.

Basil became a naturalized U.S. citizen and, in studying for his citizenship, turned into a great student of American history, adapting to and championing everything that was American. Costandina became Constance, but to her Albanian friends, she was always known as Kocha. Her aunt's and uncle's names were Sanda and Spiro Semo, and their two boys, who were some fifteen years my senior, were named Peter and Paul. The entire Semo family moved to Meadville, in Northwestern Pennsylvania, some sixty miles south of Jamestown, where they would live and work on a small farm. The boys, having grown up, would open a small shoeshine and hat-cleaning business in town, but they still lived on the farm just outside of town. Their farmhouse, painted a pristine white, was maintained beautifully and would become a regular gathering place for extended family events.

In 1928, my older brother was born and was named Herbert, after the current president, Herbert Hoover. I was born in 1932 and was named after the popular socialist, Norman Thomas. There would be another son, Robert, born in 1936, but he died one year later. The last son, Peter, was born in 1940. We three boys would be raised in Jamestown, four years of age separating Herb and me, and then eight years to Peter. We would grow up, all attending the same schools and living our youth almost entirely in our third house, a well-built three-story with a basement, located on the northeast corner of Seventh and Jefferson.

My father established his tailor shop in the Hotel Samuels servicing that hotel and, then later, picked up all the tailoring for the Hotel Jamestown, both hotels being cross corners from each other on Third and Cherry Streets. It was a short six-block walk from our house to my father's tailor shop.

The entire period of my youth can be summarized within the small extended family noted here and between the communities of Jamestown, Westfield, and Meadville.

1 Jamestown

W e had a simple routine. My father worked in his tailor shop six days a week, and on Sundays, we would visit most often with his brother, our uncle George, in the western part of the state. It was a short pleasant drive along Chautauqua Lake and then over rolling hills to his restaurant in Westfield. On these visits, we would be treated to free meals off the menu, of which my favorite was roast beef with mashed potatoes and gravy. All the while we were there, Herby and I would eagerly wait for one of two side trips we knew we would be taking. We might plead for our preference, but my father would always choose either the train station or Lake Erie, both of which were only a few miles away.

At the train station, we would walk out onto the tracks, where all boarding was done from ground level platforms. In those days, we could wander all over and had to cross several sets of tracks to get to the main lines. We would look down the tracks all the way, to where they disappeared into the shimmering distance. Images were so far away that it was difficult to understand exactly what we were seeing, whether it was a train or smoke or what. We would pick a track to stand on and wait, watching for the first signs of the coal-burning locomotives to materialize out of the mirages. Herby and I would compete to be the first to shout out that we saw a train coming. Not only did we want to be the first to see one but we also wanted our train to be the biggest and best of the day. In our impatience, we would run back into the station to look at the schedule chalked on the arrival board and then at the pendulum clock, trying to figure out how much longer that would really be.

The memories that linger are of the marble station floor, the fancy wooden benches and vending machines in the waiting area, dispensing penny Hershey bars. We finally grasped that the trains were coming in pretty close to the way they were posted. Passenger trains would pull to a stop, and conductors quickly descended from the Pullmans, placing their small step stools on the platform so they could help passengers off. At the locomotive, the engineer would pull hoses from an overhead tower to top off his water tanks. Porters, in the meantime, transferred luggage on and off the baggage cars onto large wooden-spoked, steel-rimmed wagon pull carts. Following the call for "all aboard," the locomotive would start moving slowly, the conductors walking alongside and then impressively boarding the train while it was in motion. We would watch the train disappear into the distance, whereupon we would rush back into the station to see how long it would be before the next one, hoping our father would let us wait for it. What we always hoped for was the most exciting treat of all: the appearance of a freight train, totally unannounced and passing through at full speed—turning into a roaring, belching, earth-shaking monster, just blasting through without slowing, in an unbelievable noise, shattering, ground-shaking rumble that would be so loud that all we could do was laugh. At some point, our father would call us and say that was enough; we had to return to the restaurant.

On other weekends, we would go to Barcelona, a fishing village on the rocky Lake Erie shoreline. There we would watch fishing boats coming and going from the fish factory. There were small sheds surrounding the factory, each with smoke pouring out of cracks in and around the doors and smelling real good.

On shore, the narrow beach was strewn with flint shale and other flat stones, which provided an endless supply of skipping stones. Barcelona was our favorite stop because, on occasion, we would be treated with gigantic black storm waves that would pound the shores unmercifully, challenging even the largest locomotives in their energy. Eventually, our father would say that too was enough, and it was time to go.

On both of these trips, while driving back to Uncle George's, we would cross the last bridge over the railroad tracks and past a large Welsh's Grape Juice sign outside its factory. This sign became my personal signal and a symbol that we were reentering civilization and that the best part of the day was over.

Every third week or so, we would travel to Uncle Spiro's farm on the other side of Meadville. By this time, the Semo boys had grown up and married two Albanian girls. They all lived together on the farm. While the boys helped on the farm, they spent most of their time running a small shoeshine and hat-cleaning business in town, bringing some of their hat-cleaning work to do at home. For entertainment, they played cards every night, with the girls becoming especially heartless card sharks, even when playing with their nephews. As kids, to play them, we knew it would always end in disaster. A rare win by us was sweetly cherished, even if it was only the luck of the draw. They were bad losers.

While the farm was a sixty-mile drive from Jamestown, it still took a good hour and a half to get there. The roads, while few, were actually very good—usually paved in concrete. They were mostly two lanes' wide as they ran across the rolling countryside and turned into brick streets as they passed through the many small one-light, two-stop towns. The ugly sight of automobile accidents was a common distraction. Accidents were never considered unusual and, in fact, were almost predictable at one particularly bad crossroad.

Once we arrived at the farm, we would already be at a heightened state of excitement. The farm was relatively small, having only two cows, some chickens, ducks, sheep, corn, pastures, and several acres of dense woods. Besides exploring these areas and target shooting with their .22s, our favorite pastime was to go to the lower fields in the valley and fish a small stream that meandered through. It was blessed with a good population of small fish, four to five inches long, and had a few eight-to-ten-inch suckers and bullheads that became obsessions, in our understanding of what the true purpose of life was.

Each summer, we looked forward to a vacation of a week or so on the farm. Our parents would drop us off one weekend and then pick us up on another. We enjoyed the peace and quiet of the farm, fishing in the stream or just lying back, watching falcons circling high over the valley. On occasion, a flash storm would create a new excitement, causing great turbulence and flooding in the stream. Overnight, the storm would make major changes to the stream banks, leaving sights to remind us again of the power of nature. It was on the farm that I first marveled at the blackness of the night skies and the richness of stars in the Milky Way. It was an awakening to the existence of the universe.

Often, these visits coincided with family reunions. Picnic tables would be set up around the farmhouse, on the manicured lawns, with tubs of beer and ale on ice scattered about. The wives would be preparing pastas while the men were roasting lamb on a spit—all as distant cousins continued arriving. As a kid, I would sit in anticipation of finishing off the bottom of a glass of beer from a considerate uncle. My times on the farm became the fondest memories of my childhood.

Peter was born in September of 1940, soon after we bought and moved into a nicer house on the corner of Seventh and Jefferson. This would become the house we would always refer to as "home." It was much larger than our first two rented houses, the first of which I have absolutely no memories. It offered cozy little corners for our hobbies. Herb, being the oldest, took claim to a room in the attic to build his flying model airplanes and, later, the coal storage room in the basement, to turn into a photographic darkroom (after the furnace had been converted to natural gas). My needs were simpler, as I was mostly following my big brother, carving solid model airplanes or watching Herb develop photo negatives and making prints.

One Sunday, while returning from the farm, the world we knew suddenly changed. The drive back was very quiet as we tried to understand what it meant, that *the Japanese had bombed Pearl Harbor*. As a family, our lives did not change much, but we now had a new sense of the world.

I followed the events of World War II, mostly through the *Movietone News* in our local theater or through *Life* magazine pictures on the newsstand. I also remember a grade-school classmate telling me about letters he received from his brother, who was a tank driver in North Africa and was fighting the Germans. We participated in bond drives at school by buying ten-cent stamps every week. These stamps would be dutifully pasted into savings books, which went toward the purchase of $25 war bonds. There was also an aluminum salvage drive where I nagged my mother into giving me an old aluminum pot that would gain me free entry to a Saturday movie matinee for the war effort.

As the war progressed, I was promoted on up to Lincoln Junior High (middle school). I was old enough then to take on an afternoon newspaper delivery route. That would bring me even closer to world events by way of the daily headlines. Our weekends had to change somewhat because of gasoline rationing. With only a low priority A window card, we had to cut out most of our weekend drives.

As we were growing older, Herb and I started developing other interests. Peter was still too young for us to involve him. We followed new developments in science, primarily in the weapons of war; rockets and flying were now capturing our minds. We lived only a few blocks from the James Prendergast Library, so we frequented it often, trying to learn all that we could.

With the war seemingly coming to an end, we were greatly anticipating the new society that was sure to follow. If we were to believe the magazines, flying cars were definitely in our future. With the atomic bomb, World War II came to an abrupt end. Herb was fortunate because he was about to start his last year of high school, and now with the war over, there was no longer a danger of his being drafted and sent off to war. Not only that, but it appeared he would still be able to join the army after graduation and become eligible for a free college education under the GI Bill of Rights. Everything looked great.

Later that same August, while waiting to start eighth grade, I had a strange summer fever. I experienced some stiffness and pains in my neck and muscle spasms in my legs. After staying in bed for a few days without any improvement, my parents called Dr. Lindbeck, our family doctor (who made house calls in those days). His immediate diagnosis was that I had contracted polio, and that the worst of it was over. I wouldn't need to go to the hospital but, rather, I could stay home to receive treatment. School started, and I missed the first few days, but I fully expected to start in a few weeks. The school sent someone over with homework, to help keep me up to speed. After a few more weeks passed, however, it became obvious that I would not be able to make school that semester.

In the final analysis, the polio had afflicted only my right leg. As hard as it may be to believe, the family was relieved at my good fortune, that of not having had it affect my lungs and ending up in an iron lung for the rest of my life. In my recovery, I was restricted to staying in bed and was not allowed to walk or put any weight on my right leg. The treatment of the day was called the Sister Kenney method. It would be administered by a social worker, Ms. Ohman, a nurse who would visit me three or four times a week to perform the therapy and treatment.

The first thing she did was to have my bedroom rearranged for the therapy sessions. I had been moved into the second-floor master's bedroom, which was in the front of the house, overlooking Seventh Street. Our dining room table was taken apart and reassembled next to my bed for the leg exercise therapy. She next asked for an old wool blanket that she could cut up to make hot packs. She also had some plastic-like material that she cut up into panels. These were all trimmed so that some of the wool panels could be heated in hot water, wrung out, and wrapped around my upper and lower right leg. They would then be wrapped in the oilcloth (as a moisture barrier) and finally overwrapped with dry wool panels to keep the heat in; all of this was then safety pinned together. My mother would apply this hot pack treatment, once or twice daily, to help condition the muscles.

The packs would stay warm for a few hours, after which they would be removed; and they would be left off at night when I slept. Ms. Ohman would arrive between the hot pack treatments to exercise my leg, trying to maintain some muscle tone and mobility. She would provide resistance forces for the various muscle groups, and I would try to react against them. The polio had damaged my nervous system, such that whenever I tried to apply the requested force, I could fully feel the exertion; however, the muscular forces I was able to deliver were negligible, offering little or no reaction force against her resistance. My ankle was especially weak, behaving more as if it were a loose ball joint. When not actually doing exercises, I was supposed to keep my right foot against the headboard (I was reversed in my bed position for this purpose) to keep the tendons stretched.

This continued for about three months before I tapered off on the hot pack treatment first and then the therapy. I was looking forward to the day that I would be allowed to walk. That day finally came, and everyone was there when I was asked to stand beside my bed. I arose, and as I put my weight on my right foot, a sharp jolt of pain started in my heel, shot straight up through my spine, and then bounced off the inside of my skull. I realized then that I still had a much longer road to recovery ahead of me.

As I worked to regain my strength, I targeted Thanksgiving Day to be downstairs. I did make that date and did it by scooting down the stairs on one good leg, two hands, and my butt. Shortly afterward, they provided me with a pair of crutches, and in time, I was becoming very proficient with them, progressively putting more and more weight on my foot. I developed a style that was fancy enough that, in time, I was moving about the house on arm strength and crutches alone—"Look, Ma, no feet."

There was a chance I could have returned to school at midyear, but after some discussion, it was determined I would be better off returning the following school year. For some reason, it hit me hard that my class would move on without me and that I would forever be a year behind. Once I accepted that, however, I was able to proceed in my rehabilitation without distraction. By now I knew the extent of damage that the polio had caused. I would basically be limited to having a weakened right leg with almost no ankle strength. Those muscles that had been cut off from working nerve centers had already atrophied. Of the remaining muscles, which I still had some control over, they would now be called upon to do all the work required of the leg.

That spring, I was taken to a clinic where the doctors prescribed that I be fitted with a foot brace. My mother and I went to a shoe store where we purchased a regular pair of shoes and then took them to a technical specialist, where my leg was measured and the right shoe was left behind to be modified. We returned a few weeks later to have it fitted. The technician had fashioned a U-shaped metal strap that crossed beneath the heel and was topped with two hinge pivots, in line with the ankle joint, and connected to metal straps running up each side of the lower leg, secured by a leather strap, which was laced around the calf of the leg.

The brace would constrict my foot to a pure up-and-down rotation while walking, inhibiting all twisting and side motions. The metal joints had a cam feature built in that would limit the up rotation, to keep the ankle from bending up greater than ninety degrees.[1] I would wear it that summer and be ready for the start of school in September. I had long since stopped the physical therapy, and I no longer needed the crutches.

About this same time, having graduated from high school, Herb joined the army and was stationed at Camp Lee, Virginia. Following basic training, he was assigned peacetime duties in their graphic arts group. This worked out fine

---

[1]   Later, after I got off the brace, the tendons would not stretch beyond a certain point, and that would limit the foot up motion, so I could walk up stairs on the ball of the right foot, even though the ankle muscles did not have the strength to lift my weight.

for him because he intended to go into commercial art when he got out, and he would use his college scholarship to study art.

After missing a full year of school, I was concerned about how I would adjust to returning. Outside of being self-conscious about the brace, I felt okay, and I was able to accept the kids as my new "classmates," my true class having moved on. The school made some curriculum adjustments for me, excusing me from physical education classes. I had also mentally accepted the now obvious fact that from now on, I would never take part in any varsity sports. My life—in fact—had changed.

School was several miles from home, and there was no way I could walk it, so I had to take the city bus to get to and from school. This meant I had to leave earlier to catch the bus and transfer downtown before continuing on to school—then returning the same way. I did have a pleasant surprise when I found I had taken myself to a higher level of attention in my class work, getting better grades but also improving my attendance (catching fewer colds, etc.).

By the start of my ninth and last grade in junior high, I no longer needed to take the bus, and I walked to school, winter weather and all. The walk included traversing the long Third Street Bridge, which spanned the Erie Railroad switchyard, the Chadakoin River, and the foothill at the base of the armory. My leg strength was constantly improving, yet I knew it would always be my "weak leg."

While I didn't participate in school sports, I did become active in pickup touch football games played during our lunch breaks. There was no cafeteria, so we either had to go home to eat or bring our lunches and eat outside. It was afterward, while waiting for the doors to reopen, that we would play football. Even though I wore my brace, I was still able to move at some speed, and I'm sure that at times I looked like Charles Laughton in his portrayal of Quasimodo in *The Hunchback of Notre Dame*, as I lopped out my pass patterns.

During the winter months, when we couldn't play football in the snow, we would wait outside the two main side doors, and inevitably, snowball fights would break out between the two groups. On one occasion, after having seen a movie about the crusades (during the Middle Ages), I recalled longbow men launching clouds of arrows high into the sky and having them rain down on their enemy. I called our side together and had them all collect two snowballs. On my command, we fired the first salvo of snowballs into high trajectories. Then, in a timed manner, we fired the second snowballs into flat trajectories, so that they would be arriving on target just as the first snowballs were falling. The other side at first appeared stunned by the barrage; then in short order, they collected two snowballs each and returned the favor. It was, perhaps, our first worldly lesson on the risks of weapons escalation.[2]

There was an incident that occurred one summer that would have a strong influence on me. One evening, while riding in the backseat of our car, Herb was driving and his best friend, Van Shaka, was in the front passenger seat when Van suddenly exclaimed, "There's a meteor!" By the time I looked, it was gone, but it so affected me that the next day I went to the library to read all I could about meteors. I learned that they were really quite common and that they were only about the size of a grain of sand. On a clear night, it was said that one should be able to see about six random meteors an hour. Reading more about astronomy in general, I also learned that it was possible to see the planet Venus in broad daylight, if one only knew where to look for it. At night, the planets themselves would not be all that difficult to find, because they would usually be the brightest things in the sky. Even more surprising was that Jupiter had several moons and that four of them should be visible through a common pair of binoculars! That last claim absolutely astounded me. We had a pair of five power field glasses, and I decided to give it a try. Our house had a sun porch facing due south, and from there, I could open the door and see Jupiter high up and bright in the early evening sky. I propped up the field glasses to minimize any shaking, and then with some difficulty, I was able to determine that—yes—there were four small moons visible, appearing as fine jewels that would pop in and out of view in the shimmer of the air. Their appearance closely resembled the drawings Galileo made of the moons when he first discovered them. I spent the next few evenings repeating the observations, just being fascinated by how the moons would have changed their positions each night. I was hooked. The field glasses were not very good, and it was necessary to strain to see the tiny specs so close to the glare of Jupiter, but the experience was absolutely monumental. That summer, I kept returning to the library and checked out every book they had on astronomy. In their reading room, I would pick up *Sky & Telescope* magazine to find out what was going on currently. News on the completion of the two-hundred-inch Hale telescope on Mt Palomar was the hottest item of the day. The back cover almost always had full-page black-and-white astronomical photographs. Occasionally, they would have beautiful cutaway illustrations of the two-hundred-inch telescope drawn by the architect Russell W. Porter. I was impressed by his style, which made everything look so understandable and real.

---

[2] It has been noted in life that people who become limited in some physical capacity often developed other strategic skills to offset their physical shortcomings.

I ran across his name in other publications also and found out that he was a major contributor in *Amateur Telescope Making,* a book that was a collection of articles from earlier issues of *Scientific American.*[3] Most of the articles were attributed to a small group of amateurs who subsequently founded what was considered to be the first organized club for telescope making and amateur astronomy as a hobby. They had a very attractive observing site with a clubhouse and some very large telescopes located outside a small town in Springfield, Vermont. Their site was named Stellafane.[4]

What impressed me most in the book was the fact that it was possible for an individual to grind and polish very large optics to make a good astronomical telescope, and further, the main element would be a mirror, not a lens—all of this would be done by hand, no less! The hobby flourished, following the first world war, when a lot of surplus sixteen-inch naval porthole glasses became available. These turned out to be ideal for making telescope mirrors. The only difficult part was the risky chemical process required to silver the mirror when it was done—risky in the sense that it could result in an explosion if done wrong! In more current readings, however, I learned there had been an aluminizing process developed for the two-hundred-inch telescope that ultimately replaced silvering and apparently was now available for amateur's mirrors. *Sky & Telescope* also carried advertising for telescope-making kits in six-, eight-, ten-, twelve-and-a-half-, and sixteen-inch-diameter mirror sizes. These were now being manufactured by Corning using their Pyrex cooking glass formula. The six-inch kit sold for about seven dollars.

Later that summer, before starting high school, Herb bankrolled me to buy the six-inch kit. I wrote a letter and sent a postal money order the next day. I had a strange feeling, as I dropped the envelope in the mail slot, as if somehow, I had set something in motion that was irreversible, as good as if I had already received the kit. I eagerly awaited its arrival over the next few weeks. I had also ordered a book on telescope making by Allyn J. Thompson. This would become my personal project, not having any participation by my brothers. The book arrived first. I read it thoroughly and started preparing a work area in a breakfast nook, following its directions. One of the best pieces of advice it gave was to keep a good logbook and to document everything. Another beneficial factor was that because there was absolutely no one in the area knowledgeable

---

[3]   These were monthly articles edited by Albert Ingalls, which started appearing in 1928. Later they were broadened in scope, and the series was renamed the *Amateur Scientist* and ran continuously until 2001.

[4]   The organization grew as the hobby expanded, and it became a Mecca for amateur astronomers, hosting annual conventions for the believers.

on the subject, I would have to do everything by the book or else figure my own way out of any problems if the instructions didn't work.

When the kit arrived, it was comprised of two solid Pyrex glass disks, six inches in diameter and one inch thick; about a half dozen packages of abrasives; a couple bricks of a hard tarlike pitch; a package of red rouge polishing compound; and a couple of lenses for an eyepiece. Putting my setup to work, I began the systematic process of grinding one glass disk on top of the other. The lower disk was wedged between cleats on a barrel that served as a workbench. This would allow me to walk around it as I ground one disk over the other pushing strokes from all directions.[5] A course grade of carborundum grit was first sprinkled on top of the lower disk and water added to create abrasive slurry.

After some time grinding, the upper disk began to hollow out in the center and the lower disk started wearing down around its edge. The depth of the hollow continued to deepen and the tool edge kept wearing toward the center as long as I kept on grinding. By the time I reached the desired depth, the two disks were fully ground and tightly fit each other.[6] I stopped and cleaned everything to remove all traces of the course grit. I then resumed grinding with a finer grade of abrasive, with the intent now of only removing all traces of abrasion left behind by the courser abrasive. Once these traces disappeared, I cleaned up again and repeated the process; each time changing to progressively finer and finer grits, until eventually, the glass surfaces were satin smooth and ready for polishing.

The upper hollowed disk would become the mirror and the lower disk would be converted into a polishing lap (after casting the resilient pitch onto it). The pitch was relatively hard, but it could be heated to melt on to the disk, and then channels pressed into it while it was still warm and soft, making it look much like a waffle. Heating it again, it was pressed against the mirror, which was now coated with the slurry red rouge, to both reestablish contact between the surfaces and to impress the polishing compound onto the lap. Using strokes similar to those in grinding, one could feel the high drag of the satin smooth glass surface as it was wiped over the pitch lap. This in turn would cause the glass to melt[7] on a molecular scale to start what would become a polished surface.

---

[5]   This is what would make the optical surface smooth and uniform, randomizing the strokes from all directions.

[6]   Any zones that were too high would abrade away, and low zones would be sheltered until all surfaces would be in contact, i.e., spherical.

[7]   Glass is actually already melted and is a very viscous (super plastic) liquid. The extra heat of friction causes the molecules to flow more readily and redistribute themselves over the abraded surface.

Surprisingly, only a few minutes of polishing were enough to start showing reflections, although it would take several more hours of polishing to remove all traces of fine grinding. The mirror still required some delicate tests and adjustments to meet the final surface standards called for in the book. Even at this stage, however, it was possible to prop the mirror up to cause light from our living room chandelier to reflect back and come to a focus. Holding the lens that came with the kit up to the eye and standing behind the focus, it was possible to see a magnified image of the individual glass links and fine brass chain hooks.

With more polishing, the images became brighter and I was ready for my next anticipated experiment. I made the same setup, but this time it was in the sun porch, and the image was that of Jupiter, which was again in the southern sky. The image appeared to be real, floating some sixty inches[8] in front of the mirror, as long as I viewed it in line to see its reflection in the mirror. I tried to stay as close to the center of the mirror as I could, so that half of my head would be silhouetted in the reflection (putting my eye near its optical axis).

From this position, I could bring Jupiter into focus by moving my head and the eyepiece closer, until it came into focus as I had seen it before with the field glasses. This time, the moons were spread far apart, and Jupiter had a distinct flattened look to it. Further, I could see several distinct dark bands running across the disk, representing its great atmospheric weather belt system; all of this, remember, was from only a partially polished piece of glass. The bare mirror was reflecting less than 4 percent of the light, yet it was presenting spectacular images of Jupiter—from a piece of glass I had worked with my own hands! The finished mirror when aluminized would reflect about 90 percent of the light. This was really exciting. I could hardly wait.

Before it was fully polished, however, I started encountering difficulties when the polishing lap began to lose its effectiveness, and I concluded it had to be rebuilt before I could finish. My problem was that I needed to buy more pitch, but I couldn't find any in town. Everything stopped for several months until I found a rosin material in a hardware store that was similar but much harder. According to the books, it had been used for polishing before but was not preferred because it was so hard.

With the new lap completed, I resumed polishing and started trying to bring the surface to its correct shape,[9] which was referred to as its figure.

---

[8] By design, the mirror was ground to a 120-inch radius. The focal length of that surface would be one half of that, i.e., sixty inches. The focal ratio, as cameras are measured, would be its focal length divided by its diameter, in my case 60/6 = f/10.

[9] Theoretically a parabola, but at f/10 a sphere was almost acceptable.

The test[10] for determining when the figure was right was by itself a magical process. In this test, punching a pin through aluminum foil and illuminating it from behind created an artificial star. Placing the pinhole near the mirror's center of curvature caused a real[11] image of the pinhole to form right next to itself. Here a razor blade was fixed to a sliding guide, so it could be positioned to cut into the floating image. By observing the mirror from immediately behind the razor, the out-of-focus image would appear to fill the entire surface with light, and then, by cutting into the cone of light, ghost shadows would appear to move across the mirror's surface. Cutting in front of the pinhole image, the shadow would appear to come in from the same direction as the blade. Cutting from behind the pinhole image, however, had a surprising effect. The shadow would appear to cut and enter from the exact opposite side![12] In this way, it was possible to find where surfaces were too high, or too low, by only millionths of an inch. The exact center of curvature for any zone in the mirror could be located within thousandths of an inch, and by measuring each zone from the mirror center, it would be possible to graph its exact optical profile. The test was so sensitive that one could hold their thumb on the mirror for a few minutes and then go back to look at it with the test. The place where the thumb was held would appear as a slight hill, the result of the glass having expanded from the body heat. As long as one knew where the errors were, corrective polishing strokes could be applied until the mirror surface began to respond,[13] i.e., where material could be moved predictably. After several months of figuring and testing, the surface was brought to within the prescribed limits, and I sent it out to be commercially aluminized.

---

[10]   The Foucalt test is named after its French inventor Jean Foucalt. Foucalt was also the inventor of the pendulum that carries his name.

[11]   The image we see reflected in a regular mirror is a virtual image that does not exist. An image created by an optical system, whether by mirror or lens, is real in that if photographic film were to be properly exposed there, it could be processed into an image.

[12]   I discovered that this phenomena can be exactly replicated by punching a real pinhole in a card and intercepting the view with another card, alternately from in front of and then from just behind the pinhole, while holding it close in front of one eye. Since in the test the image is considered to be a real image, in effect, we could substitute a real pinhole.

[13]   Trial and error would be the teacher here, where one could see what changes resulted from a particular stroke and then, whether it was better or worse. One could actually see visual effects that correspond to real changes in the order of 0.000010 inch.

There were other chapters in the book for the telescope tube and its mounting hardware, and I had started making some of these parts as I was nearing completion of the polishing. With the mirror now out for aluminizing, I was able to start some of the bigger parts. I had a local sheet metal shop roll and weld up a five-foot-long galvanized iron tube. The mounting design called for two-and-a-half-inch pipe fittings: tees, elbows, nipples, and such. My father helped me set a four-foot-long pipe into a concrete footing along the side of our house. Screwed on to the top of the pipe was a forty-five-degree elbow and a combination of fittings that created a German-type mounting, with two crossing axis—all motions being achieved by turning the fittings on their threads. The lower axis angle was close to Jamestown's forty-two-degree latitude. In this way, simply turning the tube saddle on those threads (about that north-south polar axis) the telescope would follow the stars across the night sky. Many of the smaller parts I made in my high school wood shop class, assembling them with standard nuts, bolts, and springs.

The greatest boon in amateur astronomy occurred right after World War II when surplus lenses and prisms became readily available at dirt cheap prices. There were two national mail order houses selling surplus optics; one of them is still doing business as Edmund Scientific—in the present day it is more of a science projects house than a surplus store. I bought several eyepieces and a diagonal prism for a few dollars each.

I lined the inside of the telescope tube with one-fourth inch sheet cork to minimize the effects of turbulence caused by heated air rising from the mirror surface as it cooled in the early evening air. All the mechanical systems were completed and assembled while I awaited the return of the aluminized mirror.

The mirror finally arrived by U.S. Mail parcel delivery on Thanksgiving Day 1949, and the telescope saw first light[14] on a cold winter night shortly after. The first star images I saw were astounding in their brilliance. I set out that night in my lone exploration of the universe, having great satisfaction in what I had created, but also with the knowledge that I would have to make yet another telescope.

While astronomy became my strongest interest, I continued in other activities with my brothers. One that began with Herb and continued later with Pete, when he grew older, was the making of rockets.[15] This activity was inspired

---

[14] In astronomy, this refers to the first time that light from a sky object passes through a telescope and forms coherent images to be seen or photographed.

[15] This interest would continue for another decade, long after we went our own ways: building and launching rockets when we got together on vacations and holidays.

by watching *Movietone News* clips of captured German V2 rockets launched from the White Sands test range in New Mexico. We made "poor boy" rockets out of paper and used match heads for fuel. All the rockets were quite small, and their distinctive characteristic was their relatively slow flight speed—a byproduct of the match's low burn rate. Our record flights were originally tape-measured inside fifteen- and twenty-foot distances. The appeal was that the visual images very closely resembled the V2 launches we saw on newsreels; they would start slowly and then accelerate while trailing a bright orange flame. My most successful launch used an electrical ignition system, and after some smoking, it rose slowly to about twenty feet while turning downrange, accelerating past a neighbor's house, and landing in the next neighbor's tree. Pete was to launch one that would streak straight up some forty feet and then fall back to bury itself near its original launch point.

When Herb completed his army service and started college in Rochester, he used his art training to introduce another activity during his summer break—it was to design board games. Baseball was one of the first games we attempted because Pete had started playing Little League and we wanted to extend the flavor, making the board game as realistic as possible. Herb bought a poster board, and we laid out a ballpark and develop dice rules to animate the game. The games then went into football, submarines, tanks, treasure island, and even a politically incorrect assassination game. Sports and stock car racing games would follow a few years later. We hoped that someday we would manufacture them under the name of James Games, but it never happened.

In 1948, when I entered high school, I elected to take the technical mechanical course, which would prepare me to become a mechanical engineer. About this same time, I also took a part-time job as an usher at the Palace Theatre, which was in the Warner Brothers' theater chain. Now that I was working and had some money, the telescope bug bit again; and I decided to start another telescope. This time, it would be a Richest Field Telescope (RFT) made to specifications I found in *Amateur Telescope Making Book II*. This was a telescope designed to use the lowest power possible! The idea was to see the largest number of stars possible in any one view—therefore, the name richest field. My six-inch telescope at f/10 was designed for high power, to look at the moon and planets. Looking at a star field under high power, on average, it would show only three stars, randomly spaced. A 4-¼ inch f/4 RFT would not see stars as faint as my six-inch, but at the lower power and wider field, it would see, on average, several hundred stars in that one view.

As soon as the 4-¼-inch kit arrived, I started rough grinding the same day. I followed quickly with fine grinding, polishing and figuring, ending with a mirror of sixteen inches focal length. While my six-inch mirror took about forty-five actual hours of optical work, the 4-¼-inch mirror took only about sixteen hours spread over a few months. It saw first light in July of 1950. The views of the Milky Way were absolutely spectacular, and they profoundly influenced my perception of man's proper place in the universe, which was very humbling.

The views through the RFT were so impressive that barely two months later I ordered an eight-inch mirror kit for a larger RFT to capture even fainter stars. The kit arrived in August, just before I was to start my senior year in high school. I started rough grinding on my birthday, the twenty-sixth and finished it in September with an elapsed log time of only eighteen hours, seeing first light on September 26. This would become my workhorse telescope for all of my astronomy during my senior year. I went on to build several devices for taking photographs of the moon and planets. On one occasion, I tested the equipment in the daytime by sending my brother Pete to a street corner, a block away to be photographed.

Other events that summer saw our routines change slightly. Pete and his friends were involved in Little League play, and I would give them baseball drills on the brick street in front of our house. When we were not actually practicing, I would quiz them on situations to sharpen their mental awareness for decision making, asking, for example, what the proper play would be under some unusual or outrageous circumstance. Beyond the Little League activity, our baseball interests included following the Jamestown Falcons, a class D team in the Detroit Tigers farm system.

My father typically worked long hours and six days a week in his tailor shop, so he was not able to become directly involved; however, he was very supportive, making sure we could go to the ballpark to enjoy the games. My mother's role, as she filled it, was to make sure we were well fed—and then some.

Herb returned to work as a bellhop at the Hotel Jamestown during his summer break from college. I had quit my job as an usher and was now also working in the hotel as a bellhop. Despite having had polio, my strength had built up sufficiently so that I could carry a full load of baggage under both arms. The hotel job, while paying more, was also better because it forced me to interact with more people, helping me to learn to live with my shyness. At summer's end, Herb transferred to the Cleveland Art Institute to complete his commercial art training.

I was doing quite well in my technical mechanical course, especially enjoying our physics and mechanics classes. My closest friend was Ronnie Swanson, who was also in the technical course but had elected to go into electrical instead of mechanical engineering. We would be very competitive in our respective technical options, trying to outgrade each other.

Mr. Panzarella, my favorite instructor, taught almost all the combined electrical and mechanical technical classes, except for the few that were elective specialized. I had an interesting experience with Mr. Harding, our machine shop teacher. Mr. Harding would usually start each long shop class with a sit-down tutorial and follow it with a small quiz. We would finish the quiz at our own pace, hand it in and, if he accepted it, proceed to the shop to pick up on our projects. I generally did well in all the mechanical subjects and was usually one of the first to finish, but one day he just returned my sheet back to me and sent me back to my seat. Well, I puzzled over it and could not find my error. I sat there until well after all the others had finished and left. Finally, I said to him that I couldn't find the error. He replied that there wasn't any, but he wanted me to be sure of myself when I turned it in.

He had one very interesting preshop session where he had a special guest. A gentleman was there to give us a talk about the General Motors Institute, where students would alternate between weeks of classes in the institute and weeks working apprenticeships at General Motors factories, ultimately taking employment somewhere in the system. I loved automobiles, collecting all the information I could on automobile design, even having started (but never finishing) two models to enter in the Fisher Body Craftsman's Guild (scholarship) competition. I would spend many of my study hall hours sketching cars. I was greatly awed to be in the presence of a real General Motors person.

———————————

The dark winter nights would always stir my interests in astronomy, time and again isolating me from the rest of the family. Pete was now too old for Little League and would have to look at a bigger league for the next season, which would put him at a considerable height disadvantage. In keeping with another season when Herb came home on weekends, he and I would play touch football against Pete and his friends. The differences we noted were that he and his friends were getting bigger and faster and we were now sensing the first pangs of ageing.

That spring Herb did something to look out for his younger brother. He knew I was interested in cars and art, even though I had gone into a technical high school curriculum. On his own initiative, he sent a letter to General Motors asking for recommendations on automobile design schools.

———————————

My graduation was nearing, and I hadn't made any real plans. I felt I had a good job and was saving money so I thought I would just skip college the first year and look around. I had been receiving some counseling in school from

Edwin P. Hartwig of the New York State Department of Rehabilitation. He was involved because I was considered to be in rehabilitation from the polio, and we had had some general career discussions at various times during my senior year.

In the final state exams, I scored the highest in the technical mechanical group, and my friend Ronnie scored highest in technical electrical. When I graduated, I felt comfortable in my job at the hotel and everything seemed to be going well. Then in July, I received an unexpected telephone call from Mr. Hartwig. He said he would be in town the next week and wanted to set up an appointment for me to see him. We set a time and place, and I showed up, as agreed. I outlined my "loose plans" for going to "some" college the following year. He was upset and angry that I had not already made commitments for the coming year. He told me that he could get me a disability scholarship for any school in New York State as long as I was able to pass their entrance examinations.

As it turned out, Herb had heard from General Motors and they had recommended two schools that taught industrial design, which would be the correct curriculum for automobile designers. The first was the Art Center School in Los Angeles, and the other was Pratt Institute in Brooklyn, New York. Under Mr. Hartwig's requirements, Pratt would qualify for a scholarship so I told him of the GM referral. He said he would help me if I could get the papers filed soon enough. He urged me to apply immediately for the coming semester and only let me go after I promised I would do so.

Herb was also reassuring, in that at the end of his junior year he was seeing graduates from the Cleveland Art Industrial Design curriculum landing very-high-paying jobs compared to entry-level commercial art graduates. With Herb's help, I requested enrollment papers from Pratt, barely a half a dozen weeks before classes were to start. When the papers arrived, Herb also helped me fill out the forms and tried to give me some quick lessons for the "art" portion of the entrance exam.

He showed me how I should vary the line weight as I drew something so that it would have a sense of direction or motion. A heavy blob at one end of the line would cause the eye to fall somewhere on the line and then be drawn toward the heavy end. He gave me a few other hints but left me to do the drawings myself. In short order, we finished the application and sent it back to Pratt. I was concerned because industrial design was listed under the "Art" school; I had no art training in high school whatsoever, and my degree was in mechanical engineering. The only art background I had was self-taught, drawing cars and things in study hall, while Herb had received formal art training through his Liberal Arts curriculum. I sent a note to Mr. Hartwig, advising him that I had completed the application and sent it in. I would check back later to see if everything was on track. Now we had to wait.

It was getting into August, and there were only a few weeks left before classes were to start; I had still received no word. One Friday afternoon, while I was at work in the hotel, Herb came in and told me I had been accepted. I had one week to quit my job and prepare for college.

It was not that hard putting my affairs together because I had none. It was more a matter of adjusting to the concept mentally. I quit my job, selected the clothes I would take, and gathered my savings, planning to find a boarding house off campus to live in. Herb and his wife Mary would drive me the four hundred miles to New York City. We planned to stop and visit with Uncle Roland (my mother's brother) and Aunt Molly when we reached New Jersey. We would depart the next weekend.

Saturday finally arrived, and it was time to start our journey. Over the past years, I had been to Cleveland several times; it was 140 miles west, as the crow flies, but still took four hours to drive over state and county roads, through the many small townships. Now we were looking at driving east four hundred miles to New York City where we could expect a good ten or more hours of driving. We would be driving my father's Chrysler, which would at least give us a more comfortable ride. With everything packed and ready, we said our goodbyes and left Jamestown in midmorning.

The drive started along New York Route 17, which was mostly two and three lanes wide, and took us through small towns whose names I had only known as rivals from our Class D PONY (Pennsylvania/Ontario/New York) baseball league. I experienced some strange feelings, like being in enemy's territory, while going through Olean and Hornell, but they passed quickly once we left the city limits. Gradually, the rolling hills became deeper and wider as we entered the Salamanca Foot Hills. Passing through Corning, New York, was a moving experience because of all the stories I had read about the casting of the two-hundred-inch telescope mirror from the *Glass Giant of Palomar*.[16]

Shortly, our path took us into the deep valleys of Pennsylvania. The roads were starting to get wider and the traffic heavier. It felt as though we were in the middle of a river of vehicles and the pull of New York City was more and more like being in rapids to a waterfall. The townships kept getting larger, and stopping anywhere to eat became more and more of a project. Toward twilight, we were into multiple-lane-divided highways. The effect New York City was having was overwhelming and yet we were still a hundred miles out. Continuing after dark, the sense of the metropolis became even larger with the vision of hundreds of white headlights and red taillights exaggerating the effect. Finally,

---

[16]   A classic authored by David O. Woodbury, Dodd, Mead & Co.

near 10:00 p.m. we were in New Jersey and only a few miles from Uncle Roland's place. We found a motel with a vacancy and checked in.

We were able to relax and spend some time with them that Sunday. Roland had been an inspirational uncle. We never saw very much of him as he and Molly were always busy. They were professional ballroom dancers and performed under the name of Rolando and Louise. They had a small trailer, which they towed while doing the road circuit from coast to coast. In our impressionable young minds, their extensive travels always seemed like great adventures.

In spite of being in show business, Roland had other high-tech interests that would awe us as kids, dabbling in photography, radio, and home movies. Now when we saw him, he was showing us his new (audio) tape recording system. He gave us some great demonstrations, and I was amazed, the first time I heard what my voice really sounded like to other people—I didn't really believe it. That evening we said our goodbyes, but I knew I would be back to visit on weekends from time to time. We returned to our motel to sleep and for me to start preparing myself mentally for our final leg to Pratt in the morning.

We were up early and found a diner to have breakfast in before heading into the city. It became memorable when Mary found a fly in her eggs; and when she complained about it, the waitress said she would only charge her for the half she ate. A short time later, we were back into the flow of the traffic and queuing up at the entrance of the Lincoln Tunnel, waiting to pass under the Hudson River. Exiting on the New York side, we got our first close-up views of the city, but were limited to what could be seen from the elevated expressways. We traveled down Manhattan and crossed into Brooklyn, appropriately by way of the Brooklyn Bridge. Following our map, we continued eastward until we arrived at the Pratt campus.

Finding a parking space, we headed to the admissions office on Ryerson—my paperwork in hand. Everything was in order with the scholarship, which was the only concern I had. I was advised of scheduled activities, given a list of off campus vacancies and a map showing the location of the Student Union Hall, where I could be helped in other matters.

We took the list of available rooms and went just up the same street, finding a likely brownstone apartment building that showed a vacancy. The landlady laid out a list of her rules and requirements, and we simply accepted the terms, as it basically looked clean. All the while we were talking, we all ignored the landlady's bulldog that was "humping" my leg. The room was for two, and I would have to find a roommate to share it. Split two ways, it would cost me $12.50 a week.

The landlady lived in the basement apartment and rented out the three floors above. My entry from the street would be up a flight of stone stairs and then through a double-door keyed entry. Inside, there was space for a stairway on the left and hallways along the right, all the way up to the second and third floors. To the immediate right was a room with a front (street) view through two windows. The hallway led us to the back where, on the right, was the vacant room, the one I had accepted. Off the hallway just to the left was the "community" bathroom. Also at this end of the hall was a stairway leading down to the landlady's basement apartment. Our room had two beds, some bureaus, a closet, and a small washbasin with hot and cold running water. After signing off on the agreements, we went back to the car to get and drop off my clothes and belongings. Being first, I staked out the bed that I wanted. With this task complete, we headed back to the student union where I found a bulletin board and posted a note saying I was looking for a roommate. There was a bookstore there also, but the word was out that some of the required books and art materials could be purchased cheaper at two private art supply stores on DeKalb Avenue. Of the two, I selected Charlie's Art Supply and purchased a heavy cast iron (base) drawing table and a Dazor fluorescent lamp that Herb recommended. I would wait until classes actually started before buying any general art supplies. We brought the table and lamp back to the room and set it up. Then we set out to find a bank where I could keep my living expense money safe and secure. There was one on Myrtle Avenue, under the El (elevated railway), and I opened an account, mostly of money I had earned in the hotel. My father would also send me small weekly checks to help sustain me. One other item, that I find hard to believe today, is that I had a laundry box that I would use to mail my dirty laundry to my mother, who would wash it and then mail it back. This seemed to work out OK—at least, so I believed.

By now it was getting late into the afternoon, so we found a restaurant to have our last meal together before Herb and Mary would start their journey home. After the meal, we drove back to the front steps of the Pratt main building, where I was dropped off; and after a few goodbyes, they drove away. It was the first time that it really hit me that I was alone and starting a new life.

Left, Norman at the Semo farmhouse. *Right,* The James family posing for Uncle Roland, *circa* 1946. Basil and Norman, seated; Constance, Peter, and Herb.

The walk to Lincoln Jr. High over the 3rd Street Bridge overlooking the Erie RR switchyard and the city power plant, as viewed from the Armory Hill.

Left, Basil skipping rocks in Lake Erie. *Right,* Uncle George at his restaurant.

The author with his 8" f/4.5 RFT telescope.

Photograph of Peter taken through the telescope from a block away.

Left, The author electrically lighting a match-head-fueled rocket prior to achieving a distance record flight. *Right,* Another memorable launch.

Rapid sequence photographs of Peter's altitude-record flight.

2   Pratt Institute

The next morning, I returned to the main building to take care of some formalities and to make the rounds of the student union center, lounge, cafeteria, and bookstore, still trying to get comfortable. Taking a break, I went back to the front entry, where I sat on the stone porch rail, observing people coming and going—all of them probably students. I would see someone with what might seem to be a familiar face, then hearing their voices, I would be startled by their strange accent, it being either from another part of the country or foreign in origin. I reviewed the papers I received from admissions, looking at them over and over, checking schedules and classes. I had signed up for industrial design, but as I now understood it, the first year would be a "Foundation Year" course, required of all freshmen in the art curriculum, regardless of their intended major. It would not be until our second year that we would enter our elected fields. The rational appeared to be that they wanted to "untrain" everyone of anything they may have already been taught and to put in place a common "foundation" onto which they would build. They also felt it gave the students an opportunity to change their elected majors, if they so desired. In a way, this alleviated some of my earlier concerns about not having had any formal art training since I now felt I had a head start.

Looking at the class schedule, I could see courses that were clearly related to industrial design; then looking at the sophomore, junior, and senior curriculums, I noted which industrial design instructors were also teaching Foundation Year classes. Most notable was the color instructor, Alexander Kostellow, because he was also the head of the Industrial Design Department. He had a lecture class every Monday in the main auditorium. Along with the paperwork I had processed in admissions, they had scheduled an appointment for me for an interview with Mr. Kostellow, since I had noted my intention to go into his department.

As my appointed time was approaching, I headed back to the Industrial Design Department in the rear of the building, starting early enough so as not to be late but moving slowly so as not to be too early. Right away, I noticed a stark cleanliness in the rooms and hall interiors. There was indirect smooth lighting in the ceilings, and glass displays were illuminated, evoking a "this is really nice" feeling. I saw beautiful models of things in Plexiglas, painted plasters, and polished brasses that really looked great. I couldn't wait to be doing this kind of stuff. At the appointed hour, I knocked on Mr. Kostellow's door and was invited in.

I sat on the chair across from his desk, still observing nice details in his office, seeing vertical window blinds (for the first time), fine non-glare reflective egg-crate overhead lighting, and an overall cleanliness of detail, minimalism as it would be called in the design world. Kostellow was in his late forties or early fifties, slightly stocky, well dressed and had a full growth of straight longish but trimmed dark hair, slightly peppered gray. Most pronounced were his bushy John L. Lewis eyebrows.

Unexpectedly, he asked, "Why do you want to be an industrial designer?" I struggled for an intelligent answer and mumbled something about having an interest in designing cars. He was ready with his next question. "What do you expect to learn here?" His question seemed phrased to solicit what great expertise I felt I was bringing to the school. My answer this time was somewhat better, in that I generally implied that I didn't know but I would depend on their guiding me to what they saw I needed. As an afterthought, I added that I wanted to have a reason for why I designed anything in any particular way.

Apparently satisfied, he went on to explain the way the school was set up and that all freshman students of the art school, including architecture, illustration, advertising, interior and industrial design had to take the same Foundation Year course to establish the basics of design. It would not be until the second year that anyone would be taking specialized courses in their selected curriculum. In my case, I should not expect to see anything related to car design until then. He then added that his department was supported by numerous corporations, each having a lab, where they could interact on various projects to bring a sense of industry into the curriculum. The main benefit was that each corporation contributed $40K each year to help cover expenses of the wood and plaster model shop facilities. General Motors, Reynolds Aluminum, and Monsanto Chemical were among the contributing members. He went on to explain that Pratt did not in fact have an automobile design class in its curriculum, since most of the graduates would go on into other design fields. But he honored the lab obligations by having after-school noncredit classes conducted by senior class members or visiting consultants.

He said he would be conducting a single color lecture class for the Foundation Year students but since it would be so large, it would be unlikely I would have any personal contact with him until my second year. Having then been excused, I went back to the front entry to sit on the stoop and contemplate all that I had just heard.

While sitting there, I heard a voice from behind ask, "Are you Norman James? I understand you're looking for a roommate." I turned, and the young man introduced himself as Eric Norton. Eric had gotten my name from someone coordinating such things, and they had paired him with me because he was going into industrial design and he also had an interest in car design. We compared our classes, and it appeared that they were the same. He seemed OK so I invited him to come and look at the room. It turned out that Eric's home was in New Jersey and that he expected that he would go home over the weekends. The room was fine for Eric, so we agreed to room together; and I introduced him to Mrs. Kane, the landlady. Eric then moved his things in, and we returned to the main building.

We made the rounds to see where everything was located. Downstairs was the bookstore, which was open and had lists of required books and materials for the various classes. Just down the hall, we found the cafeteria, which was closed. Following more noise coming from further down the hall we found the student lounge, where music from *The King and I* was blaring. The large auditorium-like room had seats, lounge chairs, and tables scattered about and a coffee shop situated in a small back room. This would likely tide us over when the cafeteria was closed.

We looked our schedules over again more closely. There appeared to be two major design classes, 2-D and 3-D, each of which consisted of two three-hour lab classes each week and both conducted by industrial design instructors Robert Kolli and Ivan Rigby. Color was only one hour each week in the lecture hall, but since Kostellow was giving it, we assumed it would be a heavy weight. Other art classes were Figure Structure and Nature Structure, scheduled for morning sessions and aligned more toward the Illustration majors. History of Art was the last of the art subjects and was scheduled for Wednesday mornings, again in the lecture hall for the entire Foundation class. The Art School dean, James Boudreou, known to all as Dean Boudreou, would personally conduct this class. A few academic classes would round out the week. One was Communications, which was basically English, and the other was Social History. With all of our books and art supplies purchased and squared away in our room, Eric went home for the weekend. We would both be ready for the start of classes the next week.

We arrived at our designated second-floor classroom Monday morning, officially starting our freshman year. The room had a high ceiling with full windows from waist high on up on one side. There were two rows of high six-foot-long-by-three-foot-deep tables, each with a pair of high-backed stools, scattered about to accommodate forty students. Promptly at nine o'clock, Mr. Ivan Rigby came in, introduced himself, and called roll. This was my first realization that I was no longer in high school, when he addressed us by our proper surnames. His first name "Ivan," was a "fooler," in that his demeanor was more reserved and very British.

He explained how the 3-D course would be structured and that it would take the full year to take us from the most basic elements of design in space to ultimately the most complex structures.[17] In the beginning, we would work with simple singular shapes and then in combinations, progressing in order from rectangular solids, round disks, or rods and then finally to spheres. There would be no free-form sculptures in this class.

On the first day, his lab technician Joe Campos handed out broken slabs of plaster that had been cast into sheets of various thickness, and we were then given our instructions. From any given slab, using a band saw, we were to cut out a rectangle, trying to make the resulting shape have pleasing proportions. We would then look at it, and either like its appearance or more likely feel that it would look better if one or more of the sides were shortened. What was difficult was that we could not make a change by adding material. Next we had to sand the surfaces clean and smooth in order to sense the effect of each face and the relationships between the faces. Finally we had to sense the effect of that particular volume as a mass. The true objective was to develop a personal sensitivity to form and shape. We were encouraged to fiddle with the proportions until we felt we could not improve on them. Then we were to set it aside, pick another piece of plaster, and start all over again.

After a few lab sessions, we were taken to the next level when Rigby instructed us to collect all of our perfect shapes and arrange them next to each other into pleasing relationships. We then received an instruction that would be repeated in many of our other design classes: to create relationships that could be classified as dominant, subdominant, or subordinate. The dominant feature could be a component or any strong relationship of subelements that would stand out as the clear theme of the group. There should also be a subdominant effect that stood out but was clearly dominated by the other effect. Ideally, it would be arranged such that it enhanced or enriched the dominant effect. There could, or should also, be other effects that would be interesting but would clearly not be

---

[17] Some of the course descriptions that follow actually carried over several years, but they have been condensed here for better topic continuity.

any part of the theme as such. An example of doing it wrong would be to have any ambiguity as to which was the dominant of several features or themes.

At this point, all the shapes would be rectangular prisms with all faces and edges square to the world. Our compositions also would be square to each other, but they could be in any relationship whatever. To fix the arrangements of a design, it would be necessary to actually intersect the shapes one into the other. Slots or notches would then cut into shapes so as to hold them in relative space to each other. When satisfied, white glue would be used to set the joints. The same sense of rules applied, in that the intent was to develop a sensitivity to know when they were placed into their best relationships to each other. What was helpful was that there was an unspoken competition between the students so that when any student had a better resolution, it provided a measure that some "apples" were better than some "oranges." It also reinforced the idea that there was room for improvement, even if it was only in sensing or understanding how the other student achieved that better composition.

With these first exercises completed, we proceeded to add the cylinder as a new element to our compositions. It could be a wood dowel cut square at the ends and painted white, a thin sheet of plaster cut into a flat circular disk, or it could as well be a short fat wood or plaster cylinder. The same rules would apply for the creation of pleasing compositions. Whose studies were best, of course, would be subjective, but the better ones would be found to comply with the basic rules of dominant, subdominant, and subordinate. Later, spheres or spherical segments were added to the allowed shapes and the exercises repeated.

In time, we were to realize that long elements would capture the eye and lead it to a different location; crossing components would stop and redirect imparted visual motions; masses of components could be distributed to affect a sense of balance, much as a small element linked at some distance would have a greater "leverage" on the other masses. Physics could almost be applied or implied as a rule in design. The eye was found to be surprisingly sensitive to determine whether or not a composition was in balance, regardless of the physics.

Much later, 3-D design would introduce the slight modification of shapes to correct for optical illusions, much as the Greeks did in applying slight curvatures to their columns, and there was a period where the shapes became more architectural in nature, but the essence of the class was its establishment of the basics of three-dimensional design.

Two-dimensional (2-D) design was taught by Robert Kolli, also an industrial design professor, as previously noted. Its format was similar to 3-D in that it returned to the building block system. Instead of solid shapes, however, Kolli had us bring in colorful old magazines. We were then directed to cut up pictures and graphics into snippets of shapes, all edges being independent of the subjective content, i.e., the edges did not follow any graphic features. They became only random pieces of colors, patterns, or textures. Our task was to arrange these pieces onto a white board until there was a pleasant relationship between all of them. There would be no subject to the composition; it would, therefore, be an abstraction. Final compositions would then be glued down and then posted for class review. As in 3-D, we were to apply the same rules of dominant, subdominant, and subordinate to the compositions. Most of this work was done in the three-hour lab class environment where Kolli would walk around and give individual comments or criticisms. I found 2-D immediately to be more difficult as I did not have a good feel for it. I found a comfortable table in the back of the room where I would be out of the way and with my own peers. As I was arranging the pieces, according to the rules, Kolli stopped by and commented, "No, no, James, it's not working blah, blah, blah." I tried again, concentrating a little harder, but my mind wanted to wander. I kept placing scraps into my composition while, as a group, our table began having some interesting conversations. Then I heard Kolli's voice behind me say, "Now you're getting it, James." My impression of Kolli immediately nose-dived as I started doubting his sense of judgment—I knew I wasn't even paying any attention to what I was doing.[18]

The 2-D classes would later evolve into pen and brushwork, where graphic elements would be created directly into compositions according to planned themes. The key turned out to be the ability to develop a sensitivity to observe one's own work in progress, to sense any existing imbalance and to determine what additional actions would be required to bring it into a state of balance. It would require a continuous series of adjustments to correct and finally complete the composition. One of the biggest problems in any design process turns out to be in judging when to stop—when is it finished? A properly developed sense in the artist will rapidly iterate through these corrections on a totally subconscious level so that no thought process is involved. In fact, the presence of a thought process would very likely derail any successful conclusion. Any disruption of the subconscious would very likely have the effect of leaving a trace or artifact in the art, much as any interruption of hand writing in a paragraph would be clearly noticeable, even to a novice.

As the year progressed, in parallel with other class subjects, we started developing compositions in various media such as charcoal, Conte crayon, pen and ink, and brushed tempera. In all cases, they involved the development of hand/eye coordination for technique and technical control in the application of colors, patterns, and textures, with an emphasis toward applying them to

---

[18]   It would be much later before I realized that my sub-conscious was following the rules and Kolli was right.

achieve desired graphic effects. Some compositions classically were contained within four borders, but I found the most interesting compositions were spot designs where the art was allowed to drop out incomplete, leaving large areas of untouched white paper (which would actually contribute as part of the composition).

For our final 2-D assignment, we were charged to select a subject and develop a mural on a theme. The key graphic objective was to overlay a structure of light and dark patterns into the composition, independent of subject matter or other natural edges. The final mural would be black and white, less than two feet long and be done in charcoal.

In both of our 2-D and 3-D classes, no attempts were made to represent realism. There was another class that turned out to be outstanding that was directly related to reality. It was figure drawing. While it was structured primarily for those Foundation students leaning toward Illustration, it turned out to be one of our best classes for teaching us how to draw. It was taught by Calvin Albert, who was a renowned and published artist.

In our first class, our group entered the studio and selected easels to work from. We had brought our prescribed charcoal sticks, kneaded erasers, and 18 x 24 drawing pads and sat on our high stools as we waited for class to begin. Albert sat in front and directed questions to the class, asking each person in turn to introduce themselves, give their art backgrounds, intended curriculums and to state what they expected to gain from the class. In the meantime, the model entered the room and sat at the back wearing a robe. We continued our introductions and when finished, Albert said, "Okay, let's get started." The model got up, walked to the raised platform, and dropped her robe, taking a pose. It was very quiet in the mixed class of former high school boys and girls as she wasn't wearing a bathing suit. After some varying discomforts, we got on with the program.

This first class was uncharacteristically quiet as she took a series of five- and ten-minute poses, ending with a longer twenty-minute pose. By the later classes, we had all adjusted to the protocols and were starting to progress. Figure drawing was not offered in later years, at least not for industrial design students, but I was to find that this was where I had learned the most about drawing and sketching.

The best exercises were those where Albert had the model take a series of five- or ten-second poses and we had to capture the essence or gesture of the pose within that time, including flipping the pages for the next poses. It taught us to observe and simplify the gestures as we committed them to paper. There was an exercise where we had to draw while looking at the model only, not being permitted to looking at the drawing at all! Details would be disjointed; however, the stroke and character totally captured the essence of the pose. It also surprisingly, contributed to adding a sense of three-dimensional space to the drawing.

These exercises also taught one not to draw from memory but rather from reality. A common fault would be where someone had to draw a known subject from memory and then have to transition into an unknown detail. The drawing would betray that the detail was unknown. The true irony was that the better the artist, the more evident the flaw would be. When drawing from life, a figure, a landscape, or an arranged setting, there would never be any unknowns.

The discipline sought was the development of the eye/hand coordination that translated visual images into strokes on paper. A surprising observation was that once the techniques were developed, details in a drawing could actually appear or be implied that were far smaller that the instrument (point or edge) that created them.

Mostly, Albert had us sketch the model from poses that varied from five to ten minutes each in length, while in a few, the poses could be up to twenty-five minutes. On longer poses, the model would take breaks to relax and then repose. Regardless of the length of the pose, the objective from the start would be to capture the total gesture of the model within the first few moments of the sketch and then to refine detail, as time was available, not necessarily for the objective of achieving a photo likeness. Albert would absolutely not allow anyone to start a drawing with the eyes and eyelashes and then move on out.

Summarizing, in figure drawing, everything is understood because it is in clear view taken from life, not from memory. The only thing that remains is to apply the artist's skill to interpret that vision. In the process of developing this coordination, skills would be developed to represent things in space, without having to resort to perspective grids and vanishing points. For a student going into Illustration, this could be the end product itself, a skill to be polished and refined. In advertising and architecture, it would serve as an aid to augment or enhance presentations of their product. To an industrial designer, the value of figure drawing would be in its developing the ability to represent things in space.

The fourth Foundation subject of importance was color. This was Kostellow's one-hour lecture series, as noted earlier. Since the full Foundation class was in attendance for these lecture classes, there were no questions taken from the floor. Kostellow would present his featured topic each week and issue assignments, which would be due the following Monday. We would execute them and place them in a drop box in the morning. Kostellow would collect, review, and return them for pickup later in the week, with comments attached if he had any. As he said, this would be the only contact we would have with him through the year.

He began his first lecture by explaining color as a three-dimensional structure: progressing from red to red orange, orange to yellow orange, yellow to yellow green, green to blue green, blue to blue violet, violet to red violet, and returning to red (as if they were spokes on a wagon wheel) even though red and red violet were on opposite ends of the physical spectrum.[19] Even though this structure does not really exist, putting them into this relationship helps explain what otherwise would be very complex material.

For our purposes, we could assume that the red end of the spectrum would blend as smoothly into the violet end, as any other color would blend into its true neighbor. Once this assumption was accepted, we could then apply simple geometric relationships to understand concepts such as complimentary and harmonic color schemes. While the colors would be disposed along the outer rim of the wagon wheel at their maximum intensities, lesser saturations would be represented along their spokes, with the intensity of the color diminishing as it approached the hub. Complementary colors (red and green, for example) would always appear as spokes on opposite sides of the wheel, and one could observe the one color transition into the other as it passed on through the hub, as an absolutely neutral gray.

The third dimension of the color structure would be brightness. Looking at the center hub as an extended axis, we would see gray; but setting it vertically, we would observe the gray above to be a little lighter and the gray below a little darker. The highest and lightest gray in the stack would be a pure white, and the darkest bottom gray would be an absolute black. Brightness would be equal for all colors at the same level, with only color saturations increasing in intensity as they reached their maximums at the rim.

This would be true for all colors, except for black and white, as the addition of any color would darken a white or lighten a black. Other observations were then noted. Yellow, being naturally a light color, would reach its highest saturation at a fairly high light value, while it's complementary opposite blue purple, would reach its highest saturation at a fairly low dark value. This meant that the most intense colors in the color wheel would be asymmetrical, vertically. Our first assignment was to assemble a Munsell Color Chart, which was a physical representation of this same observation. We had to rubber cement color chips onto a checkerboard grid according to color family, brightness, and saturation.

Having gone through this exercise, at our next class, Kostellow went on to explain the relationships of colors as they may be used in color compositions. The familiar complementary color scheme would be comprised of colors from

---

[19] The visible spectrum is linearly continuous between the short ultraviolet and the long infrared wavelengths. The marvel is that by joining these ends together (where otherwise they would extend in opposite directions into the invisible), the eye perceives it as a natural closure, even though it is contrary in physics.

one chart, and the complementary colors would be found to lie exactly on the opposite spoke chart of the color wheel. This would be true between any opposite sets of charts also across any opposite in between sets of charts, if they existed. Color schemes did not end there however. Just as it was in other classes, it was necessary to have dominant and subdominant color schemes. Then, of course, there could be additional subordinate colors comprised of any combination of chips of color, saturation, and intensity. A successful color scheme would have a pleasant, balanced distribution of all the color elements in relative proportions and intensities.

Another color scheme was Harmonic, where balance is achieved not by selection of colors from spokes opposite but rather with the dominant color on one chart and a subdominant color one chart up or down stream of the opposite chart. The subordinate color(s) then would be selected across from the missing (complementary) color. In effect, the subdominant and subordinate colors would average to be the equivalent of the missing complementary color. Properly done, these color schemes could be quite rich and attractive. The sensitivity and skill of the artist would determine how far one could drift from the complementary opposite color and still achieve the balance.

Another rule or concern was the color reversal which presumably could not be found in nature. This is where a naturally dark color is light in value and is found immediately next to a naturally light color, which is darker, for example, a light blue against a dark red. The way that nature handles this occurrence is that color saturation is reduced so that where the colors are in close proximity to each other, they are very nearly neutral grays. So unless it was for some other purpose, if one had to transition from one color chart across to the other, they would pass through the center gray zone.

As the year progressed, Kostellow brought us through more complex color relationships, adding patterns and textures. In some exercises, he would have us purchase small postcard-sized prints of old master paintings and task us to select color chips and fabric swatches to coordinate a color scheme for a room that would hold that painting—a first cut for future interior designers.

The last major class was history of art, which was conducted by Dean Boudreau. He obviously wanted to play more than an administrative role and participated by teaching the subject he loved most. As with our color class, he presented it lecture style in the main hall, Wednesday mornings, to the entire Foundation class. There was a textbook that we followed, and we had assigned readings before each lecture. His procedure was to provide mimeographed notes on what he would be covering because, as he said, he wanted the full attention of the students and didn't want it diverted by having to take notes. In a like manner, whenever he gave tests, he would identify those general pages from which the test questions would be drawn. In this way, he was able to give a good visual presentation, rich with projected color graphics. It was loosely structured so that one could easily slip through without giving full attention, but he did offer students the opportunity to learn art history without imposing too heavy of a demand on their valuable time.

Rounding out the first year, there were a few more light art classes and the two academics, English and social history. Nature structure turned out to be quite interesting. It was similar to figure drawing, in that we would be drawing from reality, going on field trips to museums, zoos, and parks. The Museum of Natural History was good for us as starters because the stuffed animals didn't move too fast. Later, we went to the zoos, which offered more of a challenge because we never knew how long a pose would last. Our media was predominantly colored pastels. Trees and landscapes also became objects for colorful compositions. Drawing from life also sharpened our senses of observation. It was here that I first observed how each limb, branch, and twig of a tree was conscious of itself in its world and fought with its neighbors for light and growing space.

Aside from the curriculum, I was exposed to other things that New York City had to offer. When Eric went home on weekends, I would break from my studies and frequent the museums, the Natural History Museum off Central Park being a favorite. Besides the many floors that could not be covered in a single visit, there was the attached Hayden Planetarium, where I would return on the first Saturday of each new program to get my astronomy fix.

I also found the subway system to be most exciting and considered it to be the most distinctive feature of the city. In a short two-block walk, I could be in the subway system at Clinton and Washington, take the Independent train two stops to Hoyt-Schermerhorn, transfer to the A Express to Columbus Circle, and then jump on to the AA local, two stops to the Natural History Museum, entering through it's own station entry in the basement. This was most appreciated on bad weather days, when I would otherwise not have even ventured outside. I really enjoyed the subways.[20]

On a few weekends, I would take the subway to the Forty-second Street bus terminal, transfer to a bus to take me through the Holland Tunnel into New

---

[20] In the 1950s, there was little concern about personal safety or crime. There were no drug problems, and gangs were not evident in the area. Likewise, there was no graffiti and very little awareness of homelessness. I would often return late at night by myself and never have any concerns.

Jersey, to visit Uncle Roland and Aunt Molly. Most often though I would just walk some fifteen blocks down DeKalb Avenue to downtown Brooklyn to a first-run movie theater. A few times, I made it to Ebbets Field to watch the Brooklyn Dodgers play. It was my first time ever in a major league ballpark, and I was overwhelmed by how plush the grass was, the smooth infield, and the size of the crowd. I watched the game from a front box seat in the left field upper deck. Everything seemed far away, but I was still thrilled. I believe the Dodgers were playing St Louis, and they were facing Stu Miller, a junk-ball pitcher that really gave them fits. I don't remember who won, but the impressions remain.

Because Eric was away those weekends, almost everything I did was as a loner. My Saturday routine would have me returning late in the afternoon, and because the cafeteria would be closed, I would stop at a local greasy spoon for dinner, almost always having franks and beans and black coffee. Sunday mornings were slow starters, going out for breakfast, stopping at the art store and a deli to look at magazines, or to pick up supplies and maybe some chocolate-covered doughnuts, pacing myself to start homework assignments by midday.

If I had a writing assignment, after breakfast, I would walk to Fort Green Park where I would find a quiet bench with a view of the Manhattan skyline to start organizing my thoughts and making notes. I would then return to my room and write a draft from those notes and rework them until they seemed right. I would then handwrite the final version onto composition paper. My spelling was so bad that it would take me up to three hours to write and check my spelling at the same time. I always expected Eric to return in the early evening, and when he got in, we would compare notes for the next day's classes.

Our school week typically would have us return to our room after classes, and we would go back to the cafeteria for an early supper. Occasionally, we would follow dinner with a trip to the students' recreation center, where we would shoot a few games of pool or bowl a few games on the two-lane self-serve bowling alley in the basement. From there, we would stop at the art supply stores and then return to our room to do homework, each at our own pace.

The radio was our constant companion, playing dramatizations of half or quarter-hour serial episodes. *Jack Armstrong, Sergeant Preston of the Royal Mounted Police, The Lone Ranger, Sky King*, and *Broadway Is My Beat* were some of the regulars. My favorite was *Gun Smoke*, with Bill Conrad playing an earthy Matt Dillon and Parley Bear playing Chester "Proudfoot," the lame deputy. Homework was pretty heavy, and it would easily take us to midnight to complete. On occasions, we had to push ourselves into the early morning hours. For those times, the soothing *Music through the Night* sponsored by American Airlines, gave us a peaceful working environment, with few voice interruptions as the instrumental pieces were presented in groups of four or five. My memories of those nights are forever linked to the classics and especially the instrumentals *Moulin Rouge* and *Green Sleeves*.

Curriculum breaks came at Thanksgiving, Christmas, and spring. Thanksgiving was notable because I had planned to stay in Brooklyn, but at the last minute I became homesick and decided to go home. I packed a small bag and took an early evening subway train to Manhattan where I got on to a ferryboat to the Erie Railroad Station on the New Jersey side of the Hudson. The overnight train ticket cost $27. Ticket in hand, I called home and told them I was coming. I then boarded the Pullman coach for the 8:30 p.m. departure. It was my first real experience riding a train, and I was fascinated at how slow it seemed to be moving, even though it was dark outside and I couldn't really tell. It was a fitful ride with many stops along the way, and I wasn't really able to sleep. By the time we were approaching Jamestown, it was just starting to get light and I could see that a light snowfall had fallen, which always seemed to mark the beginning of a Thanksgiving holiday. I arrived at 7:00 a.m., and Herb was there to pick me up. He was always in Jamestown over these holidays for the start of hunting season.

The break was good, and I was able to talk to Herb at length on how the art classes were going. With the holiday ending, I returned to the train station Sunday evening for the overnight ride that would take me back into the Monday morning rush hour traffic but with plenty of time before my first class. Memories of recrossing on the ferry are still vivid; walking under the elevated freeway on my way to the subway while merchants and produce delivery vehicles were already starting their new day. The subway ride to Brooklyn gave me the experience of a real New Yorker's commute, but in time I was back in my room to meet Eric, who had also just arrived. We gathered our assignments and began the new week fully refreshed.

The return for the Christmas break was similar for all the same events but was not particularly notable. The spring break was even less memorable because I did not go home. What was notable was the knowledge that the school year would soon be coming to an end. By now I had adjusted to the routine. I was getting along about as I had expected; my grades were average, but I was still in the running with full expectations of advancing into industrial design the next year.

Eric and I decided to stay with Mrs. Kane in the same room for our junior year, so we made arrangements to leave our supplies in the room over the summer. Closing up shop on the final day, Eric packed everything he needed to take home and I packed my personal things to tote them, just like my old bellhop days, to the subway, the ferryboat, and on to the Erie Railroad Station. The overnight train again brought me into Jamestown early the next morning.

The next few months were too short to do anything more than just try to get some rest and help out around the house. I was able to spend some time with Herb and Pete, which felt good. I had received my grades and knowing I had passed took a lot of the pressure off. Herb by now had graduated and was working in an art studio in Cleveland. He would still drive back to Jamestown to visit every few weeks. We would resume our rocket building and game board activities on those weekends. By now Pete was older and was starting to become more involved.

There was another incident of note that summer. I returned to the city library one day, feeding the old habit, and went to the reading room to look for *Aviation Week* and *Sky & Telescope* magazines. This day, however, there was a sign posted indicating that they were displaying artwork from the local third and fourth-grade classes in the back of the reading room. I giggled a bit as I thought, "this ought to be good for a few laughs." As I walked into the display area, I was stunned. Yes, there was poor detail in the simple drawings, but the graphic proportions and boldness of color usage just sang out. These kids were doing exactly what Pratt was trying to teach us! It appeared as though the third-grade students had an inborn natural sense of graphic form and color. The fourth-graders were still showing a trace of that natural sense, but you could see the detrimental effects their teachers were having, of inhibiting these natural senses, trying to teach them how to shade and make things more realistic. My experience that day was devastating and extremely humbling.

As September approached, I started thinking more and more about the coming year, and about finally starting Industrial Design. I was accepting the reality that it was going to happen, and I would be back on track to become an automobile designer. I called Eric to verify that all was well at that end, and I started packing, planning this time to return by day train to see all those things through those same dark Pullman windows that I had only imagined before.

3 Industrial Design

As we were told, one benefit of having a Foundation year first was that it gave students an opportunity to change career directions after they better understood their options. In our cases, Eric and I remained committed to industrial design. Other friends we had made in our Foundation class would now go on into architecture, illustration, graphics, or interior design; we would still see their familiar faces in public areas, but now we were part of a much smaller group of some forty students, including a half-dozen females. We were now the industrial design sophomore class, and we could look forward to seeing the same faces together in future yearbooks, progressing in identity from sophomore, to junior, and then senior industrial design graduates. The only concern, of course, was whether our faces would still be in those pictures. Some classes would be in continuation, from our Foundation year, and would have the same instructors, but the emphasis would now be placed more toward product design. This time, when we would see Kostellow, he would be teaching us more fundamental and analytical design concepts. Additional instructors would "round out" our more specialized curriculum, all of them focused and drawing us closer to "the product."

Our best overview came in Kostellow's first class. He told us what to expect over the next three years. It followed closely what he told me in my original interview the year before. The entire sophomore and junior years would be comprised of courses necessary to complete our training, i.e., developing the tools necessary to become industrial designers. The combination of exercises, assignments, and lab classes would reinforce repetitive procedures to the point where they would become second nature and automatic. Our senior year would feature photography and other presentation techniques. That whole year would really be dedicated to the single purpose of completing portfolios,[21] which we would need to get jobs in industry.

He then gave us a brief history of industrial design, telling us that he was in fact one of the founders of the field, establishing it as a new profession. He helped organize the first industrial design curriculum at Carnegie Tech with Don Dohner and later brought it to Pratt in the 1930s. He described it as the first effort to legitimize the field by formalizing its structure with a balanced foundation of prerequisite courses. He also helped in the founding of the *Industrial Design League* and was its president for several years. Their activities were in close accord with parallel activities in architecture, those of applying basic abstract and structural design concepts, under the leadership of Moholy-Nage and Mies van der Rohe of the Bauhaus School of Design. The curriculum we were currently taking was basically the same as the one he had created at Carnegie Tech, including even an identical Foundation year.

Kostellow then explained what industrial design actually was and ended up by saying it was really a way of life, as the things we learned, we would continue to apply in our personal lives during every waking hour. He made a very important clarification to distinguish the field from engineering. He said, "An industrial designer does not design for a person's needs . . . an engineer designs for a person's needs . . . an industrial designer designs for a person's wants!"[22]

He went on to described the working relationship he had with industry and how industry leaders like General Motors, Monsanto, Reynolds Aluminum, and others were participating in his "Lab" programs, supporting the department's model shops. Industry would also provide real world assignments for the students, as well as advise and critique their work, assuring that our education was current. It also gave their recruiters a "heads up" for good placement prospects after graduation.

At the end of the senior year, Kostellow would personally become involved in the placement of his students, finding good jobs for them in industry. After telling us how instrumental he was in placing graduates, he then surprised us by saying that often, after placing someone in a good job, he might later pull them out of that job and place them in a better job with another company, but not to worry, because he would make sure the original employer got a good

---

[21]   Starting even from our Foundation year, we would collect what we considered to be our best works and compile them into 18" x 24" portfolios. The collection would constantly be upgraded with replacements as better work was created, and in the end, it would be comprised of work from all four years.

[22]   This may not be altruistic (as an objective), however, there is little doubt that it could yield the greatest satisfaction to the consumer.

replacement. It left us with a warm feeling, that we would be taken care of, but we didn't know what to make of his claimed power and influence.

He then went into depth describing the specifics of the curriculum. He said his courses were laid out to develop skills in concept definition, not resolution. He would repeatedly have us begin new design projects, taking them to the point of definition and then drop them, with no further execution, so we could start yet another project. His reasoning was that the time it took to fully learn how to resolve problems would be too long, and would waste too much valuable-class time. He expected his students to learn this phase during their first two years on the job. He whimsically added that that was the reason he would never hire one of his own students, right after graduation.

We would find that the rest of the classes fit tightly within the overview he gave us. The product sensitive classes also conformed to these fundamentals, but in those cases, the department brought in practicing designers to help us relate to their fields. Instead of learning, how to design specific products, we would be exposed to how unique problems were uniquely addressed and solved in that field. The underlying theme was that all basic design processes were the same, and by understanding those processes, they could be applied within any field.

One such class was conducted by Eva Zeisel, a professional in the field of Ceramic Design—not of the pot-throwing kind, but of the manufacture and mass production of fine-dinnerware kind. She brought knowledge of the processes and the understandings of how production limitations would influence the design of elegant shapes and forms. Her classes were conducted in a lab format, with access to the plaster and modeling shop next door. In a way, this was an extension of our 3-D design class, except that the shapes conformed more closely to free forms and introduced the concept of families of shapes, containers, all varying in size but aesthetically related. Design concepts would be carried out as three-dimensional plaster shapes, using turntables and templates to turn either the forms themselves or to make the tools (molds) from which the final forms would be cast. By the end of the year, using special techniques, we would be making large, very thin plates or shells, which would then be trimmed into complex three-dimensional profiles.[23]

Another professional was Otto Hula, a furniture designer who brought formal drafting disciplines into the curriculum. I had had drafting in high

---

[23] I was pleasantly surprised in February of 2007 to read in the San Diego Union Tribune that the *Centenarian Eva Zeisel* was present for the opening of an exhibit of her work at the Mingei International Museum in Balboa Park, San Diego.

school, but it was foreign to most of the other students who came from liberal arts backgrounds. It was interesting to observe that, with the limited training the student's received, their designs were constrained directly to their ability to draft their shapes. Chairs, tables, arms, and legs all seemed to be very straight, since these were the easiest characteristics to project into three views. The single purpose of orthographic drafting is so that only one design can be built from its views (the one intended). In addition to drafting, he brought us a variety of presentation techniques that would be helpful in a manufacturing or business environment.

It would be one thing to draw a shape correctly in all views; it would be quite another to have it look good. A compound curve in space can be relatively simple, but trying to draw it in three views is difficult. A line represented in two views[24] could look different in each but must have related characteristics in each. A good example would be the path of a baseball slicing foul. Its path is three-dimensional yet very simple, as the physics of gravity, momentum, and drag define vertical and linear factors, while spin imparts aerodynamic side forces that progressively change its lateral motion.

To graphically represent this path in an orthographic drawing, it would be necessary to assure that the physics events occurred at the exact same instances in all views of that path. The difficulty comes with the need to coordinate and maintain the same line character throughout its length; each uniquely foreshortened in its own view.

CURVE IN SPACE

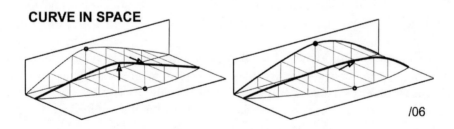

/06

Figures showing how designs incorrectly drawn in two views will show discontinuities as two uncoordinated vector arrows (left), while correctly coordinated views show a single "theme" vector.

---

24   Only two views are needed to define such a detail. There are no options for the third view, as it must follow the first two views. The designer's choice is only to select those two views that best define that detail.

In practice, a concept is usually defined in 3-D space first and then measured and translated accurately into three view drawings. The purpose of these exercises, however, was more to introduce the mechanics of drafting to the student, so that it would be easier to learn later, on the job, or at least to make one able to communicate with a draughtsman in defining a concept.

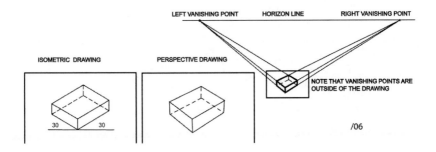

Isometric and perspective: These are the classical methods of drawing objects to make them appear three-dimensional.

There was another method for presenting picture views in drafting: isometric drawing. It was a relatively easy process as the dimensions of the objects were measured the same and presented in a single view, except that the horizontal lengths and widths would be laid out along opposite thirty-degree-angled lines and verticals only measured up or down. Simple shapes could be represented easily in this technique, but it had two problems. First, drawings with all sides drawn at thirty-degree angles would look boring—lacking any excitement. It would have been possible to rotate the view slightly to change the angle, but this would have led to a very tedious process, losing all the advantages of what was once simple. The second problem was that all lines from the same side remained parallel. There was no convergence or perspective that gives a drawing its natural appearance, similar to what the eye sees when looking down a pair of railroad tracks. Most students were familiar with perspective drawing as being a process where a horizon line is drawn first, and vanishing points placed so that each side of a box would appear to converge to its own vanishing point. This is a more natural way of drawing, and looks more like what the eye sees. It is difficult, however, to maintain any accuracy in proportions without having developed personal skills, especially when the vanishing points are off the paper.

As we were going to be Industrial Designers, it would be necessary to develop more accurate drawing skills to represent scaled objects. Hula introduced us to two methods that would do this. Using the classic French's engineering textbook, we first learned of a precise drawing technique called the Frieze Method. This would be used for those occasions where an accurate, near-photographic representation would be demanded.

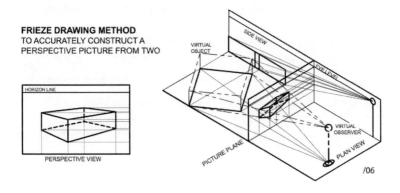

The Frieze drawing method may be used to accurately construct perspective views from two orthographic views.

In this method, a theoretical observer is placed within the orthographic drawing itself, usually within the plan and side views, and at the same scale so that the observer's eye height and distance will be dimensionally accurate, relative to the object that will be drawn. Within each view would then be created a theoretical picture plane shown as a line, edge on. This would represent the paper onto which the drawing would be created. One would then draw construction lines, in both views, from features on the objects, to the position of the eye in each view. In side view, one could then mark the height of where that point should appear on the "as seen" drawing (that point where it intersected the picture plane). Repeating the procedure for that same object point in plan view would then show where (left or right), that point would appear in the horizontal plane.

Completing additional object points and plotting their proper positions on the picture plane would soon provide sufficient drawing points to connect the dots. This could be performed to find all points of the drawing but in practice, only the basic defining points would be needed, and the student could then free style the remaining features in between. In the end, the drawing would look very much like a conventional perspective drawing with lines converging to their vanishing points, even though those points could actually be far-off the paper. Things could appear above or below the horizon line, all depending on the relative eye height. The resulting drawing would likely look very stiff, but it would be more accurate and believable in a presentation.

The second method was more akin to using the artist's natural drawing sense, but incorporated techniques that introduced checks and balances to tweak the drawing in progress. The best way to draw accurately is to draw from life, without using vanishing points or aids as such, however, when the life does not exist, as when an Industrial Designer is trying to create a new product, it is first necessary to define the space or volume in exact overall proportions and then, to construct the elements within. The second method established those overall proportions.

As to the technique, in exercises, we would practice drawing perfect cubes, where all edges look to be equal in length, the corners appear generally vertical,[25] and horizontal lines appear to converge uniformly on both left and right sides, to a horizon line that may or may not appear in the drawing.

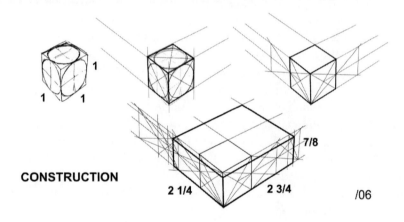

CONSTRUCTION

A construction sequence showing how to reproportion a basic perspective cube into an exactly scaled rectangular prism.

Because each side of the cube would represent a square, a circle could be sketched within each, and it should be tangent at the midpoint of each edge. The visual test would be simple—"does it look right?" If the answer is no, then the response would be to keep making adjustments until the answer is finally yes. We would not be drawing cubes but rather would be building the framework within which we would hang our drawing elements. The cube was our basic

---

25   This technique will even work with (vertical) three-point perspective.

unit of measure. We would now expand or subdivide that cube, as needed, to achieve our desired proportions.

We would select one side of the cube already drawn and construct diagonal lines between the opposing corners. At the intersection of these diagonals, a new construction line would be drawn in the direction of the vanishing point on that side as well as extending the upper and lower edges toward the same vanishing point. Two new diagonals would then be drawn, so that they crossed at the midpoint of the back edge, nicely defined by what would become the midpoint vertical. A new vertical line could then be drawn between where these new diagonals now intersected the upper and lower extended perspective lines. This vertical edge now defined a doubling of that side's length creating a rectangle of 2:1 proportions.

The beauty of the process was that it would be insensitive to the severity of the viewing angle or the artist's own personal sense of perspective. This routine would then be repeated as many times as was necessary to achieve the proportional length needed to frame the drawing. This would then be repeated for the other side for the width and then for the vertical, if that were necessary.

Logically, the next question would be, "How would you define a fraction of the cube?" The answer would be the same, except that instead of doubling each side, verticals could be drawn at the cube diagonal intersections to halve them and new diagonals constructed to quarter the halves, etc.

The perfect volume in actual practice would only be as good as our original approximation of the cube. Perspective parallel lines will not always look exactly right, and small amounts of tweaking will still have to be done until they do look right. Until these skills are developed, one will find that several adjustments will have to be made before one is satisfied. As we would find out, this technique would be very handy on those occasions where one just wanted to clean up a rough sketch before tracing over it to make a hard line drawing for a formal presentation. A freehand sketch always yielded the freshest style we could call on, and this technique retained most of that freshness.

In an overview of all we were taught, repetitive practice and observation were the main training mechanisms. It would be our choice to decide which drawing techniques were best to use for the results we wanted. As we received assignments from other product design classes, we would use those opportunities to apply and develop these drawing skills.

There was another class called aesthetics conducted by William Burger, which strangely was fit into the curriculum. It was basically a philosophy class, keyed to art and design. It seemed an odd subject originally, but in hindsight, it turned out to be very appropriate. Most notable were the discussions on Plato and his comparisons of things in the real world to concepts of abstractions that represented the ideal (in lieu of the real/in life). It brought with it a new way of looking at things, to search out the essence of an object, as detached from its physical embodiment. We would find later, while trying to create things that do not exist, that this could be a vehicle for establishing the essence of what we wanted to create. These effects would tie in later, when Kostellow taught us empathic sketching.

As for automobile design, which was why I came to Pratt, there was no formal class. Those interested could attend a voluntary, no credit after-hours class, held once each week. There were less than a dozen students from the combined sophomore, junior and senior years in attendance. Initially, they were conducted by Industrial Designer, Richard Arbib, who at the time was having black and white concept car sketches appearing in a monthly publication. Arbib would give us automobile design assignments and critique the drawings as we submitted them. It culminated with our class, putting together an exhibition of the best of these studies for a New York auto show. There were two juniors with strong credentials in that class, Elia Russinoff and Ken Genest. Russ was very quiet but highly respected and accepted by his classmates as the best prospect for GM Styling. Before coming to Pratt, Russ had won first prize in the Fisher Body Craftsman's Guild[26] model car competition, and had developed unexcelled drawing skills in the standard automotive drawing medium of Prisma color pencil on Canson Mi-Teintes colored paper. Ken was very good and respected also, but Russ was considered the Master.

There was no clear distinction between the Industrial Design sophomore and junior years, as they just seemed to blur together. I would have a few strong classes and a few weak ones, not really standing out in any way. Across those two years, however, two classes that spanned both years would stand out in their impact. They were Kostellow's "drawing" classes, by other names, and a series of 3-D sculpture classes conducted by Rowena Reed, a.k.a. Mrs. Kostellow.

Kostellow took us into the mechanics of drawing as it was taught by the old masters. He went into methods used for still life, portraits, and landscapes. He broke down the structure of these techniques into *what the eye would see* and how it could be controlled, and led as the artist wished. A line of continuation was an implied line that connected separate aligned lines, which were not otherwise related. A line in one part of a drawing would lead the eye to bridge

---

[26] The same model building competition that I had twice started but never completed, when I was in high school.

to any other feature in alignment. Once bridged, the eye would follow a path that could curve back upon itself, or bridge to other features. Such an implied line would be valuable because it could create other effects, such as building a framework for the implication of space.

The line could itself create a sense of direction. The eye falling on a line would be drawn to its dominant end or feature, then move on to the next attracting or leading feature. He used simple graphic symbols to demonstrate this, similar to a series of playing cards set in space. Line elements were drawn about, and through the cards, entirely changing their apparent relationships without changing the cards or the lines themselves. Depending on how the cards overlapped, the line could be made to appear to move through space quite differently.

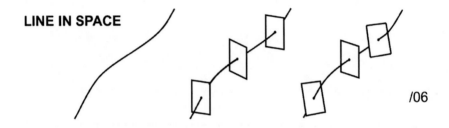

LINE IN SPACE

/06

A construction showing how a line can be changed in effect by adding "implied" spatial relationships to it.

In a painting, these lines needed not to be literal but could be implied by a juxtaposition of arms, legs, gestures, and other features to align themselves into a theme. Other elements like color, light value, and texture could be used to link and build other graphic structures. For example, accents of the same strong color repeated across the longest dimensions of the painting would create a tension linking the elements and exaggerating the sense of distance between them. Light and dark zones[27] in a painting could overlay an entirely different jigsaw structure to knit the composition together. Another way that space could be implied was to use subject matter such as the sun, moon, and

---

[27]   Light and dark would not represent the color tones of objects in the painting but rather whole zones of light and shade that fall across and mix independent of theme and form, having absolutely no relationship to edge or object features of the drawing beneath.

earth, in a context of tying several graphic elements together by use of logic. The painting could be comprised of all these multiple and independent graphic techniques, and work together to define a powerful foundation structure. The creation and definition of space would be the most important tool an industrial designer could have in his toolbox, and all exercises were sharpened to develop this sensitivity into a working skill.

Addressing the problem of knowing when a composition was finished, Kostellow provided a demonstration. It also exposed bad design or composition. Using a student's drawing as an example, he held his hand over a part of the composition, hiding a detail and asked the class if anything was missing. The answer obviously was no or he would not have asked the question. If the answer was no, it meant that the detail was not contributing to the composition and was unnecessary. If the answer was yes, then it meant it was critical to maintaining the balance. This would have to be true for all elements of a drawing, at which point it could be said that the drawing was finished. We would find ourselves, afterward, walking down the street, with our thumb in front of one eye, looking at building details and finding bad architecture all over.[28]

Another demonstration was performed to show why a particular drawing could appear very boring. Again, using a student's work, he placed a sheet of vellum over a bent elbow detail and traced out the boomerang shape of the arm. He then promptly placed the tracing over a dozen other details in the drawing, showing that even if it had to be rotated, all the other features exhibited the same general shape, size, and angle of the boomerang tracing. There is apparently a natural lazy trait in artists to repeat the same forms or strokes. It became a warning to be on the alert for this potential failing.

There was another drawing variation for the representation of space, in which Kostellow tried to instruct us. It was very difficult in that throughout his years with us, he claimed that none of us had ever mastered it. It was a methodology for perspective drawing. We were to understand that each artist had a personal (sense of) perspective that was unique and what he tried to teach was a different way of seeing our space, then representing it on paper.

---

[28] This is a very *fun* exercise to perform when finding a bad piece of art, seeing how everything is totally unrelated to everything else in the composition.

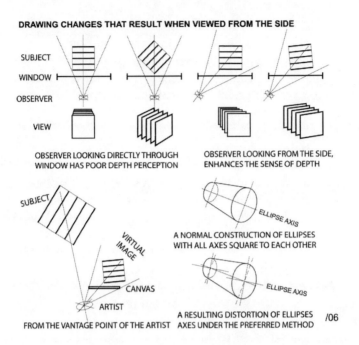

Constructions showing how to better represent space in perspective drawings.

He repeated that all the great masters used it in their paintings but that it would be most noticeable in their architectural landscapes, where the artifacts of the process would be more readily visible. As he explained it, in order to show depth, the painting would be considered to be a "window into another world."[29] In order to see space between objects, one would not choose to stand in front of the window and look directly out because any object in the foreground would automatically obstruct the view of objects behind it. In order to see the space behind, the artist had to step to the side and look through from that side.

To this day, the methodology defies analysis. It mostly seems to work for an artist when drawing from life. In painting, a portrait or a still life, the artist would stand to the side of his easel and draw it from that side. If viewed from

---

[29] While Kostellow referred to it as a window, thinking of it as a mirror may be easier to comprehend, since virtual images are abstract concepts and the mind may find them easier to accept. One may readily be able to sense these spatial relationships, when they are viewed within the expanding space behind.

the artist's vantage, to look correct, the elements would take on a particular distortion, as if truly drawn from the side. We have all seen how eyes in a portrait will follow us as we move from side to side. This means that it can be observed from any angle, but it will still be seen from the artist's vantage. An interesting exercise would be to look at old masters paintings and try to determine which side of the easel they were painted from.

Not surprisingly, it became apparent that Kostellow himself was very skilled and capable on the subject. In his work, he had developed other methodologies, and now he would present us with yet another drawing technique, which would become a cornerstone for Industrial Designers, the empathic sketch. This was a methodology, he advocated for capturing the essence of an idea only, not for defining it. The media used was Conte crayon (usually black, square in section and about the size of a cigarette) on 18 x 24 inch (blank) newsprint paper. Sheets would be stacked and clipped to a drawing board many layers deep, so as to provide a soft-padded surface to draw on. The crayon would be held between the thumb and two fingers, and could be used to lay down various lines on the paper depending on how it was held. A broad line could be created by a crossways stroke along one flat side, or conversely, a crisp line by drawing the crayon, knifelike, along one edge. The resulting lines would usually favor one edge over the other, and vary in intensity or boldness throughout their lengths.

The key factor was that these variations could impart particular emotions as a by-product of the strokes, creating the *empathy* in the empathic sketch. A skilled artist, in a series of strokes, each with its encoded data stream, could convey meanings far beyond the stroke itself. The first exercises were to develop a sense, or relationship between the stroke and the effect desired.

To create an empathic sketch, it was first necessary to identify the feeling or emotion that was desired before the stroke. We were required to visualize or personify particular qualities such as steel, envisioning a component made of steel, placed under tremendous pressures, causing it to bend, flex or yield—all these thoughts evoked while placing the stroke, giving it meaning.

After dozens of strokes, a new theme would be selected, moving on to glass, wood, silver, gold, etc. Later, we would experiment with feelings of elegance, power, grace, etc. Surprisingly, while at first it was difficult to achieve specific effects, one could readily see that the different line sets were at least different in character from each other, so at least something was happening.

As the class became more familiar with the objectives, we would attempt other materials. For glass, the senses would try to impart forms or line characteristics that would be glassy in nature, reflecting on the forms glass takes under blowing pressures or sagging, showing characteristics of the nearly molten materials. The same process was applied for steel subjects, envisioning different stresses and pressure loads, trying to imagine deformations or other characteristics that would be appropriate for its manufacture. The exercises continued for other materials, emoting characteristics unique for each.

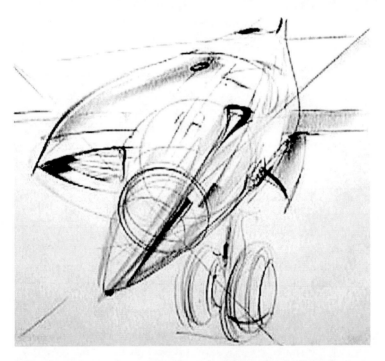

A Conte crayon on newsprint paper—*empathic sketch* of a turbo-prop engine nacelle drawn to capture the essence of the nacelle form.

The drawings would not look labored because it only took a second to create any line. Line after line would be put to paper until the sheet was filled up. Then it would be ripped off, and the next sheet started. Looking at the lines, we could see they were directional, in that the lines did not just sit there; but if the eye fell on one, it would be "picked up" and led to another point. Most lines would be observed to have a crisp outer edge and a soft inner side, almost creating the effect of a surface, rolling out of sight over the edge. Surprisingly, sometimes a crisp inner edge feathering to an outer edge could imply a soft smooth rolling surface, not of the line itself but rather to the clean paper inside of that edge, almost as if it were a defining shadow. This meant that the character was encoded and created by the line, independent of what it was representing.

The exercises were intended to develop an automatic response to deposit conditioned line character on demand. Practicing the strokes by the hundreds, if not thousands, was a prerequisite for applying them in earnest. We would sketch shapes until the material selection was obvious to an outside observer. We would carry these exercises into our model-making classes where we would try to convert our elegant shapes into white plaster.

In our lab classes, we learned how to turn plaster shapes, and this gave us our first opportunity to see what the shapes we had been developing for Kostellow really looked like. There were large two-foot diameter cast iron turntables in the model shop onto which we would build up an armature of dry plaster scraps held together with fresh splashed plaster. For a given design, we would cut a template to one side of our shape. It would be trimmed to the outside of the profile and nailed to a plywood backing to stiffen it. We then clamped the template to a vertical post outside the turntable and adjusted it until it was just inside of the final form, as measured from a vertical centerline. The armature we had built up would be fixed to the turntable but would remain entirely inside of the template as we turned the table by hand. We then mixed a batch of hydrocal (industrial plaster) by filling a large bowl with water, surprisingly almost to the quantity of plaster we needed. Then dry plaster, much like cooking flower, would be sifted over the water, kneading and breaking up any lumps, to sink to the bottom until it filled up to the level of water, ending as small islands scattered across the surface. We would then dip one hand into the batch and start working it, blending it to a uniform consistency.

The plaster had strange properties. We had to wait for it to start setting before we could use it and then we would have only a few minutes to complete the application before it solidified. When applied to the armature, it would have sufficient stiffness to hold its shape. By stirring the mix, we would speed the process to start it setting, but as long as we were stirring, it would not set. If it was left alone and started to set, we could start stirring it to restore it to a pliable state, but of course when we stopped, it would return to set with a vengeance. Needless to say, there was an eager period waiting to start applying the plaster. If we started too soon, it would just run off.

Pausing to observe the batch after occasional stirrings, we would see the shiny wet surface, then, in one moment, it would start to take on a dull matte sheen, meaning it was about to set. It was ready and we had only minutes left with this batch. Reserving one clean hand to turn the table and adjust tools etc., the other hand would dip into the plaster for a small batch and throw, or backhand slap it onto the armature where it would stick. Working very fast, the plaster would be built up, and we could then start turning the turntable under the template. Where the plaster was excessive, the template would cleanly sweep it away, leaving a perfect profile behind where it hit. Additional plaster would be applied to fill in the low spots until the plaster was fully built up to the template. Hopefully, the plaster would not have completely set up before all the holes were filled and the shape was well defined.

By plan, the first turning would have been made slightly inside of the design profile so as to allow space for a second coat. The template would then be reset to the exact (design) diameter and a skim coat of plaster easily applied, filling all remaining holes, and leaving a clean smooth profile. There was one small problem: at some point, a decision had to be made, to stop turning, and there would always be a residual line of plaster, on the template that would remain in contact with the finished shape. The procedure was to leave it alone, as removing the template would dig into the soft-finished surface. Once it was determined that the final plaster coat had set, the turntable would be given a very short turn, no more than a quarter of an inch, and cause the buildup to shear away clean. It would leave only a trace mark on the finished surface, but this could be sanded smooth a few days later, when it was dry.

As to the finished shape—more than likely it would be ugly—nothing at all, like what we had expected, based on the grace and elegance of our template. It was a very important lesson, proving that it was necessary to retune our senses, to figure out what the shapes were really going to do in 3-D space. It would be a lesson repeated often as we learned how to adjust and correct to compensate.

As to the empathic sketch, the fault was not in the drawing because it faithfully created the feeling we wanted to have in the finished design. It became necessary to develop the skills to nurture a design until it delivered that feeling. The sketch was the purest abstract definition, identifying our objective, but in no way telling us how to achieve it.

There was another aspect related to empathic sketching that Kostellow stressed. It was in the way that designers should approach the design process. It was not taught as a subject, but rather introduced as concurrent to any other instruction we might receive. It was the concept of an abstract equivalent. He repeated it often, in the sense that we were not to think of design elements as physical things we could put our hands on, but as abstractions, to simplify and reduce an element to its absolute essence. By doing so, we could resolve problems abstractly and then seek numerous mechanisms to deliver the resolution. Doing it the other way, we would find a solution but not really understand the reason for doing it that way. It was on this track that I recognized the relationship to our Aesthetics class. This approach offered a tremendous flexibility for creative solutions. This was, perhaps, the "silver bullet" for Industrial Designers.

Another aspect that must be addressed was Kostellow's class-side manner. As a first cut, John Houseman's portrayal of professor Kingsfield in *The Paper Chase* would almost bring us there. He could be a little rough—enough so that there would always be a touch of fear in his classes. We found that if a student responded poorly in one of his assignments, Kostellow would heap verbal abuse upon the poor soul and totally rip them apart, using them as examples for what not to do. It would be typical to enter his class in a high state of anxiety, hoping you would not be the one selected for sacrifice.

He was very demanding in that everyone had to conform to his standard, accepting his philosophy that industrial design would be a way of life, not an occupation that could be turned on and off from 8 and 5. He would constantly remind us of just how bad our class was, comparing us again and again to the veterans (of WWII) who had just graduated and were so dedicated. He constantly challenged us to raise ourselves to those levels.

His methodology for conducting classes was to issue assignments, usually for the preparation a dozen or so 18" x 24" Conte crayon sketch studies. These would be relatively loose drawings, focused on the theme of the day. Each student would pin his or her work up anywhere along one long wall, picking either an upper or lower position and forming a single stack, each sheet on top of the next. Their location on that wall would be of their own choice, the better students always up front, closer to Kostellow's usual lecture and starting position. The rest of us would pin them where we felt comfortable, meaning that our review would be not too early or too late in his lecture, to draw unusual attention.

After his opening statements or comments, he would start from the front of the room and progress down the wall, critiquing one by one. He would go from one student's stack to the next in progression, starting with the upper stack. Having completed his comments on the first sheet, he would then give it a sharp downward tug, tearing it free of the corner pins, dropping that sheet to a convenient ledge, and begin his critique of the next sheet and so forth until the stack was completed, then he would move on to the next student.

I always felt traumatized while waiting for him to come to my stack and experienced relief when he only commented on how bad it was. It was not unusual for him to stop during a critique and ask why a student even bothered to continue the course. A common story he related (but always about a different student) was on how he so chastised and embarrassed a student for working so poorly that they would stomp out of class and disappear for several days, only to return after going through a day and night drawing binge, mastering the technique, and returning in triumph. It made one wonder at times if that was why he was so vicious in his critiques.

Except for academic classes, the department had instituted a different process for grading. A procedure was adapted where each student would be allocated a display space, in which they would present all their class projects in any manner they wished. In this way, all their class productions would be visible at one time to all the instructors who would then be able to judge a student's work in context of the whole. Privately, the instructors would gather to review all the work as a single body where they could comment and in turn influence each other's critiques. The process was called judgment and of course, the day became known as "Judgment Day." These reviews were held for both the mid and end-term periods.

As the end of my sophomore year was approaching, I experienced a strange sensation while preparing materials for my judgment display. I was looking at an interiors model I was just completing and then looked at several drawings and other completed models I had made when I was struck by a strange out-of-body experience. I was seeing a common thread or an indescribable pattern of some "other person," unseen, that had created these. I was seeing myself as that third person. It was not a sense of style, but rather a feeling, as if I had entered a room and realized that another person had just been there but left, then, going into another room and finding that I had just missed that same person again. After a while, the feeling became continuous, that I knew the person, but would never see him.

At the end of the school year, Eric and I decided that we should move to a larger apartment for the next semester. I would leave my drawing board and Dazor lamp with him, to hold in New Jersey, and he would search for a new place later that summer. I was confident in his judgment and gave him my OK to deal.

When I returned in September, Eric had found a larger apartment and had moved in. It was another brownstone, as were almost all the other buildings. This time, ours was a large room on the third floor in the front of the building, with two windows overlooking Washington Avenue. We would be taking on an additional roommate, Larry Haji, who was also an ID student from our class, and Larry would take the remaining small room next door, also with its own window out-front.

We still had the inconvenience of a community bathroom for all tenants on the second floor in back. The plumbing was early 1900s with a cast iron tub and a jerry-rigged freestanding shower curtain over it. The commode was operated from overhead, by way of a classic pull-chain.

The back room tenants had two windows, just as Eric and I had the previous years. Eric, Larry, and I had the entire front half of the third floor for ourselves. There was another tenant in the large room in back, whom we never saw, and there was another small-unoccupied room in back used for storage with a single window overlooking back yards of the entire block, each lot partitioned by small fences and further defined by cloths lines and hanging laundry.

When I arrived at the new apartment, Eric had already brought my drawing equipment in and we allocated and set up our own spaces. Larry had the single room, but we would all use the large room as our work area. The rooms were furnished with single beds, some dressers, a lounge chair, and basics-like carpets and curtains. An antiroom had a small washbasin and some cupboard space. We found a place for a coffee maker, but would not try anything more ambitious than that for cooking. We further divvied up the room for drawing boards and work areas because we would be making a lot of models there.

The arrangement was much better than before, being higher up and in front brought us back into the world. It was noisier—much noisier. In addition to the traffic of the busier boulevard, we were near the Washington Avenue subway stop of the Independent Line, which was the loudest noise source. There were ventilation gratings just below our windows and we could hear the constant screeching of steel wheels on steel tracks, every time a train went by and came to a stop. This went on around the clock, but surprisingly, we adjusted to it and it turned out to be no problem at all.

With our accommodations set, we focused on the start of our junior year and were at an elevated state of excitement. We had just passed the halfway point, and while our grades were not that great, we at least knew we could hold together long enough to finish. With the comfort of the two years behind us, we could settle down to an easier pace, with the classes taking on a slightly different character and tempo. We were finished with Koli's 2-D class and Rigby's 3-D class was replaced by Rowena Reed's Sculpture class, which was also in a lab format. The product design classes would be more demanding and would involve a lot more model making. Richard Arbib no longer conducted the automobile design classes. They would be taken over by Russinoff and Genest, who now, as seniors, were in their homestretch for going to General Motors.

Just as Kostellow was to deliver the heart of the drawing classes, his wife Rowena would do the same for 3-D through her sculpture class. Her classes would incorporate more free form in their modeling than they would the abstract solids of Rigby's classes. The media was different also, in that rather than starting from basic geometric shapes and removing material to achieve effects, we would be working in clay[30] and mainly add material to build up the forms. Previously, our instructors had us structure our compositions with dominant, subdominant, and subordinate elements. Under Rowena, the procedure was to first develop a theme by the creation of a miniature space sketch. This would be

---

[30] The clay used here was not of the type that was fired to make ceramic shapes, but rather, it was permanently pliable but rigid enough to be scraped and smoothed. Its pliability could be improved by kneading it between the thumb and forefinger. We were told this plasticine was identical to that used in the automotive styling studios.

an approximation of the simpler elements in the composition and their general relationships to each other. The reason for being small was to discourage any attempt to get into too much detail—the size would not allow it.

The sketch would then be placed on top of a small turntable. With the model centered, the table would be rotated slowly so that the model could be viewed from a constantly changing vantage point. The first rule or lesson we learned was that it would not be viewed from a front, back, or side because there were no sides. There would be no differentiation between views because all the elements really existed in true space. Features would be free to develop and recede, relative to each other—not as a function of any particular view.[31]

In orthographic drawing, we found that lines in two views had to be coordinated to properly represent the single line in space. Working in 3-D, this was no longer a problem as its shape could be seen and formed directly. By rotating a composition on the turntable, any kinks or irregularities in a line would clearly jump out. Studying the space sketch further, all the motions and forces could be seen in total. Imbalances in some elements could be counterposed by other singular or multiple elements. The aggregate of elements would constitute the theme of the space sketch. Rotation of the sketch on a turntable caused a modulation of those elements, almost like a dance, causing new and interesting dynamics to be revealed at an art tempo.

The turntable would also reveal flat spots or dead zones where there was a discontinuity in pace or of interesting events. That would suggest that adjustments or changes could be made in the sketch before progressing to a larger or final construction. As a rule, no design was considered complete until all of its elements were in place. Conversely, when all were in place and it was finished, no additional elements could be added without upsetting the resolution. In practice, if they were simple enough, several space sketches could be developed before the selection of a theme to proceed on.

The next step would be to go to a full-scale rough, to resolve the finer details. With an idea of what the mass distributions would be, an armature for the clay build-up could be made, and that would give a first hint of the true design mass. Sometimes with the change in scale, things would look different and small design adjustments would appear to be in order. Starting the buildup, small pea-sized pinches of clay would be kneaded between the thumb and forefinger to soften them, and in one motion, applied to a selected spot, so as to slowly build up the surface. Once cooled to room temperature, the buildup could be scraped and shaved into tooled surfaces. The ideal tool turned out to be a pencil-sized

---

[31]   An exception might be in the sense of the vertical, since a sculpture could elect to acknowledge a gravity vector.

steel instrument with sharp spade like, double-edge blades at each end. The edge on one side was smooth and bent slightly at the tip, while the other edge was the same, except serrated with fine teeth. The toothier edges left the best surfaces, since they planed through irregularities cleanly, without skipping or sliding, and left a fine furrowed surface behind. This toothed surface also left a clean visual trace of implied flows that the eye would follow, just as it was lead by line strokes in graphics.

An eye following such a surface would be attracted to and led in the same direction as the surface was created. This could become a style in itself, if the entire surface were tooled to this texture. Our basic objective in these sculpture exercises, however, was to consider the arrangement of the shapes rather than the dynamics of the surfaces. This is actually a danger, frequently exposed in failed art forms, where the art is entirely in the surface alone. The true objective of a good resolution would be to create and reveal the mass forms that exist within. Done properly, none of the excitement of surface interplay need be lost.

When done boldly, the application of clay by thumb alone can result in a very powerful style. A sculpture built up entirely in this manner will have a strong texture of elongated hollows created by crisp stroke edges. Because of the way it is deposited, each stroke will have a pronounced direction and flow, and the surface will be composed of hundreds of strokes. When the form remains visible within the texture, the sculpture may be considered complete. In one technique, molds are taken from the clay sculpture, and the final art piece is cast in bronze. Alberto Giacometti's sculptures are perhaps the best examples of this style in modern art.

This could have been the end of this particular lab session, if a piece of art was our objective, but in our case as students, we would take our scraping tool and plane down the surfaces, agonizing over the loss of their dynamic excitement. As the surfaces became rendered smoothly, clays sometimes had to be added or removed in response to unexpected changes. Bulges and hollows would appear where none existed before. The nice sense of flow the eye saw before now seems to have disappeared, and the surfaces seem to have lost their purpose.

At this stage, Ms Reed, using a knifepoint to communicate, would scribe lines on the surfaces, to point out visual flows or accent features. This was not in a destructive sense, since they could be easily burnished away, but they would become surface features that the eye could follow. They would show the flow path the eye would take on that particular surface, or they would indicate the desired path that the eye should take, meaning that we had to rework that surface to achieve that effect. Being a work in progress, this communication method was most direct because it was tailored to each student's unique sculpture. Trial, error, and critique would in time bring each student's work to near completion.

As the sculptures began to approach solutions, plastic slicks would then be used to burnish away all tool marks, leaving a smooth, shiny surface. The sculptures could be considered finished at this point, but they were really of no further use, since it was only the exercise that mattered.

After struggling through all the mechanics of developing forms in clay, and feeling them comfortably under our belts, we were then introduced to, perhaps, the most important concept of sculpture in 3-D space. The surprising thing was that we had no idea that this other concept existed, or even that something in our previous training was missing. After it was introduced, as artists, we would never see a sculpture again with the "old eye." That concept was of *negative space,* and it would turn out to be one of the artist's most powerful tools.

Just as we were taught to see form inside of a mass, we were to learn that as sculptures increased in their complexity, and masses were being played one against the other, a condition was being created where vacant spaces began to exist between those masses, and they became sculptural elements in themselves. As it became more obvious, all the painstaking work we had put into developing the masses within, they could be equaled or even overwhelmed by the impact of the negative spaces created between them. As material was added or removed, lines of visual flow became complemented or opposed by flows of negative spaces. The resolution and interplay of these relationships had an enormous impact, and for the first time we understood what sculpture really was.

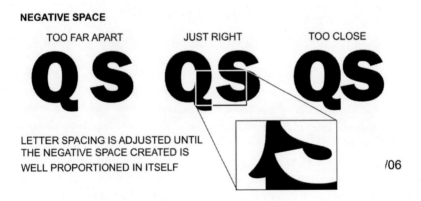

NEGATIVE SPACE

TOO FAR APART   JUST RIGHT   TOO CLOSE

LETTER SPACING IS ADJUSTED UNTIL
THE NEGATIVE SPACE CREATED IS
WELL PROPORTIONED IN ITSELF   /06

Another way of visualizing negative space is to consider its 2-D equivalent. Looking carefully at a type font as found in a line of text, especially in a large bold style, one may see the abstract letters only, which give meaning as words, or one may look only at the spaces between those letters and see that they create other abstract shapes. In the latter case, one would be observing negative 2-D spaces. The test of a good font is to see how well each letter works next any other letter in that same font (as it would appear in a body of text). Another example would be, when one is placing large type, like stick on letters, one letter at a time. The typesetter will play with the spacing between each pair of letters until they look just right. This would be when the negative spaces and letter shapes have just the right balance between them.[32]

As applied to sculpture, a form or group of forms may contain dynamic elements, which in themselves are unbalanced, but when combined with other imbalances, are offset so as to bring the whole into a balanced state. A common theme found in many sculptures is the use a human or other figure in a near horizontal "flying through the air" attitude, but where the art is cantilevered and supported entirely from one end. Obviously one knows that the entire weight of the sculpture is not balanced over that single attachment, but when the eye views it, a usually slight upward inclination implies a tremendous flying force, sufficient to make it appear natural and not in need of any counterbalancing force. This would be a good example of how implied dynamics can become part of a sculpture. Negative spaces can contribute strong driving forces to help create these effects. In changing from the single dominant mass of a simple sculpture, negative spaces have changed from being the garments adorning a sculpture to where they can become the sub or even dominant elements of the sculpture. Some of the best examples of negative space in sculpture will be found in the works of Henry Moore.

The same design exercises that were performed earlier with simple forms have now become compounded, as the act of adding or removing real material from a piece has also impacted the negative space surrounding it. The surprise is that while the lay public may not be consciously aware of negative space, their subconscious is and will respond to it.

In the winter of my junior year, I had my first encounter with the dreaded Kostellow wrath. It was during a critique. It was not really that severe, but it was after I had just become comfortable with the knowledge that, one way or another, I would survive another year—then it happened. The class had been given an assignment to bring in a series of Conte crayon sketches, on real life

---

[32] A simple 3-D exercise to demonstrate this, while waiting for dinner, is to play with a place setting of knife, fork and spoon; to position them next each other, trying to find their most pleasing arrangement as a group, seeing how the space between the edges looks either better or worse.

city or street scenes. On Sunday, the day before the assignment was due, I went to the vacant back room of our brownstone and made a series of sketches from the window overlooking the checker-board-fenced yards and spreads of hanging laundry. That Monday I posted my stack of sketches along with the rest of the class, and I was properly apprehensive. From start to finish, Kostellow was extremely dissatisfied with everything he saw, even from his regular top students. When he completed my stack, which was the usual bad, he added that I should not have done all the sketches from the same spot, "lazy" being one of the words I remembered "but go out and explore other scenes."

At the end of the critiques, he repeated his extreme dissatisfaction with the class and reassigned us to do it all over again. He gave us two weeks. I thought about it a great deal. In fact, I had thought about it enough so that it was again another Sunday, and the assignment was again due the next day. So I gathered my drawing pads and crayons and trudged back to the same rear window to repeat the same sketches. The only thing that was different this time was that a light snow had fallen and the scene looked somewhat fresher. I did my sketches again and had a difficult time sleeping that night, totally dreading what would surely be a "bloodbath" the next day.

Before start of class, I picked a spot, a little short of midfield sort of, like being offered a choice of where the slaughter would be, and then pinned them low and out of the way. When Kostellow arrived, he passed on the lecture and began his critiques immediately, starting directly and working his way from right to left. He seemed to be in a better mood, yet when he came to mine, I was still dreading what his reaction would be when he recognized I did exactly what he told me not to do. He paused and lifted the corner of the page, adjusting his glasses and read aloud, ". . . James." A long pause and then slowly said, "these are very good." He went on to ask the class what it was that made them good, and finally answered his own question, that the line quality exhibited a sensitivity to the subject. This apparently was an important quality in a designer, the ability to be responsive to the subject. My moment of glory was short lived, however, as he would often chide me when critiquing my work with comments like, "I don't see that sensitivity I once saw in your work." I basically had blended back in to the rest of the class.

On the good side and at about this same time, our automobile design classes were moving along. Russ and Ken were doing well, having taken over the classes from Arbib. Through both years, so far, our main activity had been developing the drawing skills we would need to get jobs in the automotive industry. Under Arbib, we were into watercolors, which yielded spectacular results when done by skilled hands, but at our level, Prisma color pencil and brushed-white tempera for accents were more appropriate. Russ and Ken were good teachers in this technique.

In this drawing style, the basic color of the paper (Canson Mi-Teintes) created a general colorcast and color-coordinated pencils would be used to bring out highlights, shadows, and reflections. Shapes would be "ghosted" in place, and crisp sharp lines added to cause features to jump out in stark contrast. The true skill turned out to be where the pencil shading was applied. Color tones would be laid in and feather out to nothing within the body of the car, i.e., into the pure color of the paper, needing only a minimum of pencil strokes. A beginner would tend to use the pencil too long, allowing it to get dull (because it would cover the surface faster). This, however, would leave a pronounced rubbing effect, where the grain of the paper became prominent. The true craftsman always worked with a sharp pencil, requiring more strokes, but this gave more control and a finer resolution.

The resulting "magic" was that while the greatest portion of the car's surface had absolutely no pencil strokes, the car appeared to take on a high-gloss-painted look of the paper color. One could look at the same bare paper on the car, and in the untouched paper in the background and declare they were two different colors. With only a few bold lines in a foreign color on the far side of the car, it could be made to appear illuminated by another light source from behind, like the moon or something else, and it would create a special effect, appearing to lift the car off the paper.

The next step in the drawing would be to add reflections and highlights. It turned out that they didn't need to be studied; the application of arbitrarily stretched, elongated, packed, and distorted shapes literally created an appearance of a highly "waxed" lacquer surface. These reflections were followed by numerous pure white tempera "firefly" dots and dashes, teasing of glint reflections of the sun, spotlights or other mysterious sources. The true surprise was that all these spontaneously drawn strokes were symbolic only. Apparently, the eye was satisfied in seeing the attributes of a reflective surface to determine it was in fact a reflective surface.

Sometimes the drawings were done on black Mi-Teintes because it yielded more dramatic reflections and highlights, but this was at the cost of losing the color benefits. Having Russ's drawings available to actually see it work was very helpful. One could readily see that the drawings with the fewest line strokes were the most effective.

In these classes, I experimented with several concepts, one of which was a panoramic drawing of a car. I used the Frieze method but applied it as if it had a curved picture plane. It ended up with three vanishing points, all on the same horizon line. Plotting the coordinates into the view made it look like a fat bellied mackerel, but when the drawing was bent and viewed from its center of curvature, it straightened right out and looked three-dimensional.

Our class continued to refine its drawing skills. As a junior, I was trying to learn all I could while Russ and Ken were still with us. The other seniors were working in earnest to complete their portfolios by the end of the class year. Russ, and probably Ken had a lock on getting jobs with GM, but the others would have to work hard and only hope. The weekly meetings under their leadership did help in another way. It served as a bridge to establish a common bond, breaking the usual class-year barriers and creating a sense of brotherhood for those of us hoping to go on to General Motors to design cars.

There was another strange separation that existed in the department. A division existed between the automobile design students and the pure art or design students. To be proficient in automotive design, a highly developed skill was required to render (create drawings) in a very tight style, while on the pure art side the driving force was to be able to sketch in a rapid loose style. We had our own self-classification system where we considered ourselves to be either renderers or sketchers. I knew I was a renderer. Of the two classifications, rendering was considered to be the lower class of the two. The trade magazine *Industrial Design* routinely ignored automotive design as a profession, except perhaps if they were Raymond Lowey's Studebakers. The 1953 Studebaker did make the industrial design highlights with an innovation that would go unnoticed today, by the addition of a concavity: a negatively shaped indent in each side panel. The design convention of the day was to pile convexity on top of convexity like a wedding cake. In that day also, it was a nice coincidence that style and design were just coming into the general public's awareness, as we were entering the ground floor of the trade.[33] Make no mistake about it; those of us that were looking to go into automobile design were considered to be no more that just "prostitutes," that we would sell our design principals to become captive corporate designers. This, however, was exactly what we wanted.

Coming to the close of the junior year, Eric and I had completed our academic exams and had to work through the night several times to complete our project displays for Judgment. We finally felt relief when we recognized there was no time left to do any more, and we just had to go with what we had.

Judgment Day came—and passed. We would know our fates later but we felt we did okay and knew we could finally relax. We paused, while knocking down our displays, to casually talk and think about packing it in for the summer. While we were in this relaxed state, in the now near vacant lab classroom, we

---

[33] Shopping centers were just beginning to show a style consciousness. Home living rooms no longer had lace curtains and doilies on sofas. Design was just beginning to be featured at some of the more advanced stores and the new shopping malls.

were aware of the anxieties the seniors were experiencing. We understood that several recruiters from industry were around, and we could see the tension building among the seniors.

The summation of their four years at Pratt was now in their portfolios, and for some of them their future was now. We had heard that there were some GM people in, looking for design prospects. They apparently were in Kostellow's office, and the seniors were being called in one by one. We knew that Russ and Ken had received offers, but they apparently were still interviewing. As seniors kept coming out from their interviews, we would get more bits of information on what was going on.

The afternoon wore on, and it was becoming apparent that GM was here for a "pretty big buy." They also had a sizeable product development group in Frigidair,[34] which designed refrigerators, washers, driers and other appliances as well. These products were actually more in line with what the "bread-and-butter" Industrial Design course at Pratt was tailored for, and we saw several non-automotive students also being interviewing and apparently receiving job offers.

By late afternoon, we noted a real slow down in activity and got serious about wrapping things up and getting something to eat before packing up to go home. Just about then, I saw Vic Canzani, who was one of my favorite instructors, come into the lab from the far door, then after only a few steps he shouted, "James . . . You're going to Detroit . . . Get your portfolio and take it to Kostellow's office." Not fully understanding what was going on, I gathered my folder of artwork and proceeded to his office. Being invited in, I found Kostellow, Bill Mitchell (Harley Earl's right hand man) and Tom Christiansen (GM Styling's Administrator). All were smiling, and after a few pleasantries I showed them some of my drawings including some wild concepts, to which Bill Mitchell commented, "Spooky"—which was considered flattering. I held up my curved drawing, giving each a chance to stand at the center to see it right. I was able to figure out that I would be going as a summer student and that it was a "done deal" before I had even entered the office.

Then I was almost "floored," when from out of a clear blue sky, Kostellow said to the GM people, "I give you my personal guarantee." I floated out of the office thinking of little else except that I would be working for GM that summer—for real—and I would have to change what few insignificant plans I had already made. Before leaving, I got Russinoff's telephone number and address, since he lived in Detroit and became the logical coordinator. With our

---

[34] Frigidair, at that time, was a GM Division and had significant exhibits in the GM Motoramas, featuring "The Kitchen of Tomorrow." Kostellow and Rowena had major involvements in these shows, all under their contracts with GM.

contacts finalized, we separated to go our own ways; we would all meet in Detroit to start work on June 14, 1954. All in all, there were about a dozen students going to Detroit, a full quarter of the senior class, and I as the summer student.

The week before we were to report, I received a letter from Russ advising me that several of the guys were booking themselves into the Fisher YMCA on Grand River and West Grand Boulevard, about a mile west of the GM complex. He suggested that I also check in there. They figured they would base there for the week or so until they found permanent apartments and I could likely room with some of them through the summer. Russ said he would come by to see us there before we reported. It sounded like a good plan so I called to make reservations. I finished the few things I had to do in Jamestown and arranged to have Herb drive me to Detroit that next weekend.

The Saturday drive from Jamestown to Cleveland was familiar since we had done it dozens of times before, but it took on a strange and exciting feel as we continued on past Cleveland, never having been that far west before. The Ohio Turnpike had not yet been completed, so our route took us through many small communities along the lakeside highway. At Toledo, we took a distinct turn northward, and it reminded me of my first trip to New York, except that the traffic was not so heavy and the surroundings had a different industrial character to them. I watched for telltale names on buildings to assure myself we were really going to Detroit. We finally entered the Detroit network of streets and radial boulevards, Grand River apparently being the main northwesterly drag out of the downtown hub. A series of east-west-mile-named roads marked the progressive northern march out of town. West Grand Boulevard was the four-mile east-west marker, above the downtown hub.

Ford Country was to the southwest, in the Dearborn area and Chrysler to the northeast, along Grosse Pointe Shores off Lake St. Clair and the Detroit River. GM generally was to the north, headquartered in the fifteen-story GM Building on West Grand Boulevard, just west of Woodward Avenue, which was the main north-south corridor. We understood that GM had started building a new technical center on Twelve-Mile Road, but it would not be complete for yet a few more years. On this day, we proceeded up Grand River Boulevard until we reached the "Y" where I signed in and dropped off my things. We had lunch, and then I saw Herb and Mary off, as they returned to Cleveland, and I went back to the "Y" to see if any of the others had arrived.

By Sunday afternoon, a few of the guys had shown up and we called Russ. He said he would drop by that evening, pick us up, and show us the area. He arrived as it was just starting to get dark. We got into his car and rode down West Grand Boulevard to the GM complex, which spread across open public streets. The

GM Building was comprised of four attached fifteen-story towers and couldn't be missed because it had "GENERAL MOTORS" blazed across the top in giant red neon lights. The entire ground level was an automobile showroom with giant floor-to-ceiling windows, displaying the entire GM automotive product line, all of it open to the public. Across the street was another and taller skyscraper, the Fisher Building, a twenty-eight-story office complex of a grand style. At this time of night, it was all lit up and was very impressive. Russ then drove us around to the back, on to Milwaukee Boulevard; to a pair of common looking brick buildings that Russ said contained the GM Styling and Research Laboratories on the upper floors. This was where we would report the next morning. I was overwhelmed, much as I felt when I saw my first major league baseball park. Russ returned us to the "Y" and my thoughts were only of tomorrow.

Left, The author and Eric reenact a Kostellow Color Lecture for the camera. *Right,* Larry and Eric taking a work break in our brownstone apartment.

A mural study prepared for Robert Koli's 2D Class. Charcoal on paper media with the objective of inter-lacing light and dark patterns to knit the composition together.

A tempera and Prismacolor pencil rendering on Canson Mi-Teintes paper, prepared for the automobile design class.

A double-bubble car concept prepared for the same automobile design class, 1953.

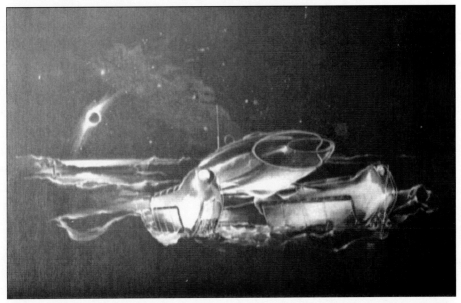

A Prismacolor pencil on black paper study for a lunar roving vehicle shown as if seen during a total lunar eclipse.

4   GM Styling

Daylight finally arrived, and I got up to start the day. I shaved, showered, dressed, and went outside to meet the others as planned. Since this was an important occasion, I had borrowed one of my father's ties and was able to put it on somehow. I didn't do a very good job of it, but the guys were nice enough to show me how and retied for me it. The tie had a painted outdoor sports theme of a pair of trout jumping out of a stream. The guys must have liked it because they were all smiles. We then hopped on to a local trolley, which took us to the GM complex where we got off and walked to the buildings in back. In the lobby, we were directed to take the elevator to the seventh floor. Stepping off the elevator, the receptionist sent us to personnel where we were processed and then directed to the Orientation Studio for our indoctrination. The studio was comprised of two large rooms, one being a corner with windows facing north and east. The building itself was rather old, having a brick and stone facade. In each of the windows were air-conditioning units working hard to bring the temperature down to tolerable levels in what would become a hot Detroit summer.

As we and other new employees from other schools began to collect, we introduced ourselves. I turned out to be the only summer trainee. Most of the others were from the Art Center School, a name we all recognized at Pratt as our chief rival in automobile design. Two of the Art Center placements were Stan Mott and Bob Cumberford.

Before much time passed, I was surprised to see Kostellow walk into the room, although I should have realized that he would have had some consultancy relationship with GM. As it turned out, he would be leading the orientation class, preparing all the graduates for their introduction into the production studios and I, of course, to return to Pratt for my senior year.

Getting down to business, large drawing pads and Prismacolor pencils were passed around, and we were given our first assignment. We were to draw any car we wished, but it had to be done entirely from memory. I selected the 1954 Buick and did a monotone blue-pencil drawing on vellum of it. It was really only a "get loose" exercise, but it served its purpose. The next day they passed out several sheets of acetate and told us to make our own drawing sweeps and curves. Unlike ships' curves, which are sets of progressive radii, our curves were more like French curves, only longer and slimmer. They would be more in the character of fender lines than teacups, and we would each make about sixteen templates.

We made them by double face taping a master template to a piece of acetate, then scribing a fairly deep score around its perimeter, making several passes. The acetate was then bent along the score mark to break it free, and then the sweeps were sandpapered around the edges to make them smooth. Unfortunately for Russ, we all used his personal sweeps for masters.

By the end of the first week, the guys had scoured around and found an apartment with a bedroom, kitchen, bath, and a studio area in a nice building on Euclid and Second Avenue, about a dozen blocks up from the GM building. Four of us—Ken Genest, Paul Deesen, Pete Regner, and I—agreed to share the monthly lease on the apartment, and we moved in. They were all Pratt graduates, and all had participated in the same automobile design classes. It would be an easy walk to work and at the halfway point, if the weather was bad, we could step into the New Center Building, enter the underground concourse and, in order, go through the Fisher, GM, and then the Research/Styling buildings. The Fisher Building was a grand twenty-eight-story ornate Art Deco complex[35] that totally contained a mall-like central shopping center, and a huge beautiful movie and stage theatre deep inside of it. Except for our apartment building, all the housing in our area was old residential. There was a good-sized grocery market across the street that had a lounge and piano bar attached next door, a mom n' pop family restaurant a block north and a laundry and dry cleaning shop along our way to work. It was hard to ask for a better setup.

Also moving into the residential area were two other Pratt graduates, Al Nakata and John Hayashi. They had been hired as Industrial Designers and were placed directly into the GM product and exhibit group. We would variously hang around together, with Al Nakata being central figure because he had the family car. Evenings, after work, we would go out to eat together and afterward,

---

[35]   Designed and built by Albert Kahn in 1927-28, it remains as one of the best examples of Art Deco architecture and was designated a National Historic Landmark in 1989.

on average, take in about four or five movies a week at the big screen downtown theatres. On other evenings, we would cruise up and down Woodward Avenue, between the Totem Poll and Big Boy drive-ins. Those who knew would point out the small Sundberg-Ferar Industrial Design office across the street. This was a novelty for us because Industrial Design, as a profession, was not well-known to the general public.

At work, we quickly settled into a routine where we didn't see all that much of Kostellow. He apparently had other responsibilities—attending to the Product Design groups, which would have been his first love or perhaps he was working with Rowena on another Kitchen of Tomorrow project. We understood that Styling was again well underway preparing for the next Motorama show, although none of us had any sense of the scope of the effort, because of all the secrecy that permeated the culture. We went about our own business, receiving training as GM saw fit to prepare us.

We were just now realizing the difference it made, being able to work with unlimited resources. As students, we had to restrict our color schemes to the media we had in our drawers and be concerned about how much paper our money could buy. Now the sky was the limit, and we were able to requisition whatever we wanted, not needed. We would do pastel on vellum studies by the dozens, working at one-fifth scale, which made each drawing about four feet long, torn from rolls. Through their purchasing agent, I bought two and four-inch ellipse template sets, which of all tools, were a must for any aspiring automobile designer.

Another nicety was that we had access to archives of old drawings and studies, in all different media and styles. The most spectacular styles were the watercolors because of their brilliance in color and the smoothness of their grain-free transitions, ideal for renditions of glass and highly polished surfaces. This apparently was no longer the media of choice because of the skills necessary to work it and the need to crank out concept after concept at a high rate in a very competitive design environment.

We met a young MIT graduate, Chuck Jordan,[36] who gave us one of our more interesting assignments. Jordan had designed the Aero Train, which was a streamlined Show Train for the GM locomotive division. He was now doing work for the Euclid earth moving (equipment) division, and threw us a "design bone" to chew on. It turned out to be an excellent exercise because it employed

---

[36] Charles Jordan was later made the studio head of Cadillac Exteriors (designing the 1959 classic), and much later was named the GM Vice President (VP), head of Styling, from 1986 to 1992.

an entirely different kind of physics, and therefore, the shapes that evolved were altogether new.

I befriended several of the Art Center students and was surprised one day when one of them complemented me on my sketching style. This came as a total shock because, as I have noted, I always thought of myself as a renderer. *What was going on here?* I found myself working several projects with Stan Mott, whom I enjoyed because of his spontaneous sense of humor and his great cartoons. We would later send each other corporate publications through the mail, where we had doctored articles or pictures in some discrete but outrageous manner, trying to see how long it took the other to find the forgery.

As a part of our training, GM arranged field trips to the GM Proving Grounds in Milford Michigan and to the Cadillac Assembly Plant in Lower Detroit. Both were extremely exciting—the proving grounds especially so. We had heard that Chevrolet was coming out with its first V8 engine and perhaps we would see it there. Previously, their top engine was the Blue Flame 6, which even found its way into the first Corvette flagship. We kept our eyes open for it all the while we were there.

The main function of the proving grounds was to test all of GM's cars, but it also tested most of its competitor's cars, in what were called endurance or durability runs. Each model under test would be driven around the clock by three shifts of drivers, taking time out only for refueling, meals, rest stops, and to make any repairs necessary. The cars would take three laps around the high-speed oval and then exit to an exact route over a mixture of road surfaces: dirt, washboard, gravel, asphalt, winding; a Belgian Block that would hammer cars apart; a San Francisco hill climb; through water troughs and simulated rain; executing planned panic stops and spin outs on a skid pad. Having completed this exact route, it would return to the high-speed oval to repeat the sequence again and again and again. It would be the same continuous routine for all the models under test until they had completed twenty-four thousand miles, at which time, they would be completely disassembled[37] for engineering review.

---

[37]　A large garage was set up for twenty or so cars to be completely taken apart and having their parts displayed on white-paper lined picnic tables. The welded sheet metal body would head a column of tables, which would have spread out on them the engine, disassembled to engine block, heads, pistons, rings, plugs, and radiator. Following tables in line would have the transmission, drive shaft, differential brakes, etc., until all the basic parts were laid open for inspection.

By this time of summer, however, the endurance runs had been completed, and they were only running specific tests, so we were only seeing a small mix of test activity. It was while standing inside the banked turn of the high-speed oval that I heard someone shout out, "There it is!" Looking up, I saw a dirty black car screaming around the banking and trailing a shrill whistling sound, apparently coming from the clean-cut wheel openings. The general shape of the '55 Chevy coupe was non-descript, but the panorama windshield was very noticeable. Some things had been taped around the headlights and other body features to disguise its appearance from prying Ford cameras. We were all abuzz after it disappeared. It was followed shortly afterward by a similar Pontiac model, sporting the common "A" body and having the same whistle. We kept watching as they came by again several times before we were finally dragged away to our next stop. The memories linger, of having seen what would be a future classic while it was still secret.

As the days raced on, some of the students were called and placed into production studios, having been considered ready to start earning their keep. The production studios were structured either as Exterior or Interior studios, with each of the five divisions having at least one of each. There were several "Body" studios which would be working years in advance, laying out the basic vehicle architectures for the next major body changes; delineating and defining

---

The last table would contain all those parts that had been removed and replaced. They were tagged with the mileage at which they failed and had added any comments that would be appropriate. These tags would be red to indicate that they had failed and were replaced. You would often find the same part several times, indicating it had repeated failures. On the tables containing the rest of the dissembled parts, there would be other colored tags. A yellow tag denoted a failed part that was only discovered upon disassembly. These would be replaced upon reassembly (because the cars would later be sold as used). Blue tags were added to call attention to unusual wear or some other condition engineers should be interested in. Typically, any particular car would be seen all in one column, spread out across half a dozen tables and some floor space. This would be repeated row by row for all models tested. All similar components, like engines, would thus be located at the same table positions in rank-and-file fashion. In another oddity, GM would often start running Ford or Chrysler cars in the tests even before that year's model had been introduced to the public. Later, these endurance tests would be increased to thirty-six thousand miles in order to expose more failures.

such things as the roof and "daylight openings," i.e., windows. These areas had to be established early so that manufacturing could get a head start, in advance of any design commitment. Those divisions that had to share the same body would then have to start their own styling studies, to create distinctive features that differentiated one common body from the other. Chevrolet and Pontiac would share the "A" body. Buick, Oldsmobile and an upscale Pontiac shared the "B" (or "BOP") body. Cadillac had its own "C" body, at least at that time. There were also a few special studios, a truck studio, an Interiors Color group, and a small sculptures group that did hood ornaments and other trim details to round it all out.

At the start of a major body change, rather than just a facelift, the division exterior and the body studios would literally compete, trying to come up with a theme that would be accepted, and from which a baseline would ultimately be developed in the body studios. The body defined would be only of the passenger compartment, truncated in front from the dash and running back to the rear window, which would include the fixed roofline, floor/rocker panels, door sills, and inner sheet-metal door, including window mechanisms. Once defined, the division studios would then develop their own external sheet metal anew, even if it were based on their original winning design concept. The fact that different divisions had to share the same body was a major reason why Detroit was so dependent on the use of chrome in the '50s. A simple sweep-spear and a set of portholes in the front hood could make any body into a Buick and multiple parallel chrome stripes could make a Pontiac.

One day in August, we were buzzing along on our projects and Kostellow called me, saying he wanted to talk about something. When we met, he asked if I would be willing to stay and work at GM for one year, then return to Pratt for my senior year and assist him in teaching the automobile design class, taking on the same role that Russinoff had performed—mentoring the younger students. It sounded like a good opportunity, since I was really enjoying myself—with all the resources and all—and I didn't want the flavor to stop. I agreed to do it and assumed that he would formalize the details with the GM people. That evening I phoned my family and Eric, advising them of the decision. Then I wrote a letter to Hartwig with the same information because I had to send an interim report to his department anyway.

A few weeks later, on the Tuesday following the Labor Day weekend, I returned to work to find everyone there unusually glum. It was then I heard that Kostellow had had a massive heart attack that Saturday, August 31, and died. He was fifty-three years old, and the attack was his first. Services would be held later in the week. His death was totally unexpected; however, as I understood it, I had made the commitment to stay at Styling for the year.

It wasn't long after that, that more and more of the guys were being assigned to the various studios. As I was no longer a summer student, I also received word to report to one of the body studios, headed by Pete Wozena. While the studios normally worked in support of one of body programs, I found that the studio was actively working the LaSalle II sedan, a show car for the upcoming Motorama. The clay model was about 80 percent complete, and they were working six and seven days a week to finish it. Another studio was doing the sister car, a convertible roadster, for the same show. The two cars would represent the corporation and not be associated as belonging to any particular division. They would not be running vehicles, but to all outward appearances, they would look real.

This was my first opportunity to learn much more about GM Styling and the Motoramas. Normally, automobile design can be very trying when working under pressure and, after a period of time, can become a very drab task. Harley Earl found that he could recharge his designers by exercising them to design and build no-holds-barred "dream cars." These also served corporate purposes for exciting the public with GM's product line. The Buick LeSabre was the most famous of the show cars. It was also a running vehicle, later becoming Harley Earl's personal car. Dream cars[38] were usually built to represent each of the divisions, to push the styling envelope, and somewhat to test the public's response to new ideas. Occasionally, general models like the Firebird would be built to represent the corporation in aggregate. The Firebird, which I saw in the 1953 Motorama when I was a student at Pratt, was a true running car; because its gas turbine engine was a feature, reality demanded that it run. The LaSalle II models, now being designed, were to be corporate theme cars also, but they determined that they did not have to run. The LaSalle, at one time, was a GM luxury car and perhaps they were thinking of bringing it back into their product line.

The Motoramas were traveling road shows and always opened in the Waldorf Astoria ballroom in New York. The free auto show offered to the general public, used exciting dream cars to draw them in and then they would be exposed to the new GM production models. It was good advertising and was GM's promotional signature of the decade. Here now, in Wozena's studio, I would appear to have a role in this GM drama. I was eager to find out just exactly what it would be. I

---

[38]   Today these cars are called Concept Cars and are developed for other purposes, as the Motoramas ceased in the late 1950s. GM Styling itself was once called Art and Color. Later yet because Styling was still considered to be too "sissy," in 1972 it was renamed as Design Staff, and again in 1992 it was renamed the Design Center.

also found myself in a perfect position to observe the players and see how the system worked.

I saw firsthand, many of the design techniques I had only heard about before, applied now by professionals. The sketches and the beautiful tight renderings impressed me. Another media that was used in the studio was airbrush; here full size drawings would be executed on black construction paper. I bought a Thayer & Chandler airbrush through the system, but I was never fully able to master it and never in fact enjoyed it.

The various roles of the studio people began to emerge in more clarity. The studio head, Pete Wozena, was responsible for all that went on in the studio, and an assistant head was assigned to facilitate that activity. Several senior and junior designers would be assigned to support as directed. Secrecy was at a very high level between the studios and designers only had access to their own studios. Only Harley Earl, Bill Mitchell and the Design Committee (composed of a few select studio heads and design consultants) could enter any of the studios. On some occasions, several studios could be called on to work competitively on the same project. Originality, the search for new ideas, was the reason for this structuring. Styling was a very young organization, with senior studio people being in their forties and most of the designers under thirty.

As noted earlier, we were doing the sedan version of the LaSalle II and another body studio was doing the roadster; so obviously, much of the lower bodywork that was common had to be coordinated with that other studio. The clay models had been started earlier that summer and by now, they were well along, expecting completion in the fall, when plaster casts would be taken, fiberglass laid up from those plasters, then trimmed, fitted, assembled, cleaned up, painted, and then polished into for all appearances real cars with custom interiors, rubber tires, mirrors, trim, and all.

Typically, this was an exciting period—designing and building these cars—and it did entail heavy overtime and long weeks by all the studios. Toward the end, it became standard practice to load the cars into their Motorama vans, along with mechanics, carpenters, and painters to finish them on their way to New York.

These were the stories we had heard, so we knew what to expect. In my case, I was not a key player and didn't work that much overtime—in fact, I was given mostly make-work tasks to keep me out of the way. I had no training in letter font graphics, as had graduates of the Art Center School, but my first assignment was to do some gas gage instrument studies and paint them up for the interiors instrument panel mockup. I had to letter brush the *E, tic mark, ½, tic mark* and *F* on to the Plexiglas dials. They were really pretty bad, but it didn't matter because they never intend to use them anyway. I was also asked to do some sketches on some exterior trim. This was where I learned the studio protocol.

The way it worked was that the studio head directed all of his designers on what to look at. The designers would then crank out dozens of ideas in any media they thought appropriate, or more likely to attract attention, then, they would pin them up on the walls or moveable display boards. Anyone could steal from any idea already posted and try to improve on it. Usually the studio head, a design committee member, Bill Mitchell or perhaps Harley Earl himself, might see the idea and direct further studies be made along those lines.

The best concepts would then be rendered in full size on the vertical boards for final evaluations. These were boards that stood on castors so they could be easily moved around in the studio. Shorter boards would be used for the front and rear views, and they could be placed to the left and right of the long boards so they all could be viewed together. The main reason for the vertical boards was that the drawings were so large that it was necessary for designers to be able to step back, in order to see the whole view.

By this time, the basic lines of the LaSalle II had already been well defined and the full size airbrushed-drawings had been replaced by fifty-four-inch high, by twenty-foot long sheets of vellum, the backsides of which had been marked off into a five-inch square grid pattern.[39] The clean front side was then covered with sweeping lines, defining every critical surface feature of the car (in that view). The front and rear views were similarly prepared, except that there were additional lines representing cross-section cuts, as if the car had been sliced, like a loaf of bread, into ten-inch-thick sections. These drawings now were used to control the development of the full-size clay model, which now dominated the center of the studio.

Most notable in this state was the bright steel platform that surrounded the model. It had flat rails about a foot wide that ran full length along the sides of the model, and capped by rails at the ends, altogether creating a flat level reference surface. Each rail had another smaller rail along its inside edge, marking off five-inch increments, each tagged with corresponding station or butt line numbers that matched the grid lines of the blackboard drawing. Moveable vertical angles were placed on the platform so that they could be slid to a station and then, using its vertically adjustable shelf, they could precisely positioned features or templates, relative to the clay, to within hundredths of an inch.

For the clay model, a wood lath armature would have been built to within two inches of the design surface and then hot clay built up onto it.[40] Templates of the key features would then have been accurately positioned from the platform

---

[39]   This was so erasures of design lines on the front side would not remove the reference grid.

[40]   This was the same clay we used at Pratt. At $2 a pound, a full-size car model could require up to two tons of it.

by station, butt, and waterline settings. The templates would then cut a profile into the soft (when hot) clay by flexing it back and forth. Then a line would be scribed from the platform using a mouse (a flat-sided stick with a point at one end to project the vertical plane of the reference angle), defining that exact section station. Once sufficient sections had been defined, the clay would be built up between them and the clay modelers would begin splining and fairing all the surfaces together. After sufficient adjustments and corrections had been made, both the clay model and the master drawing would now be brought into some kind of agreement with each other. It was actually after this stage that most of the design development would be performed. A concept that looked good in a sketch never really worked out in three dimensions. As problem areas materialized, designers would perform additional studies on them and post possible solutions.

It was during this period that I heard more about Harley Earl, whom I had yet to see but whose presence was felt throughout the building. Stories about him preceded the man himself. As to the actual influence he had on Styling, absolutely nothing got on to a clay model unless Harley Earl personally directed that it be put there. While Earl was clearly the designer, he never laid hand to pencil. Typically, a studio head would work to implement directions Earl had already given him. With a clay model underway, Earl would come into a studio and take a chair in a dominant central position in view of the vertical boards where the drawings were being developed. Each studio had a "blackboard man" that did the actual drawings. This name was a carryover from when cars were designed on blackboards in white chalk. A five-inch grid system[41] was used to control conversion of these lines into templates for ultimate transfer to the clay model

The blackboard men in general were old-timers who either excelled in this kind of work or were designers that didn't make it to higher levels. Another measure that had to be considered was the pressure they could handle, working directly under Earl. There was no question as to whose mind was moving the hand. Earl relied on the drawings to control the clay. He had an absolute rule that a change to the clay model could only be made, after being first defined on the board. It was his way of working and maintaining absolute control.

There were many stories that demonstrated how acute his eye was in reading lines. He would sit in front of a board and dictate, "raise this line one sixteenth-inch here, lower it an eighth there," etc. He was so into detail that all studios posted and maintained a card of principal dimensions and special features of a design, in order to quickly respond to any of his standard questions.

---

[41] For accuracy, the five-inch grids were considered as absolute, and all features were measured by their distances from the nearest five-inch grid lines—never as a distance between features.

He was a dominant presence at 6 feet and four inches, which was mostly in his legs, and he was always addressed as "Mr. Earl," by absolutely everyone at Styling. Needless to say, he was also very much feared. There was a story that one lunchtime, he came into a studio and in order to get a better view of a drawing; he pushed a moveable board back for more room. One of the workmen had been sleeping behind the board, awoke and then pushed it back. Earl pushed it back again only to have it pushed back yet again, along with some cussing from the other side. He fired the man on the spot.

I first saw Mr. Earl, one Saturday, while we were still working on the LaSalle II, and discovered he also had a subtle sense of humor. Earl came into the studio with Bill Mitchell, who was his right hand man. On this occasion, Earl chose to just sit and talk about things in general. All in the studio were obliged to stand by, attentively, and listen. He spent about ten minutes just running down Ford and the way they did things over there. Then he said, ". . . why all they've got around there are a bunch of yes men." After a short pause, he looked up at Mitchell and added, "Isn't that right, Bill?" to which Mitchell responded, "Yes, Mr. Earl." The funny part was that everyone understood what was going on, but no one even dared to smile.

Not long after the Motorama cars were finished, I was reassigned to Advanced Body Design Studio #3, headed by Fidel Bianco. Another new designer from Art Center, Wayne Takeuchi was also assigned there, and we became involved in a few studies—none of which were noteworthy. We did get a better sense of the system, understanding that there were a lot of automotive concepts developed at General Motors that never saw the light of day. There also seemed to be a lot of groups doing the same thing. It appeared that GM would do preliminary or background work on something they thought they might need in the future, but the probability was that it would just end up on a shelf. Our studio engineer, Al Aldrighetti, pulled out some old drawings that were done years earlier, on something known only as "the little red job" and I was surprised that none of it had ever reached the public. It became obvious that one could spend a career on a great project that might never see the light of day.

I did have an opportunity to try my hand on a few housekeeping tricks, learning from the old timers. At that time, preprinted five-inch grid paper was not manufactured so twenty-foot lengths of clear vellum would be rolled out, stapled to a vertical board, cut off, and allowed to normalize to the moist air. After half a day, the paper would be taken down and placed on to an aluminum-faced table, which had five-inch grid lines scribed into its surface. The new vellum would be taped down and the task was to freehand trace the grid pattern with a sharp hard pencil, using the "feel" of the groove below. Needless to say, this was a disaster for us newcomers, but it offered the old-timers an opportunity to "showboat."

A short time later, our studio was joined by a design engineer with an aeronautical background, a Californian from Cal Tech named Bob McLean.[42] McLean, as it turned out, headed the design of the single-seat Firebird gas turbine show car, which had impressed me, as a student, when I saw it in the 1953 Motorama. By late fall, McLean was named to head a special project, and most of us were transferred to his Special Studio No.2. His assignment was to design another gas turbine car, this time a four-passenger family car with an advanced regenerative gas turbine engine. It would be the Firebird II, and it would represent the corporation in celebration of building its fifty millionth car. It would have to show a similarity to the original Firebird, and of course, it would have to be larger.

McLean became directly involved in its design, having a one-fifth scale clay model made to develop details of the wider bullet form and defining exactly how the larger canopy blister would interface with the body. We would also work out some of the fender details. Before we were very far into the project, Wayne Takeuchi was loaned out to one of the production studios and would eventually be permanently transferred. To replace Wayne, McLean hired a mechanical engineer recently graduated from MIT, Stefan Habsburg.[43] Stefan and I were to work well together—he for the mechanical systems and I for the aesthetics. Stefan had studied under Professor John Arnold,[44] and I would learn a lot from him in what he called "systems engineering," where the scope of a problem was studied from a far wider perspective. By this time, our studio also picked up another engineer, Byron Voight, who had worked on the original Firebird, and clay modelers Larry Simi and Joe Henelt. Al Aldrighetti remained as our studio engineer.

We did one thing that was out of the ordinary: to mount the clay model armature onto a spit so that at discreet end points it could be lifted up, turned upside down, and then lowered to a new fixed position, all remaining within the modeling platform. In this way, we could model the entire body, including

---

[42] Surprisingly, I only learned, decades later, that McLean had laid out the original design of the Corvette.

[43] Stefan Habsburg-Lothringen was archduke of Austria, but you would never know it unless you asked him.

[44] Arnold subsequently moved to Stanford and headed a similar creative engineering department there.

the underside. This worked well for our purpose, but we almost had a tragic incident when it was hoisted up for the turnover. It was common practice when the modelers were shaving clay off the model to recover and reuse any clay that fell within the platform rails. This area was always maintained and considered clean, so there were no impurities in these scrapings. Anything that fell on the rails or on the floor was swept up and discarded, as it would have invariably picked up dirt. Styling had one man, Eddie Mathews, the proverbial fly on the wall, who serviced all the studios, keeping this area clean, and maintaining all the clay ovens with fresh clay. As such, he had access to see what was going on in all the studios, something that few others at Styling could do. Chain hoists were used at each end to lift the spit, and on the day we were turning the model over, Eddie crawled under to sweep up all the clay below. As we were lowering the model to reset it, with two inches yet to go, the hoist on one end failed and the model dropped. We all realized what close call we had.

McLean was the main man resolving the design of the Firebird II, interpreting what Earl wanted. Each of us had small sub-elements of the design that would be ours to work, but our main effort was to resolve the clay model surfaces that were now in full scale, but closely following our one-fifth scale development model. There were only a few items on the Firebird II that I could eventually lay claim to; these included the nose inlet spinners, the wheel drums, and the aesthetic execution of some of the surfaces. One thing that surprised us was that Harley Earl didn't spend much time with us, leaving much of the modeling for us to resolve; he only looked in on us from time to time. On a few occasions, we made small changes to the clay, and then brought the drawing into compliance (as we looked over our shoulders), this, of course, was in direct violation of Earl's rules. Completion of the clay model occurred when Earl came in one day and bought it off. The Styling shops could now proceed to build the body.

It turned out that we needed very few drawings to make the parts because they could be laid up in fiberglass, directly from plaster casts taken off the clay. The first step in the process was to scribe all the cuts and openings that would be required in the body, and then have the Plaster Shop start taking casts. They would take strips of clay from the extruder and stick them to the clay model, along the scribed trim lines. Brushing turpentine on one side of the extrusion would soften the surface and make it sticky. Sticking them along the scribed lines created a perimeter dam around each part making it ready for casting. A thin skim coat of Hydrocal plaster was then splashed on, covering the exposed surface area, building it up to the dam wall. After allowing it to set, a larger batch of plaster was then prepared and handfuls of loose manila hemp fiber were dipped in to wick up the plaster and then were applied over the original skim coat, giving it body and fiber strength once set. Next, the clay dams would be removed, and adjacent surfaces dammed off and the process repeated, except the second cast would butt-up directly against any previous plaster castings (coated with a lard-like parting agent).

The shop would have previously built up 2x4 mahogany frame structures, and now would plaster them directly to the separate plasters, the frames having been bolted together while still on the model. They would then remove the casts with their frames, and reassemble them into their same relative positions, no longer needing the model to support them. The plasters would be baked out to dry, sealed and sprayed with a parting film so they could start laying-up the fiberglass. This was the same procedure used to make all their preproduction (prototype) cars for internal division review and for all show cars.

For the Firebird II, they wanted to do something else—in addition. A decision had been made that a dominant feature of the car would be that it would have its body made of titanium, the new wonder metal. For this purpose, metal-forming tools had to be made from these same plasters, and the body panels hot formed from that tooling. This proved to be quite a challenge, but they were able to complete the task, working at the forefront of materials processing technology. With that technology not really quite established, most of the titanium panels were assembled using adhesive bonding techniques. The final body would have a brushed-finish metal surface.[45]

The Firebird II would be loaded with demonstration show features, and it was anticipated it would be fairly complex, so another decision was made to make a second car, one of fiberglass that could be driven and in that way, reserve the titanium car for show only. The running fiberglass car would be fully operational with research staff's recently completed regenerative gas turbine engine. This, the second car, would be taken to the Arizona Proving Grounds to make a movie that proved that it really worked. There was a third body shell[46] made of fiberglass, strictly for the purpose of shooting a few close-up shots for the movie. Research staff had already begun fabrication of the engine, chassis, and running gear by the time we were making the bodies.

Near the end of this period, other things were happening. As summer approached, I advised Tom Christiansen that I intended to return to Pratt to complete my senior year. His response was, "No, no, you're good enough, you don't need any more schooling." I insisted that I had to go back to get my

---

[45]   Years later, when Bob McLean left GM, he joined John DeLorean, and may have been instrumental in the selection of brushed stainless steel for the body finish of the DeLorean automobile.

[46]   This third shell was later modified and fitted with an experimental free-piston engine and chassis. It was released to the public as the XP500.

degree, and he followed with, "Hold on and let me see what we can do." He called me later and said he had talked with Kolli, who was now the Industrial Design Chairman and that they could set up an arrangement where I would get "on the job training" credit for my art subjects and needed only to attend a minimum of forty days for my academic classes. GM would fly me to New York every other week, some twenty times, so I could attend classes on Fridays and Mondays, then they would fly me back to Detroit to resume work on Tuesdays. They would also cover any moderate apartment expenses I might have at Pratt. It sounded pretty good, so I agreed and called Eric later to figure out the logistics. Eric would be graduating shortly, so I could share his current flat in Brooklyn with Ralph French, another ID student who still had two more years to go at Pratt. That way, Eric could leave my drawing board and equipment in the same apartment, and I would just move in for those weekends.

Eric also told me that he had received a job offer from GM, as had several of my other former classmates, including several of the girls. GM apparently was making another "big buy." The girls would mostly be going into the automotive interiors groups and a few of the others into the graphics and exhibits groups. Eric would need a place to stay in Detroit, and I told him that I was moving into a larger apartment in the same building and we could take him and someone else in so four of us would split the $90 a month rent.

From here on, things seemed to move very quickly. The Firebird II was well into construction, and all the moves happened as planned. Our new apartment was much larger and had a better view from the third (top) floor. Eric moved in, as did Vince McPherson, another ID graduate. Vince was several years older than us and did the cooking whenever we wanted to eat in. It worked out to be very convenient; all we had to do was learn to love garlic. Other graduates from the class of '55 came to Detroit and scattered about town. Four of the girls moved into a duplex in Royal Oak, a few miles west of the GM Technical Center, which was still under construction. It was north of Detroit on 12 Mile Road. We would all be working there within the year.

One evening that summer, McLean called me at home from California, where they were shooting the Motorama film and asked me to fly out and assist them in developing the instrumentation graphics that they would need for the movie. The next day at work, I arranged for a flight to California, my first. McLean was at the airport to pick me up, and we drove to the Beverly Hills Hotel where we would be staying. The memory of meeting him the next morning in the open patio breakfast room and seeing palm trees gently blowing in the breeze was a pronounced change from life, as I knew it. We drove to the studio where they set me up in a vacant room, and I started doing some sketch studies. The memories that remain, however, are of the evenings' dining out, steaks, sukiyaki, bar hopping, rum drinks, Black Russians, tequila, and flamenco guitarists, and then suddenly it was time to return to Detroit.

With my Firebird II work almost finished, I started my commute to Brooklyn that September. I was used to flying between Detroit and Cleveland, when I was visiting Herb, but my first night landing into LaGuardia was a shocker. New York at night was spectacular, but I was not ready for the pilot to lay the plane on its side for a sudden drop to the river, only to be saved by a runway that came out of nowhere to greet us. I took a cab to the apartment in Brooklyn where I met Ralph and settled in. Having only academics to worry about, took a lot of pressure off, and I was able to enjoy New York again on the weekends, doing the same things, but more of them. On Mondays, after class, I would take an evening flight back and put my Detroit hat back on.

Having completed work on the Firebird II, we began wrapping up our studio in preparation for our move to the new Tech Center. Dedication of the center wouldn't be until the following spring but Styling was ready to move. Research and a few of the other staffs had already moved in. Our Special Studio 2 was new, and not in the original architectural plans so they had to convert what would have been a storage room into a design studio, complete with all the same amenities as the other studios, except for having no windows. We would also be renamed as Research Studio. By moving day, we had packed everything we needed except for the furniture, since all of that would be new. Those of us still in the Euclid apartments decided to stay there and commute to the Tech Center, at least until we figured out where we wanted to move to.

The school year was not that eventful, in that all I got out the twenty trips was a diploma. One exception was that I had an opportunity to meet Karl Ludvigsen, who was studying at MIT and then changed to Pratt to become an Industrial Designer. Karl had known Stefan when he was at MIT so we had much to talk about. Karl was unique in that concurrently, as he was attending Pratt, he was writing sports car articles for different magazines, under several names, including his own. I remember one ride in his Porsche, through what were then the "boonies" of Idlewild, doing timing and high-speed acceleration runs.

Of course, I was also there, to see the Firebird II at the 1956 Motorama. It was the same Waldorf Astoria, but it was different this time. The only other notable memory was of a Saturday, late in the school year, when I was writing a final paper for my Great Books class. It was on *Dante's Inferno*. Following my old habit, I had a nice restaurant breakfast and dropped by the art store, then the deli, where I picked up a box of chocolate covered doughnuts. I went back my to apartment and settled down to finish the paper. I was working my way down Dante's levels of Hell, when I came to, the Gluttons, at which point I stopped . . . looked up and . . . yes . . . ate all the doughnuts. Graduation followed not long after. I said my goodbyes to Ralph, packed up my drawing board, lamp and supplies and returned with Herb and my parents, who had driven down for the graduation.

Harley Earl had been a major influence in Alfred Sloan's creation of the GM Technical Center. The Center would house Styling, Research, Engineering and Manufacturing Staffs, as well as the Service Center for running the facilities. It was situated on the north side of 12 Mile Road, between Mound Road and Van Dyke, with the main entrance on the Mound Road side. A north-south railroad spur divided the site with an older Chevrolet engineering facility mirroring the Tech Center on the east side. The small town of Warren bound the north end.

Eero Saarinen was the chief architect of the Tech Center. The two-story buildings had full glass walls running their entire lengths and ends of solid, brightly colored brick glazing, each facility in its own distinctive color. The styling building had high-ceiling studios, each well lit and appointed. One end wall would hold two sets of vertical boards, each comprised of a fixed 22' x 6' high drawing board and two similar floating boards in front, counterbalanced so they could be raised clear or lowered to view any of them. The designers' drawing tables were lined along one long wall and the remaining space allocated for clay modeling platforms, as might be required. There was a small door entering each studio from a central corridor running the full length of the building. The studio doors had keypads for coded access. There were also large bifold doors that were big enough to move full-size clay or real cars through, to extra large elevators, leading to the subterranean passageway and the display auditorium. Each studio had a lavatory, a utility room with sink, clay ovens and cabinets for flat and roll drawing storage. Styling had two cafeterias—one in the basement, that was a good place to have coffee and warm up after a difficult morning drive through sleet and snow, and the main cafeteria, upstairs overlooking the twenty-two-acre man-made Tech Center lake. There were also private dining rooms beside that cafeteria for the executive staff; and of course, Harley Earl had his own private dining room. On occasions, for variety, we would walk to the large central cafeteria near Manufacturing Staff or the length of the lake to the Research Staff cafeteria. There was a landmark stainless steel water tower at the north end of the lake and dancing fountains designed by Alexander Calder in front of the Research Staff building.

Settling in to the new studio, we executed a few studies for a front-wheel-drive vehicle with a transversely mounted engine/transmission package and having a metal sandwich floor structure, in lieu of a conventional frame. We were also experimenting with some lounge-type contour seating concepts (similar to present-day dental chairs) that were championed by Bill Dennis, from one of the advanced interiors studios. Our activities were more to keep in practice than for achieving any objective. Since we were not actively making clay models, we loaned Larry Simi and Joe Henelt to the production studios, until we had a need for them again.

We were still living near the old GM Building and commuting to the Tech Center, holding to the thought that we would move after that winter. Formal dedication of the Tech Center was scheduled for that June, and we expected we would move to someplace closer about that time. This had only a minimal impact on our "boys' night out every night" routine. We also met some new Japanese American designers that joined GM Styling, Larry Shinoda, who surprisingly came from Chrysler (rare at GM), and his friend, Eddie Kidasako. They would be added to our social and party circles.

By only a short time after the Tech Center was dedicated, our whole gang had moved north. Vince, Eric, and I moved to a barracks-like housing complex, just south on Mound Road, and the others found apartments, all within a few miles of each other. Late that spring, as the Pratt school year was ending, Eric announced he was going to marry his high school sweetheart and obviously would be moving out. Marlan Polhemus, another Pratt ID graduate, moved in to take Eric's place. Marlan had accepted a job in Harley Earl's own Industrial Design office, which was not part of GM but was located immediately across Twelve-Mile Road, on the south side. After my graduation from Pratt, Ralph French, who still had one more year to finish, took on another Industrial Design roommate, Jim Pirkl,[47] to take my place.

---

[47] Jim would graduate the following year and be hired by the GM Product Design Group. He would become a close personal friend.

Advanced Body Design Studio #3 *Back row*: Wayne Takauchi, Norm James, Al Aldrighetti, Larry Simi, and Joe Henelt *Seated*: Robert F. McLean, Fedell Bianco, and Joseph Hrabak. *Photo courtesy of GM Media Archives*

Harley Earl and Firebird II at the GM Proving Grounds in Mesa, Arizona. *Photo courtesy of GM Media Archives*

Above, Firebird II. *Photo courtesy of GM Media Archives*

Right, The author, waiting for NBC cameras to pan by on *Wide, Wide World* presentation of GM's 50th anniversary celebration telecast.

Flint, MI, 1958. *Photo courtesy of GM Media Archives*

Below, During a holiday visit to Jamestown, Pete, and Herb disagree on the proper interpretation of rules for a new board game.

5 Firebird III

Early in 1957, we began hearing that GM was going to feature another corporate show car in the next Motorama, and that we would be involved. Since we had moved into the Tech Center, Bob McLean had become more active in building his organization, adding an advanced engineering and a marketing group. As a result, he was spending less and less time with us. His executive office was in the front administration building, a short distance from Harley Earl's second floor corner office. One morning, McLean came into our studio with an assignment. It would be to develop a new design concept for the next Motorama, some eighteen months hence. It had yet to be decided whether it would be a running or a nonrunning vehicle. Our studio had been asked to prepare some original concepts, but they would only need to be done at a low level of effort because of our reduced staffing.

As we were set up at the time, apart from a few supporting people, Stefan and I did all the basic design and development work for our studio. Stefan handled all the technical/mechanical aspects, as well as schedules and interdepartmental memos. Essentially, he was acting as McLean's assistant studio head without title. As the only designer, I was responsible for all the styling. We all freely accepted inputs to our work from other team members, regardless of what hat they were wearing.

On this particular day, McLean called Stefan and me into a closed-door meeting to advise us that from now on, his participation would be strictly administrative, performing in a purely managerial function. He told us that he would give us an assignment and a completion date, and that he would not personally become involved in the design process. As he explained it, it would be as if he were a customer in a fine restaurant. He would place an order for what he wanted and that we would prepare and serve it to him. If he did not like what we served, he would send it back to have it prepared correctly. He then added with emphasis, "I will not go into the kitchen and cook it myself!" With this preface, Stefan and I then set out to develop some ideas for the new Motorama car.

At the time, electric vehicles were becoming "hot items" so we set about doing a small electric "sporty" vehicle, all in good taste, i.e., without tail fins and having very little chrome. After playing with a few full size front and side views, we felt we had a good configuration. I prepared drawings and had a full-size space-frame wood mockup built. It was of notched egg-crate type construction, similar to that used for flying model airplanes, except without a skin covering. McLean scheduled a review of our model with Harley Earl shortly afterward.

When Earl entered our studio, he selected a nice comfortable Bertoia wire chair in the center of the studio and sat down. McLean started going over the design features of our design in meticulous detail but Earl didn't even appear to be paying attention. When McLean finished, Earl began talking, describing the characteristics and features that the new car would have, totally ignoring what had just been presented to him. It was evident that a lot of other discussions had already been carried on and decisions made.

He indicated first that it would be a running car and, in fact, it would be the third of the Firebird series of cars. It had already been designated as the XP-73, in accordance with internal project naming protocols. Working with research staff, we would incorporate a regenerative gas turbine engine, very similar to the one used in the Firebird II. Engineering staff would also participate, by building an auxiliary power unit (APU) comprised of a small 10 HP four-stroke two-cylinder combustion engine driving a 115V AC three-phase electric generator, a 1,000 PSI servo hydraulic system, and a 3,000 PSI hydraulic spring suspension system. The clever feature was that when it was on the show circuit, they could run the generator backward, as an electric motor, from readily available "house current." In this way, all the electrical and hydraulic subsystems depending on the APU could safely be demonstrated indoors without having to run the gasoline engine.

As to its appearance, he wanted it to be similar to the Pontiac Club de Mer show car of the 1956 Motorama (a two-seat open roadster with twin windscreens), but of course, it would have to be a little bigger to accommodate all the mechanical systems. He then went on to describe the show environment he wanted to create. He explained how all Motorama tours started at the Waldorf Astoria in the main ballroom, offering New Yorkers a free auto show and that GM would also exhibit its new product line. He said, "People will stand in line, four abreast, completely around the city block, just waiting to get inside. Once in the ballroom, it will be so crowded around the car that they will not be able to see it all and will have to stay for the next show, just to get a better view." This would make for a bigger and better crowd. As to the visual impression he wanted the car to make, he wanted it to be spectacular; it should be "what you would expect the astronauts to drive to the launch pad on their way to the moon." Stressing what he meant by spectacular, he added, "You know, when you go to Las Vegas to see a stage show, you don't expect to see your wife on the stage . . . you expect to see a real 'floozy.'"

As Earl was describing this, he was still seated and we were all standing around in a circle, listening attentively. As he was talking, I was trying to visualize the images as he was creating them. I apparently had a silly grin on my face because he suddenly stopped talking, looked at me directly, and innocently said, "No, I'm serious," and then he continued with his monologue, as a cold chill came down over my face.[48] When Earl finished, he and McLean left the studio; Stefan and I looked at each other and based on his Las Vegas showgirl comment, I said, "Well, if we don't put fins on it then someone else will."

/06

This is a reconstruction of the first Firebird III sketch prepared following Harley Earl's "vision."

While we were waiting for technical specifications to arrive from Research Staff, I started making a few sketches, the first of which was a literal attempt to capture the image of a crowd scene around the car, as Earl had described it. Rather than just showing a "blob" of people, I tried to add graphic interest to it by placing breaks in the crowd, showing glimpses of the vehicle rising high enough to be seen through those breaks. These could be fins, open hoods,

---

48   One must remember that Earl was a very feared man and he had little tolerance for fools.

Mercedes 300SL-type raised doors, etc., that would create an attractive crowd composition. Part of the rational was that protruding fins or things, toward the crowd, would threaten their personal space and help create those natural breaks, teasing observers beyond.

There were other sketches, some showing a moon rocket in the background. I had recently been inspired at an air show by a Nike surface to air missile, mounted on its launch rail. It was a two-stage missile and had tandem sets of quad fins, one set in back and the other set midway up the missile. What struck me was that because it was lying on its launch rail, the arrays were clocked forty-five degrees out of square, while the paradigm was that rocket fins were square to the world (horizontal and vertical) so my sketches started taking on this new look.

Shortly, details started arriving from the staffs on the chassis specifications such as wheelbase, track (tire separation), profile drawings of the APU, engine/transmission packages, the joystick controller that Research Staff had been developing, and tire sizes (the rear wheels were larger than the front). We added our ninety-fifth percentile Oscar and started to size our basic vehicle, working full scale, and placing the cardboard templates of these items onto the vertical boards. The engine/transmission/differential package was positioned amidships behind the passengers and made for some very difficult proportions to work with. Following Earl's direction, we adapted the Pontiac Club de Mer theme. Neither of us was very happy with the way it was working out, so we started considering some of the earlier theme sketches I had worked up.

This is a copy of the original sketch that set the Firebird III theme.
Image courtesy of GM Media Archives

The most attractive sketch I made was inspired by the North American F-100 (nose inlet), and by the Nike angled fins set at its midbody. Because of the side-by-side seating, the body section was stretched to an exaggerated width, giving it near surfboard proportions and terminating with a stark "stovepipe" front end. Another sketch on the theme was a three-quarter rear view, showing the car suspended from a hoist, the wheels partially retracted—a moon rocket standing in the background. In these versions, the Club de Mer twin windscreens had evolved into twin blister canopies, separated but astride an upwardly flared center body section, coming in above the shoulders in the interior. There were only a few sketches made around this theme, and these were now the ones that Stefan and I were thinking about trying in full scale.

This also appeared to be a good time to try another idea—I had been mulling around with for some time; that of developing a way to create something original by changing the (design) process that defined it. The standard method of starting a new design was to stretch out a large sheet of vellum on the long vertical board, then, working with a soft pencil, sketch out the design features with bold heavy multiple strokes. One would then have to step back some distance, in order to see what it looked like. The designer would then return to the board to erase bad lines and sketch in better ones, repeating the process until they were satisfied. Then a clean sheet of vellum would be overlaid, and hard sharp lines traced over, using sweeps and curves. My concern with the process was that the eye would integrate the eraser smudges as contributing design features; however, these "effects" would be lost in the final hard line drawing.

Committed to trying the new technique, we requisitioned an assortment of heavy brightly colored yarns (which they had to go out to buy) and several boxes of pushpins. These materials arrived a few days later and we were ready to give it a try it. We began by again pinning the cardboard cutouts of the Oscar, wheels, engine train, APU, etc., on to the girded vellum. We then created lines by tying loops at both ends of a string of yarn and pinning them at the start and end points of the intended line. There was enough stretch in the yarns so that they could be made to represent curves and shapes by placing intermediate pushpins, transversely stretching the yarn into multiple short cord segments. In this way, we were able to sketch out the design line features around the components. It was surprising how quickly the general proportions were laid out, and how easily they could be changed. Of course, there were no longer any residual traces of erased features to detract from the design.

Photo courtesy of GM Media Archives

I also found that, aesthetically, I could more readily see the mathematics or the purity of the line by judging the pin placement and spacing (progression). A line could be accelerated to imply motion or direction by uniformly diminishing the spacing between pins while keeping the same angle, or by progressively changing the angles between pin segments or by combinations of both. Where I wanted to relate a surface to some feature below,[49] I would create an "event" at that feature by symmetrically or asymmetrically causing the mathematics of the line to mirror or change as the line passed the event within.

---

[49] There is a design axiom that form follows function. The logic is that a prominent feature or characteristic should influence all elements or surfaces near it. With the pushpins I could have a line or surface mathematically converge as it approached, say the corner of the APU, and just like a comet approaching the sun, I could mirror the line character as it passed from its nearest approach. This exactly related surface features to interior components.

Lockheed F-104 Starfighters at an air show. The most striking feature of the F-104 was the downward cant (anti-dihedral) of the wings.

It was the first time I had ever tried this technique in a study[50] and found it to be surprisingly easy to use. The yarns were arranged, trying to replicate the primary theme with the Nike quad fins. A slim body profile evolved with a large overhang at the front end because of the APU. I was also trying to achieve a lightness that I observed at the same air show, of an F-104 Lockheed Starfighter, as it was taxiing along an apron, its needle nose bouncing lightly and the free space below it making it feel light, as if floating on air. The midship location of the engine/transmission package posed another problem, however, since it pushed the rear wheels too far back. The quad fin feature was keyed to the concept that I wanted the fin roots to absorb most of the rear wheelhouses in order to make the body slimmer. This placement, however, resulted in a very long, "barren" extended rear overhang.

Stefan and I were concerned about this very large plank after body, and I was having trouble getting the form right. At this point, Stefan walked up to the board and said, "What if we try something like this?" and proceeded to

---

[50]   I heard that this technique was picked up and used for a short time in a few of the other studios, but it was quickly replaced by black 3M photo tape drawings because they had a stronger graphic impact. My personal preference remains with the yarn technique, precisely because it is more abstract and more perfectly defines lines in a digital/mathematical sense.

add on a large central dorsal fin and two trailing lower fins. As he was doing it, I thought, "You can't do that! You can't integrate a three-fin feature with a four-fin feature." However, I also noticed that it created the mass balance that the design was crying for. I went up and reproportioned the tail elements, then we both stepped back to see what we had created. It was starting to look good, so I developed string drawings for the corresponding front, rear, and (half) plan views, reworking all the line events so they would all occur correctly in all views. Once it was worked out, we called McLean to come down and see what we had.

He arrived shortly and appeared pleased with what he saw. From Earl's last instruction, we were obligated to show him the upscale Club De Mer so McLean told us to continue with it, but he also authorized our building a second mockup to the new design.

My task now was to convert all the stick lines into lofted surfaces. I first penciled in the straight segments between the pins and outlined the cardboard template features on to the background vellum. Then, putting a clean grid sheet over the work sheet, I began to develop smooth equivalent lines with sweeps and curves, trying to maintain the character of the stick drawing below. The fin lines and other crisp features were correctly positioned in the end views, and holding those points, I developed cross sections, fairing into these points. The station cuts for these sections were first selected in the side view, based on which grid stations would best represent the body in form and character.

In the front view, I placed two passengers in what would be a tight sports car-like cross-section so as to leave me enough room to develop the midbody quad fins and stay within the maximum eighty inches street-legal width. The design philosophy taught at Pratt was to have a high wide point in the body cross-section so as to make it appear light. The ideal GM look was basically long, low, and wide. I knew that in no way would we get away with a high section, so I tried for an optical illusion. The predominant body section was made to have a low pear shape, essentially throughout the whole length, but I structured the upper set of quad fins to flair into the body shape, almost as a catenary curve to appear to be lifting upward at the shoulders to lighten the form. The lower sets of fins were developed for a different effect. They were placed at and opposing the pear-shape bulge, behind the engine inlet scoops, with their shapes vectored to give an apparent upward supporting push to again, help lift it.

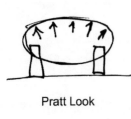

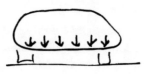

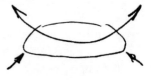

Pratt Look   GM Wide/Long/Low Look   GM Shape Lightened

Resolution of Quad to Tri Fins:
Quad fins grow from body shoulder features.
Center dorsal fin rises from the centerline
and side fins extend from widest body
section points. Upper and lower aero-brake
flaps mirror tri fin array.   /06

Placing the side scoops at this bulge, at the lower forty-five-degree highlight line, offered additional benefits. Stefan had explained to me that aerodynamically it was not necessary to "scoop" the air for an inlet. A simple opening at the side would suffice if we were to stand a small blade outward, downwind of the air stream. This would create a high-pressure zone over the inlet and divert the flow into the inlet. The leading edge of the scoop was made to stand out from the body by a small amount to effectively function as the small blade. The amount of body material that was removed ahead of the scoop also had the equivalent effect of removing a three-quarter-inch layer of fat, thinking of it as a living creature. In the rocker panel area (normally below the door opening), the apparent body section would also appear about half-inch higher from the ground, where the scoop rolled under. The eye would see the inset body section as the real form and effectively mask the real bottom.

Since the quad fins would hide the largest body section, the eye would visually read the "fifty-inch section,"[51] at the passengers, as the defining character of the vehicle. My driving design objective was to achieve lightness by maximizing the (negative) space between the ground and the underbody, trying to capture the grace of that fighter plane I saw on the taxi strip.

With the rocker panel, section tucked in so deep and door openings cut in low, it was necessary to define a healthy center spine for primary, and a shallow

---

[51] McLean had a theory that any design could be characterized by its fifty-inch section, i.e., a section cut taken about fifty inches behind the dashboard and used to show passenger head, shoulder and elbowroom. The most distinguishing characteristic would usually be the tumblehome or the tip in angle of the side windows.

outrigger platform for secondary structure at the door. I had envisioned that some kind of Mercedes 300SL type upward swinging door would have to be developed, but that it would have to be more complex because of the blisters. The door and blister trim openings would also have to be optimized to reduce the actual door size to an absolute minimum.

Working again in the end views, I set out to refine the body sections, which was more a matter of establishing a design protocol to control the design. Two focal points were defined, roughly through the passenger abdomens,[52] which would be about at the center of their body masses, and about these axes, all sections would be related aesthetically, much as planetary orbital mechanics are all related as a function of the Sun's mass and their distances from it. Holding the same focal points for all sections, in effect, created a set of straight parallel axis (like rails) running through the vehicle. The straightness of these theoretical lines would actually be judged by the visual integration of the body surfaces or sections in their final form. Any section out of character in the stack would create a wiggle or sag that would detract from the strong directional theme. In the final resolution, these theoretical lines were tuned to have a slight upward and forward thrust. Directionality cues from the side view were achieved by having the equivalent axis of the forward fender/wheel opening, blisters, quad, and tail fins all progressively sweeping further and further backward, the further aft they were. One problem that remained was that the backward tilt of the passenger blisters was contrary to the normal teardrop shape expected in good aerodynamic form.

/06

Constructions with a progressive "rake" in design elements, as shown in end and side views.

---

52   I found it was helpful in design to establish a rational or basis for doing things in a particular way. It could be arbitrary, but it would apply a uniform standard in the decision making process, necessary to achieving a coherent design. What I found odd was that it worked, even though it was not necessary for the observer or art critic to know or figure out what that control was.

The sections were all developed and crosschecked in three views, until all the basic forms were pretty well defined and conformed to the design protocols just defined. I would next have to design a mockup to these lines.

Usually, mockups were made up of plywood templates located ten inches apart, each following the surface contour and being one inch deep. The inside trim line would represent the engineering clearance allowance for the mockup components inside. These templates would be assembled on top of a stiffened plywood platform, mounted on castors. A five-inch grid pattern scribed on top would help locate the section templates and components inside. The Club de Mer version was built in this typical construction.

Mockups were usually made for engineering purposes, but this time, my objective was to create a full size "space sketch," Rowena Reed style, to assess the visual impact of the mass relationships. For this, we again deviated from the GM practice. Because the underbody area was so critical as "negative space," I elected to build a freestanding central cruciform frame from 2" x 10" beams and have them totally contained within the body form supported on four large castors. The beams were scribed with five-inch stations lines to locate the body templates. The cross beam was positioned so that Bill Dennis's long contoured passenger seats could be hung tightly ahead of the cross-member. I made a drawing of the cruciform and sent it to the shop to be fabricated.

For the body templates, clean vellums were placed over the developed sections and separate tracings made for groups of templates. The body sections were those already selected for their defining characters. The fin and fender edge features, by their very nature, were strongly definitive, but they had to be reproportioned to their true size because of the foreshortening that occurred in the side view. For all templates, the exterior edge was maintained at the surface, but the internal edge was selected strictly as it would enhance the specific visual characteristics of its features. Another housekeeping protocol had to be established to determine how the templates would be notched out, egg crate fashion, so they would nest to each other and not try to occupy the same space.

Some of the features like the nose and side inlets were considered to be more dominant as design details and so I drew them up more carefully and precisely, so the wood shop could shape them three dimensionally out of a soft poplar wood. These parts would then be painted to a high-gloss white finish, while the rest of the templates would be painted in a flat light gray. The reason for this was that I wanted the eye to linger on these scoop details a little longer[53] as dominant design elements. On other details, the blisters were simply

---

[53] I once observed that when something goes wrong in a design, and it requires a great deal of attention to correct, the eye will stop and linger on the correction because it assumes it must have been something important to have required so

defined by thin cutout Plexiglas sections. The wheels and tires were standard painted fiberglass replicas with flat spots on the bottom so they could just stand free—directly on the floor. As the final drawings were going to the woodshop, the cruciform frame was delivered to our studio, and the first body templates were starting to arrive. I could expect the rest of the templates over the next few days and the fancy painted parts a few days later, but we had enough so that we could start assembly.

I called the shop and request that two woodworkers be assigned for the next few weeks to assemble the mockup. They sent two good men, Ray Domkey and Don Schlack. They would stay with the project for as long as we needed. We had the parts but no overall layout so I had to identify each part as it came in and tell them where it belonged. The form began to take shape over the next two weeks. The cruciform frame proved to be very effective, as the mockup literally detached itself from the floor and took on life, yielding back valuable negative space. As new parts were added to the mockup, they would be hand painted in a latex paint. The high quality poplar details, after being fit, were sent to the paint shop for their high gloss lacquer finish and were then reinstalled. At the same time, of course, we continued to develop the Club de Mer mockup. We finally progressed far enough that McLean felt it was time to schedule a review with Harley Earl, so he told us to get ready and he set up the meeting.

To our knowledge, Earl had not been in our studio since that kick off meeting, however, it was generally understood that he made the rounds of the studios after hours, and knew everything that was going on. Both mockups were freshly painted, the studio cleaned, and the data sheets posted for both designs. We were ready.

The mockups were arranged so that when Earl entered the studio he would see his Club de Mer version and then, as he cleared into the general area, our mockup would come into view on his right. I was standing beside our mockup at the moment he came in, and clearly remember his brisk straight-back strut, with a slight forward lean, his tall frame, then entering into a right lean as he swept into banked turn, coming full round to a stop beside our mockup. There was no mention or discussion at all about the other mockup. He smiled and appeared pleased. His comments were direct and positive—this would be the Firebird III!

---

much attention. I concluded, therefore, that by placing labor-intensive details into the mock-up, I would be establishing the dominant elements within the dominant/subdominant/subordinate matrix.

/06

The original form of the mock-up as it was presented to Harley Earl. The most noticeable differences from the final mock-up (shown below) were the flat "stovepipe" nose inlet and the flared-up body between the blisters.

This photograph of the mock-up was taken after incorporating Harley Earl's suggestions, and installing Plexiglas blisters made from the clay model. *Photo courtesy of GM Media Archives*

He did offer suggestions, and of course, we would incorporate them. The body form between the passengers had the slight freeform flair, halfway up the blisters, as was already noted. His suggestion was that we run the body form straight on through. The front end had the flat wide "stovepipe" intake. He said, it should be brought forward about five inches in plan form at the center. He then gave us his approval to proceed directly to full-size clay. He and McLean then left the studio together as Stefan and I celebrated.

McLean returned a short time later and said that Earl had told the design committee to stay out of our studio and not to bother us. This was extraordinarily good news because we were aware of the damage the design committee could do. We knew that we were already violating several GM design rules, which Earl had apparently allowed to stand, and perhaps, working with only one master, we would be able to get away with a few of them. As it turned out, Harley Earl would make very few appearances himself and did not play his customary role of directing minute design changes. This also allowed us to make changes to the clay first, then, adjust the drawings to match afterward, something we wouldn't dare to do if Earl was around.

Our studio engineers started designing the armature for the clay model and meetings began between the Styling, Research, and Manufacturing Staffs so that vehicle specifications and functional interfaces could be defined. In the meantime, I began incorporating Harley Earl's recommended changes and refining some of the mockup details. I redesigned the nosepiece, moving the centerline forward to a sharp peak, and sent the drawing to the shop to have it made.[54] The body flair between the blisters was also removed, and the blisters redesigned accordingly. Because we were looking to have a large structural spine running down the centerline, we thought we would be able to reduce the side rails and lower the door opening to make it easier for exit and entry. We cut both the body and the overhead blister openings to reduce the door size cutting it on a bias to absolutely minimize the hinged mass. The hinges in the body were installed at a skewed angle to achieve a compact open position. The door mechanics were redefined following Earl's changes and new swing-up doors built and hung. As progress was starting to become evident, McLean began staffing up our studio for the task ahead.

Larry Simi was brought back as our head clay modeler, but this time he would have three student modelers assigned to support him. A young designer, Jim Ewing, was assigned to help me with the styling. Jim would be given the entire instrument panel and joystick controller to design. I would still design the seats and the vehicle interiors since they would be integrally related to the exterior forms. Bill Dennis of the advanced interiors group developed

---

[54] Years later, I learned that Harley Earl had intended for us to bring the nose forward in an arc, not to a peak, as I had erroneously interpreted it. The final nose form had the peak.

the actual seat contours. Dennis was the primary advocate of contour seating for automobiles at that time and would later become part of the McLean organization.

The steel-modeling platform was reset for our vehicle size, and the clay buck (armature) set up within it. On the Firebird II, we had the skewer running through the armature so it could be lifted and rotated to model the underside. This time, Larry felt that the skewer added little value and that we could do just as well if we had the ability to reposition the model about a foot or so higher when it came time to do those lower surfaces. We planned to fabricate the "belly pans" out of sheet metal any way, so we could engineer and tool this area from drawings. I'm sure the memory of the near accident we had with the Firebird II influenced Larry's recommendation and our concurrence.

The clay-buck was built up of wood bulkheads and rails with wood lath strips spanning the bulkheads. The fin armatures were of 3/4-inch plywood, drilled through like Swiss cheese and each having 1/16-inch sheet aluminum templates cut to the exact edge profiles and positioned accurately to drawing coordinates. They could be recut if we decided to change a profile, but I was assuming (correctly) that we needed only to play with each fin thickness, until it all looked right.

While the modelers were building up the clay, I was developing template drawings off the original section views. Half-inch plywood templates were cut for a whole series of sections at 15- and 20-inch separations useable for both the left- and right-hand sides. Once the clay was roughly filled in, it gave us our first full sense of the design mass.

The right side of the model was selected to be the master, and Larry and his team began working the surfaces. The clay between the template stations was slightly overfilled so that it could be scraped down to the final surfaces. Long splines were then sprung across the existing surfaces, with "hits" marking the high spots and indicating further removal was required.

As the surface became refined, irregularities (errors) in my original layout could be readily seen, as high or low zones, when the splines crossed three or more of the template stations. Larry and I closely discussed these to determine which ones to change. Later, he used a bubble inclinometer to analyze highlight lines. This was a tool that when the bubble was level, and its gage blade was set at forty-five degrees, he could tick off a series of marks down the length of the model, where the blade came into tangent contact. Connecting these points with a scribe line would give us another reference for revealing the dips and high spots between sections. These surfaces were then reworked until all the highlights for the various angles ran clean.

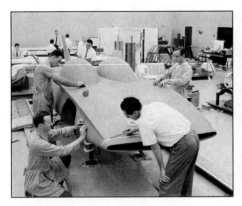 

Photos courtesy of GM Media Archives

With the body coming along nicely, we did find an area where we had some concern—the root flare surface around the upper quad fins. The rear wheels of the vehicle were larger than the front wheels, and we were trying unsuccessfully to swallow the wheelhouse within the root flare. We sent a query to Research Staff, asking if they could move the rear wheels forward three inches closer to the center of the fin. We were more than disappointed to hear their reply: "Sorry, but we have to move the wheels back two inches." This would forever give the Firebird III a slight hippy appearance in this area.

After several weeks of surface refinement, Harley Earl stopped by to review our progress. He recommended a few minor surface changes, more along how to make them crisper and more readable. First, the front hood had a slight crease down the centerline, which he suggested be changed to have a widow's peak, i.e., a slight filet upward on each side of the centerline, to make a distinct feature out of it. This would run constant from the nose, continuing on back between and past the blisters, eventually flaring into the dorsal tail fin.

/06

The other recommendation was to sharpen and embolden the forward fender edge, then to carry a crisper shoulder in the body section between that fender and the trailing quad fin. This made the features a little stiffer than I wanted, but I could live with it. Someone was nice enough to reminded me that we were already getting away with breaking a GM design rule, that of interrupting the forty-five degree highlight line (by the central quad fins), a major no-no. We incorporated those changes and continued refining the surfaces. As they became better defined, we began to scribe in cut lines, door openings and so forth, since they would have an impact on the shape of the individual panels. At about this time, we had progressed sufficiently, so that we could bring in more engineering support to develop and detail the body shape interfaces to the vehicle structure. One man would be tasked for a full year to develop the swing-up doors.

All the while, we were modeling; we were having some second thoughts about the backward shape of the blisters because it was contrary to aerodynamic convention. At a lull point in the modeling, we decided to add some armature behind one of the blisters and clay in a true aerodynamic teardrop. It made the blister about three feet longer. Even before Larry was finished modeling it, we all could see that it really looked wrong. With everyone finally satisfied, it was torn out and the blister restored to the original backward profile.

With that question mark removed, we had plaster casts taken of a blister, and Plexiglas canopies were vacuum formed from them. A set was cut to our bias trim angle, and fitted to our original space-frame mockup. The full transparency gave us a better sense of what the car would really look like, and it also helped us assess how easy it would be to get in and out.

We then entered a period best described as the long grind, where many little problems appeared and needed to be resolved. At times, I would sit on a small stool beside the clay model for hours, just staring at a problem area while trying to figure out what it was trying to do.[55] The temptation was to make an easy fix by changing a design constraint; however, I had accepted the premise that the original mockup was sacred and I could not deviate from it, even though I had originally designed it. In practice, this seemed to work and it was nice having Larry's counsel on what could be done. The solutions did not always work well, but I found that the residual faults seemed to fade in importance if they were not taken that seriously.

---

[55] Rather than trying to figure out some original way to solve a problem, I assumed that a solution already existed and I had to discover what it was. I looked for the design to lead me to its solution.

Once the blisters were firmed up, we could build the interiors armature and start the interior clay model. The contour lounge seats were to be molded in segments with a vinyl skin coat first, and then filled with urethane foam. This gave us quite a bit of design freedom for shaping the interior. Jim Ewing, meanwhile, continued to work the instrument panel and the joystick controller. With the blister trim, door opening, instrument panel, and center console interfaces defined, I started one of the junior modelers on the seating. The clay buck was rather confining, and my directions were not in the classical GM format so I had considerable difficulty communicating. I was giving directions for the forms as if we were at Pratt and trying as hard as he could, they still came out looking very stiff. I knew it was not his fault, and with Larry's approval, I borrowed his tools and rough in the whole interior, designing it as I went along. With one side mostly defined, Larry Simi helped direct the modeler to clean up the forms and copy it to the other side.

When it came time to define the engine deck opening, Larry handed me his big modeler's knife and said, "Norm, where do you want to put it?" It was a fair question; so after several tries, I was able to freehand scribe the hourglass path between the upper quad fins. Larry then put his "eagle eye" to it, cleaned it up, and laid a nylon fishing line into the scribe and burnished it into the surface.[56]

There were a few more events worthy of mention that happened leading up to the completion of the clay model. As noted earlier, Harley Earl had prohibited the design committee from entering our studio, but there was a conflicting incident that happened that summer. Earl went to Europe for a combined business trip and one-month vacation leaving Bill Mitchell in charge. Inevitably, Bill Mitchell and the design committee came by and offered their help.

The committee was in complete agreement that the three rear fins were excessive and had to go. McLean was not able to dissuade them, so we removed them and cleaned up the surfaces, ending up with a long plain overhanging plank in back. The changes were completed in time for Earl's return.

We were placed on Earl's busy schedule for a status review of the Firebird III. It would be in the auditorium so the model was transported down the long

---

[56]   This was the method used to fix a line to the surface. As a side note, one winter a few years later, the Firebird III was driven on the Detroit freeways for a promotional event; and I saw it in our studio shortly afterward. I was startled to observe that the airflow behind the blisters and between the fins, as revealed by the road salt spray, followed exactly, the hourglass lines delineating the rear deck opening.

underground passageway and set up on the center turntable of the elevated stage. McLean and the design committee gathered around it and waited for Earl to appear. Stefan, Larry, and I, with a few other studio people huddled down below on the main floor, out of sight behind some boards.

Earl finally arrived and took a position at center stage. McLean drew the task of presenting the change to Earl. McLean began his pitch. "After review . . . it was clear . . . we all agreed," while Earl very quietly and politely waited for him to finish. After a pause, Earl began speaking. "You know," he said, following with a pause, "when I came into the studio that day—for the first time—and saw the mockup . . . I actually saw the finished car in the Waldorf Astoria . . . and it was exactly as I had pictured it." After another pause, he continued, "Now, why don't you all take the car back and put it back to the way it was when I left." With that, he turned and walked out. Stefan and I, out of view in back, were ecstatic. We would have been doing high-fives, if we knew what they were.

On another day, when things seemed to be going smoothly, we received word from Research Staff saying they were concerned about the engine overheating and that they needed an additional inch of clearance above the turbine engine to improve the ventilation. This hit hard because we had just completed the topside, and normally, it would mean that we would have to raise everything. This would also add considerably more mass to the vehicle than I felt it could take, since we had fought hard to keep it slender.

We had put in a lot of work delineating the two-piece hourglass engine deck opening (over the engine/transmission package), and after some thought, I suggested to Larry Simi that we add the inch above the engine but confine the change to be entirely within the engine deck panel. We would start the surface flair upward exactly from the side, and rear trim lines, and allow the engine deck to run out a little higher behind the blisters. Larry implemented the change and I was surprised to see that the cut lines masked the change and it was virtually invisible. The other event of note, again—courtesy of Research Staff, was when they finalized the solid-axle front suspension, and located frame anchor points for two trailing arm links outside of the underbody surface, just forward of the front wheels. Again, reluctant to enlarge the body, I elected to flair a pair of local wedges from the existing surface, to absorb the fittings and thus, was able to retain the tight body section.[57]

Nearing completion of the clay model, we began delineating more of the panel breaks and openings that would be necessary, just for the fabrication of

---

[57] The design theme was to maintain a trim, but muscular, high-density body mass appearance. Any excess material would literally be considered to be fat.

reasonably sized panels. Most of the transverse cuts were made at true station lines and were functionally, or proportionally located so that each panel would have its own distinctive character. The topside panel breaks were framed by a symmetrical pair of lines, flowing continuously from the nose bumper to the rear bumper. They started with a gentle expanding sweep, curving past the blisters, then reversing directions, going into the hourglass shape (between the upper quad fins), then finally reversing to converge around the aerodynamic speed brakes.

The panel between these two lines for the front hood, forward of the blisters and door openings, turned out to be too long, so I elected to split it, creating a small bow tie patch panel forward. The main hood would open alligator fashion, but the patch panel would have to first swing clear to allow it to open. This would become a safing feature to keep the hood from opening at speed. With these trim lines defined, our exterior clay model was complete. The final body form ended up quite close, in character, to that defined by the original space-sketch mockup. It vindicated our rational of not deviating from the mockup. When the clay model was finally bought off,[58] we entered a new phase.

We began receiving technical details from Research Staff to start setting up other clay armatures to help develop surfaces for the engine inlet cross-duct and the engine deck underside. The main fuel tank was positioned immediately to the right of the turbine engine, and all the electronics were immediately opposite on the left side.[59] The engine was separated from these by vertical insulated stainless steel fire barriers on each side. A gas turbine engine normally cools itself by the air it ingests. To cool the compartment, however, the aluminum underpan would be louvered so that air could rise on either side of the engine and then vent outside, through oversize openings in the engine deck. The engine exhaust would be directed through these same openings, creating a Venturi effect that would help pump out the compartment air.

The armature for this clay model was a plaster cast taken off, of the body surface (including the trim lines), and set up vertically in a modeling platform. I elected to flare this underside surface downward, to seal against the fire barriers astride the engine. The shapes worked out nicely, fairing out to the engine exhaust openings. The underside of the engine deck would subsequently be

---

[58] From the earliest days, the Firebird III design had an air/oil suspension that would allow vehicle height adjustments. The intent was that for the Motorama, it would be exhibited two inches below its running height. Its best appearance, in my view, was actually at its running height—where I had intended it to be. I just didn't bother to tell anyone.

[59] The hinge-out electronics module was accessed through the left rear wheel service panel. It contained all the electronics (mostly mechanical relays) for remote controlled Motorama special effects as well as for the vehicle systems.

formed in stainless steel and polished brightly (turning out to be one of the nicer details of the car). Two short exhaust ducts from the engine heat exchangers were modeled in clay and then fabricated in bright stainless steel to match. These duct exhausts functioned as the venturi injectors.

We learned from McLean that instead of the usual fiberglass fabrication procedure the corporation had decided go an extra step with the Firebird III and make a plaster master model from our clay.[60] We waited in great anticipation as the day to start pulling plasters finally arrived. The only job we had this day was to stand by and watch.

The master plaster model is shown here being lifted out of the tool. *Photo courtesy of GM Media Archives*

---

[60] Fiberglass panels were usually laid up from plaster casts taken directly off the clay model. This time these casts would be taken off the refined plaster master model.

The styling plaster shop was made up of, and run almost exclusively, by members of the Bogarelli family, who had brought their trade with them from Italy. They started by placing clay extrusion dams along sharp fin features of the car, delineating those features. The dorsal tail fin was cast first and then removed from the model, to allow the entire top to be cast in one clean shot. The casting process otherwise was exactly the same as that used for the Firebird II.

Back in the plaster shop, the casts were reassembled and a plaster replica of the original clay was cast inside. Working through the open underside, a supporting frame structure was built up. After it was oven dried, the separate plaster fin details were added, and the craftsmen began to refine the surfaces. When they finished, the surfaces were sealed, sanded, painted lacquer black, then waxed, and buffed to a high-gloss finish. Black was selected because it was better for revealing any surface irregularities that might require further work. There was never any thought of painting the car black, but we were all really impressed, it really looked awesome.[61] It was determined that no changes were necessary, so the plaster shop began taking new splashes, which would become the tooling to make the fiberglass panels.

Almost by default, a secondary design theme was that the car was almost devoid of chrome or bright work, except as required for technical purposes. It would have to depend entirely on its sculptural body form for its visual impact. The only bright areas were the engine exhaust ports, the wheels, the blister-canopy edge retainer, and the grillwork inside the front end.

More and more people were now becoming involved in building the car. George Pollard, of Interiors, selected the exterior color to be a basic gold base with silver metallic content, followed by a pearlescent glaze overcoat. The color was named Lunar Sand. The pearlescent finish was a carryover from the original Firebird I. The Firebird II skipped this detail because it was fabricated of and featured brushed titanium. The interior would be a bright vermilion. The Graphics Design and Exhibits people developed the multicolored Firebird emblem for the hood and grille.

Before the exterior color had been selected, there was a period of experimentation, trying to find a really exotic finish for the car. One of the samples created by the Research Labs was prepared on a small-shaped fiberglass section. It was process finished in a "liver of sulfur," giving it a polished black

---

[61] Photos of this model appear in C. Edson Armi's *The Art of American Car Design*, The Pennsylvania State University Press, 1988.

silver look. We went no further with it, likely because of its high cost and the difficulty of maintaining uniformity across all the panels. The sample was very impressive. Later, after seeing the master plaster painted in gloss black, I wondered, "What if?"

At Research Staff, under Joe Bidwell, the mechanical systems, including the chassis, suspension, and the joystick unicontrol steering system were entering into their final hardware phase. The electronics for the controller included a wire in the road automatic guidance capability. Bill Turunen headed the gas turbine lab and was moving right along on the engine-transmission package. Tom Mitzelfeld of Engineering Staff, was developing the 10 HP APU package. At Styling, we switched our attention to the production aspects of the Motorama show.

GM had contracted with Maurice Evans, the venerable stage and screen actor, to plan and manage the entire Waldorf Astoria production. This would include: music, dancers, the slick presentation of the Firebird III on a futuristic stage and turntable.[62] As with the previous Firebirds, a 35mm movie would be produced to prove it was a running car. On the turntable, the Firebird would be fully automated to demonstrate all of its features by remote control.

The first meeting with Evans was held at the Tech Center, to work out a general plan for the film production. The day was dark and overcast, and we all met at Styling—in the second floor lounge overlooking the Tech Center Lake. Evans was there with his staff of young assistants, and Bob McLean was there for GM, with his staff (Stefan and me). Oddly, the most distinctive recollection of that meeting was of looking at Evans, in his elegant three-piece continental business suit, and then looking at his young staff, in their three-piece business suits. I then looked at McLean, in his gold (metallic thread) business suit, then at Stefan, in his bronze suit and then looked down at my stainless-steel suit. Of all that transpired that day, this is the one clear memory that survives.

However, there were decisions made, and they would be implemented. Evans would bring in a professional Hollywood crew to make the 35mm film. They would begin shooting in our studio, starting with the design sequence, taking it from its inception, and following it all the way through to its testing (yet

---

[62] My good friend, Jim Pirkl, had graduated from Pratt and was hired by GM to work in their Exhibit group, in time to receive the assignment to design it. It was done in the style of the then new, LAX International Airport Restaurant.

to occur) at the GM Proving Grounds in Mesa, Arizona. The stage production and the dance choreography would be handled entirely by Evans' people. With assignments made, they went off to do their planning, and we returned to support the building of the Firebird III.

While Research Staff had the chassis pretty well under way, they were testing its joystick controller in a modified Chevrolet. The steering wheel and column had been removed, and the controller was mounted in the driver's side door. The joystick motions were: left or right for turns, forward for acceleration, and backward for braking. The heart of the controller was in its mass motion physics, which was integrated into the vehicle electronics[63] system. Roy Cataldo, the lead engineer for the system, was driving the car around the Tech Center one day, and stopped by to offer us a ride. While we were taking a spin around the Lake, he gave us a startling demonstration. We were going about 40 mph up the three lane open road, when he slapped the joystick to hard left and let go. The electronics interpreted the command as a "go to the limit—maximum left turn." It read the vehicle speed and calculated the greatest steering angle the front wheels would accept, without losing traction (at that speed), and initiated a hard left turn. We were all thrown violently to the right, because of the centripetal force, but the mass atop the now free joystick was also thrown hard to the right, affecting an immediate right-steering correction and causing the Chevy to lurch right back to its original heading, straight down the road! The mass of the joystick in the hand also served to create an artificial feel, replacing the resistance normally felt in a steering wheel while driving through a turn. Roy's task was to optimize the mass physics and to integrate the servo controls across these complex sets of conditions.

We were each given an opportunity to drive the Chevy. As noted, the steering command was very sensitive to vehicle speed, so that it would not over steer at high speeds. When it was my turn to drive, it was excitement turning to near panic. I was about to pass a parked car when I noticed another car approaching from the other direction. I naturally slowed down to aim for my center lane and immediately felt the car starting to hunt as the steering reacted with more and more sensitivity. It was scary, but it worked out okay; and in general, it was a positive experience. Roy told us that he found a secretary who had never driven a car before and observed that she had no difficulty in learning to drive it feeling, in fact, that it was probably easier for her than a standard automobile would have been.

---

[63]   By electronics, think in terms of mechanical relays, performing and initiating all the logic and actions.

As all things appeared to be coming together, we received word that the shooting script had been written and the Hollywood crew would be arriving shortly to start their Detroit shots. The chassis was coming along well, and we were asked for inputs on what colors we wanted for the interior mechanical systems. The Skydrol hydraulic fluid was new, having just been introduced in the aircraft industry, and apparently it was murder on conventional paints. We would have to use another new paint for the mechanical parts, a urethane-based paint system. At least we would be able to have custom colors mixed rather than choosing between uglies. We settled on a simple buff beige color for everything. They had a batch mixed up and began painting the chassis frame and all the hardware as they were being completed. Research Staff also built a second chassis that would become a show chassis only. All the mechanical components would be distinctly painted and installed in the stand-alone exhibit. They never asked for color recommendations, and their chassis ended up painted in all kinds of wild contrasting and garish colors. I was concerned that the public would credit Styling with that color scheme and praise Engineering for their no-nonsense running chassis.

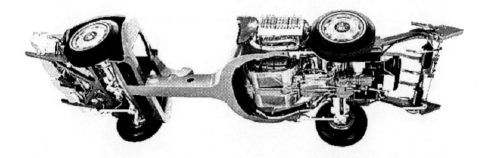

The research staff show chassis—note the centerline structural spine that enables the easy exit and entry to the vehicle. *Photo courtesy of GM Media Archives*

The film crew arrived on a Monday morning to start the film production. They had scripted the shooting sequence and gave us a copy, so we could prepare our studio and start collecting the support props they would need. Hal Moore was the director; Harry Wolfe the cinematographer. They also brought along their writer and a few other support people.

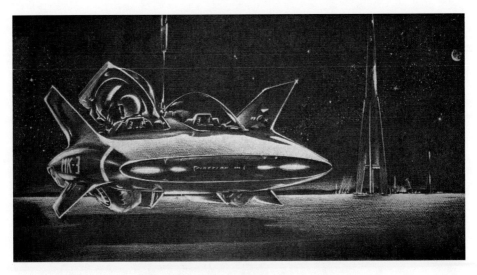

Image courtesy of GM Media Archives

The storyboard opening shot would be looking over my shoulder as I made the original concept drawing. They would show it in progression, starting with a stroke for the horizon line and fading in and fade out in stages, as the drawing materialized in front of the camera. I created the finished drawing first, showing the car suspended from a hoist, with a moon rocket in the background and another, of the same drawing again but about halfway completed. I then practiced drawing the single line on a clean sheet, trying to match the horizon line in the finished drawing. When I had it down pat, they filmed the first stroke, then faded out and back in again, blending in the drawing in progress and then again at the completion. After the design was generalized, they took shots of Stefan and me recreating the string drawing sequence.

Later, they transitioned to a tricky shot, using stop frame motion, as they dollied alongside our engineering mockup with all the mechanical components popping themselves into place. They wrapped up the Detroit filming with some heroic "low camera looking up" views of our team, walking along the Tech Center Lake with the blue sky in the background. The crew then packed up their equipment, and the next time we would see them would be in Arizona for the live action shots. I remember thinking at the time, "My God, we don't even know if the car will work yet."

It wasn't long after that that word came down that the chassis had been completed and sent to the turbine lab to have the engine installed. While it was discouraged, we found an excuse to drop by and see it in progress. A few days later, we received a phone call from friends at the lab, exclaiming that the bare chassis was being driven around the Tech Center. We all rushed outside, just in time to see it as it passed by. Very little of the body work was in place, and there were a couple of extra Research Staff people riding on top, behind the driver and passenger, holding on to whatever they could get a grip of. A nice photo of that scene was printed in the next Research Staff newsletter.

Firebird III's first run with Joe Bidwell, head of the Engineering Mechanics Department, in the driver's seat. *Photo courtesy of GM Media Archives*

A few days later, I saw the chassis in the Styling machine shop. It was raised on blocks, and they were starting to fit the rest of the bodywork. It was a very strange, and moving moment for me, as I watched them fitting the right front fender panel to its supporting framework. It was the same shape I had seen so many times before, but this time, it was not clay, and it was slipping on to a dense assembly of mechanical muscle and the creature was now coming to life.

As the car was nearing completion, there was a new sense of urgency. While we knew they would first have to checkout the mechanical systems, we were also painfully aware that the car would have to be placed on a truck shortly, for shipment to Arizona and the final checkout would have to be done there.

Firebirds I and II would be no problem, and they would be ready for shipping at any time. Research Staff prepared their list of parts and support people that they would need. Stefan developed a master plan to get the right people to Arizona at the right times. We would have a two-week window in August to complete our movie, but our biggest concern would be that a press conference had been scheduled with a hard date at the end, for the formal unveiling of the Firebird III. Finally, we heard the word, "all three Firebirds had been shipped," and, "all systems are GO!" An advance crew would fly out in a week, to shake out any problems the car might have. I would be flying out later to catch the last week of the schedule.

Arriving in Phoenix, I was picked up at the airport by a Firebird team member. On the way to the proving grounds, I heard that the Firebird III was down, and in the shop. Apparently, they were having problems with a small gear in the turbine accessories power train. A gas turbine depends on the natural flow of incoming air to keep cool. This is no problem as long as it is running, however, when it shuts down, it enters a soak period when heat from engine hot spots migrates into adjacent engine parts. What was happening was that this particular gear would heat up above its operating limit, and if they restarted the engine before it cooled down, it would break and have to be replaced. With the engine buried in the center of the vehicle, this turned out to be a five or six-hour job. They had extra gears but they found it more expedient to just keep the engine running, or if they had to shut down, allow it to cool completely before restarting.

Even with this problem, they were okay on their schedule to start shooting the action shots for the Motorama film. They brought in a Hollywood camera truck, which, in addition to the truck bed, had shooting platforms hanging off both bumpers and on top of the cab. Harry Wolfe, the cinematographer, would be behind the 35mm Mitchell camera and Hal Moore would be seated right behind him, when the action started. Any spaces left on the truck were fair game for anyone.

Most of the shooting would be done on the five-mile main track, which was circular and slightly banked. There were a few other roads within and others outside servicing the garages and engineering facilities. While the Motorama film was the main production that we all came to Arizona for, GM Photographic also had a small film crew taking 16mm footage as targets of opportunity made themselves available. The still photographer was Chuck Ternes, who had been with us at Styling, documenting the Firebird III from its first days as a mockup. I was shooting 35mm black-and-white negatives and color slides with my Nikon S2.

The circular track provided the setting for the opening shot. The camera truck drove on the inside lane, with the camera looking back to see the Firebird

I, in the same lane. Panning slowly outward, it would find the Firebird II in the next lane then continuing the pan, pick up the Firebird III in the top outside lane, all while zooming and framing to keep all three cars in that same view.

With the main shot secured, they continued filming over the next several days, taking breaks where they had to reconfigure the car or setup for special shots. One such break was when they needed a camera shot, looking down into both canopies from above and behind. The canopies had special aluminized coatings applied to protect the interior against the sun. Since the reflective coating would have defeated that high-camera view, we also had two canopies made, without coatings, strictly for this one particular shot. Emmett Conklin, the Research Staff engineer who was doing all the driving, said afterward that for the first time, the heat from the Arizona sun was almost unbearable. The Firebird III had a high capacity air-conditioning system that served it well, but only now did we realize how important a function the aluminized coatings had been performing.[64] I felt vindicated, first for going to the trouble of aluminizing the canopies, but most of all, for staying with the short (backward) blisters, instead of changing to the longer teardrops. That would have doubled the heat load on the air-conditioning system. Perhaps it was that intuition that said the teardrop did not look right.

Several times, during the shooting, they had to stop to attend to some mechanical problem with the car. They would pull the car in, under a tent, to shield it from the sun, then open up anything that had a hinge to cool it off. Large fans were set up to blow into the engine compartment while they made their fixes, hoping there would be enough light left to get another action shot. One evening, the shooting ended at dusk, and with its lights on, some of the best photographs were taken. Afterward, we—the lucky ones—could go back to the motel and wash up before a nice night out on the town, while our counterparts at Research Staff had to hunker down and work through the night to be sure the car was ready in the morning.

Our motel, the Sands, was very new and quite modern by the day's standards. It was the first time I had been in Arizona, and it was like nothing I had ever seen before. The days were hot, some ten to fifteen degrees hotter than anything I was used to, but it was dry and surprisingly bearable—I loved it. The Firebird team was provided with half dozen or so Pontiac convertibles that we divvied up, I, pooling with Stefan and Bob McLean. We drove around by day under

---

[64] The Firebird III was restored in recent years and is enjoying renewed public exposure after having been hidden away in the Research Staff lobby for several decades. The car, as it is now displayed, is fitted with these two clear canopies, which were made for that original movie shot.

clear skies and a burning sun with the top up, and the air-conditioning going full blast. Almost every evening, huge thunderclouds would build up, and we would have horrendous lightning storms, followed by flash flooding through the downtown streets. The rains cooled everything down for a balmy top-down Detroit-like evening. Then, almost as suddenly, the clouds would break up in time to see a gorgeous sunset.

We would usually look for a nice steak house to have dinner and discuss the events of the day. Afterward, some of the team found relaxation swimming in the motel pool at two in the morning under the pleasant balmy sky; definitely, this was not Detroit.

In the morning, after a nice breakfast, we drove back to the proving grounds, eager to see how the night crew had performed. We always found the "bird" ready. We couldn't help thinking about the coming Saturday. Hopefully, the filming would be behind us and we would be ready for the press conference, wondering if the car would be okay, hoping that some other small mechanical problem would not ruin our day.

Emmett Conklin was Supervisor of Testing for the Firebird program and drove the Firebird III for all the action footage and Mauri Rose was the man in the second seat, mostly for face recognition, as a three-time Indianapolis five-hundred winner, but also as the GM staff engineer that he was. There had been a lot of earlier press footage of him as the driver of the high-speed Firebird I that truly was his forte. Harley Earl appeared toward the end of the week, as did Lawrence Hafstad, VP of Research Staff; and they were both given rides around the track. Our spirits were up because we had completed all of our Motorama footage and all that remained were shots of opportunity—formal and informal—of the team members and the bird. My best shot of the week was of Chuck Ternes, the photographer, about to take the (now classic) photo of Harley Earl and the three Firebirds.

The press arrived early Saturday morning. All of us were hesitant but feeling better because of the good day we had Friday. The Firebird III was shown to the press, first as a static display, then with all of its hoods, decks and doors open so they could get a good view of all the stuffings, more than had ever been done for a Motorama show car before (or concept car since). The engine was then started, and it began a continuous series of rides for VIPs and the media. By noon, the press conference was over, and it was an unqualified success; the car performed flawlessly and we were all ecstatic. Now we could get our own personal photos, posing with the birds. This time, all the big smiles were real

On Sunday, after the press conference, we all had an opportunity to relax. McLean, Stefan and I took our convertible for a ride in the Arizona high country, along the Apache Trail. McLean, the westerner, filled us in on the story of the Lost Dutchman's Mine and the treasure of gold that was supposedly buried nearby. Going up the trail, I was surprised at how the landscape slowly changed from the arid desert with the Soccoro cactus to the rich green pines of the plateaus, as we rose in altitude. It was also the first time I had been exposed to the effects of low pressure at altitude, and how peaceful and quiet it seemed.

From the high ridges and mountain trails along the plateau, we would stop at lookout points for grand views and to take pictures. I was astounded to be able to see so far, and to observe the effects of atmospheric perspective, as the haze diminished the contrast of the distant mountains.

It was at one such stop that I had another strange *déjà vu* moment. For some reason, I started wondering about my shyness and that perhaps the girl that I would marry, might just happen to be out there, somewhere in that grand Arizona view. I then realized it was a silly thought, and tried to rationalize why I would think of such a thing. Very likely, I was impressed with Arizona and really enjoyed my last week, thinking that I could see myself moving here and to this life style. In that context, it was not too unusual.

With our task in Phoenix complete, the team began returning to Detroit. McLean and Stefan would fly back earlier and I would leave a day later. At the Motel, as others were already departing; I found myself split from my usual group, and being hungry, was surprised to find myself sitting down and sharing a pizza, one on one, with Mauri Rose. This turned out to be one of the high points of my trip.

Back in Detroit, we found ourselves waiting for the press release date for the Firebird III. It happened on Sunday, September 14, and the *Detroit News* magazine section had a full color cover and four inside pages on the design and building of the car. I was fortunate to be spotted in several places and even named in one, but the full credit properly went to Harley Earl, as he was the one that inspired it and saved it (on the day he returned from vacation).

The rest of the year was waiting in anticipation for the 1959 Motorama. I was more than disappointed, however, when that day arrived and I was not on the list of those assigned to go there. I felt better later when U.S. Design Patent No. 185,843 was issued in my name for the Firebird III.

August 1958, at the General Motors Proving Grounds in Mesa, Arizona, preparing for the start of the Motorama production film.

Hollywood Director Hal Moore and crew planning the day's shoot.

Left, Chuck Ternes of GM Photographic was responsible for almost all of the photo documentation at Styling for the Firebird III. Also visible in the picture is Stefan Habsburg. *Right*, Cinematographer Harry Wolfe is behind the camera.

The GT-305 Whirlfire engine installation. An insulation barrier separates the engine from the electronics compartment on the right and the fuel tank with a similar barrier on the left.

Above, The Firebird III opened up for service access. *Right*, Bill Turunen, head of the Gas Turbine Lab, babysits a late night fix.

View showing doors and access panel openings. The "bow tie" panel in front secures the front hood until it is powered forward to clear it.

Rear view shows the "hourglass" rear-deck access panels. The two square panels on either side of the tail fin are aerodynamic brakes that work in unison with a large central panel below when the brakes are applied at speed.

A high vantage point offers a complete view of split lines and service access compartments. *Photo courtesy of GM Media Archives*

Above, Firebird III all opened up at a midday stop. The two-piece front hood splits to provide access to the APU.

Left, Emmett Conklin, research staff's main driver for the Firebird III.

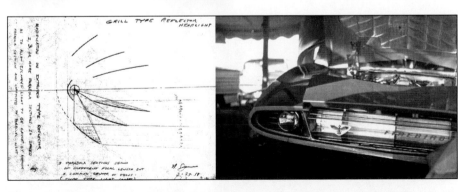

The original concept sketch (left) of the Firebird III's low-beam headlight reflector. The elastomeric nose-bumper has been removed for service access in this photograph. Note also the medallion in the grillwork that has since disappeared.

Chuck Ternes about to take the classic photograph of Harley Earl and the Firebirds.

Left, The author with the Firebird III during a shooting break. *Right*, Accessing the electronics compartment in front of the rear wheel and under the skirt.

Left, Harley Earl exiting after a ride. Stefan Habsburg is looking on from the right. *Right*, Harley Earl and Bob McLean having a discussion.

6 Moonmen

The Firebird III was a real high for me even though I wasn't able to see it in New York. That bothered me, but I tried to not let it show. I was also starting to return to the real world, becoming aware of other things that had been happening. Over the year and a half that I was preoccupied with the Firebird III, McLean had continued to build his empire, adding another research studio and still more personnel. Within the styling organization, it was now clear that, with Earl's retirement coming up soon, McLean would be one of the contenders for Earl's job. The politics at Styling—if anyone was paying attention—was that people would align themselves with particular leaders and then their fates would be sealed by those selections. Mitchell had been Earl's right-hand man, and it had always been assumed that he would be the natural heir; but no one was really sure because Earl had started bringing in a lot of new high-tech aerospace people over the last several years and McLean's name headed that other list. As it turned out, once Earl retired, he did pass the Styling/GM VP position on to Bill Mitchell.

Mitchell began restructuring the organization into his own image and in the process capped McLean's threat by redirecting his groups to provide less freewheeling and more direct support to the bread-and-butter production studios; this, however, would still leave us in a good position to explore new vehicle architectures and new body styles. One such activity was our continuing work with the structural sandwich platform floors, in lieu of conventional frames. This allowed us to consider an unlimited variety of interior arrangements, including a front-wheel drive system that got rid of the drive shaft. One variation was a sedan-sized vehicle with a raised rear roof and a Vista-Vision (Greyhound Bus) scenic roof window. This gave us a lounge-type rear seating arrangement where passengers could get up and move about. Later yet, this led us to explore larger camper-sized vehicles, with lavatories, kitchens, and sleeping provisions. We built several full-scale wood-frame mockups so we could fully assess their spatial relationships.

One Monday, upon arriving at work, I received some devastating news, almost as had happened with Kostellow. Someone had heard from Jerri Habsburg that Stefan was in the hospital. He apparently had come down with encephalitis, which was an inflammation of the brain. It was very serious, and she was told that there was only about a 20 percent recovery chance. She was further advised that he should receive his last rites. A few days later, he was still alive and there seemed to be more hope. After a week, they expected he would survive and then that it would be okay for him to receive visitors in a few more days.

The hospital staff cautioned us not to have any expectations of normality. As we started hearing from people that had seen him, the message was always the same. Stefan would be quick to recognize any visitor as they came into his room, but then he would begin to ask, "What happened? Where am I? What day is it? What's going on?" Then after a pause, "What happened? Where am I? What day is it? What's going on?" This would continue throughout the entire visit, with little change in his questions. When I visited him, I had heard that Karl Ludvigsen[65] had just been there, and that they had carried on extensive technical discussions, dating back to their days at MIT. Once, Karl left, however, Stefan did not remembered that he was there, nor would he remember my visit after I left. Apparently, it was only his short-term memory that was affected.

When he was released from the hospital, Jerri took him back to family in Massachusetts, for a rehabilitation program that would take the good part of the next year. When Stefan returned to Styling, it was, in part, for his rehabilitation. His assignments were eased, as he could no longer manage complex problems. When he drove to work, he had a map affixed to his visor—showing the route to and from work. He also had a small orange ball pierced on to his car's antenna, so he could find it in the parking lot after work. After adapting to his circumstances, Styling assigned him to training new designers in their Orientation Studio.[66]

The loss of Stefan as a partner was a severe blow, and I had to adjust to new studio teaming relationships. McLean moved me to his Research B Studio, next door, to lead a small group, exploring a potential future production project, a

---

[65] Karl joined GM after graduating from Pratt and served several years in many capacities. Since leaving GM, Karl distinguished himself in the automotive industry and in automotive literature.

[66] While Stefan would ultimately retire from Styling, he was never to realize the full potential he once had.

small sporty coupe. They gave me a lead role, obviously testing (or trying to develop) my capacity to handle it. We made a gallant effort, trying to give it a new aerodynamic look, but when the design committee came by for a review, they dumped all over it, saying, "It doesn't look automotive." We regrouped and tried to figure out exactly what they meant, so I went back to the classic forms and gave it a very long hood with a small cockpit, set way back. We went through the routine again, reworking the full size clay model to our new theme and scheduling another review.

This time, when the committee came back,[67] they were outraged. Before they stormed out, one of the key inquisitors exclaimed, "This is not a car. This is a caricature!" These comments appeared to be based upon our disproportionately long hood. The true irony was that the very next day, in March of 1961, Jaguar came out with the new Type E and Bill Mitchell immediately went down into the secret basement studio and had Larry Shinoda lengthen the hood of the new Stingray Corvette by ten inches! Not long afterward, I was to hear that Bill Mitchell had referred to our group as "a bunch of Moonmen." Inwardly, I took it as a complement, but I also recognized it as the end of my future with Styling.

Perhaps it was fate, but not long afterward, McLean called to informed me that GM was going to team with the Radio Corporation of America (RCA) in a response to a NASA Request for Proposal (RFP) for the Surveyor Lunar Soft Lander. In the team, GM would be responsible for the mechanical systems and RCA for the electronics. GM was putting a group of people together at their Allison Division in Indianapolis to prepare the proposal. They would be drawing from all their division and staff resources to collect the skills they would need. I was being assigned to the team to provide presentation and graphic support. It would likely last a few weeks. I figured I was selected because I was research oriented, and as an amateur astronomer, had some familiarity with the moon and space.

I flew to Indianapolis and reported to the Allison facility, where I was directed to the team area. It was my first experience working in this kind of multidisciplined engineering environment and with the proposal process itself. Herb Karsh was the GM team leader in Indianapolis. The RCA team would be working their part in New Jersey. There were several meetings called to bring us all up to speed. We were then broken up into several smaller sub-teams to work our individual tasks.

---

67   Bill Mitchell was not in either of these groups.

Yes, it was too good to last. One day, the following week, Karsh called us all together and told us that RCA was pulling out of the proposal. He said we would continue for a few days to wrap up what we had developed so far but GM would end up no bidding it. I returned to Styling disappointed but still happy to have even been able to participate. Hughes Aircraft eventually won the contract and built the soft-landers that went to the moon.

On the home front, our small group began splitting up and changing. New graduates from Pratt began arriving from the newest class, and we started shuffling roommates and apartments. One of my roommates from the Centerline barracks, Marlan Polhemus, found a nicer apartment in Royal Oak, and we moved into it. Then when Harley Earl's industrial design office sent him to San Diego to work on the Convair 880, Carl Olsen moved in to take his place. Later yet, we moved into a carriage house that Carl found on a Bloomfield Hills estate, on the corner of Woodward Avenue and Lone Pine Road.

A year later, Carl married a lovely English girl, Sonia, and moved to another carriage house in the area. This time I kept the place to myself. It was only $90 a month and was in a nice quiet location in the back of the estate. I was able to get some decent astronomical viewing from the estate grounds with my 8" telescope, which I had reconditioned. I still "bachelored" around with my few remaining single friends, Al Nakata and Jim Pirkl, and occasionally would go to the parties thrown by the younger GM crowd. On summer weekends, we would drive to Canada to swim at Ipperwash Beach, on Lake Huron (a two-hundred-mile round trip). Often, we would each drive our own Corvettes, in a convoy—sometimes doing it twice on a weekend, and occasionally three or four times—if it was a long holiday weekend. On the way home, we would stop at the Wish-You-Well Tavern, near the Tech Center, and have beer and a Roberto's pizza to complete the day.

As I found myself having more idle time, I resumed telescope making, although it really only involved the optical grinding and polishing part. I started grinding a group of mirrors, all at the same time, thinking it was more efficient to do all the same stages together. Before I went too far, however, I decided to pack them all up and start a ten-inch Cassegranian telescope. It would be more like observatory telescopes, in that it would have an additional convex secondary mirror on top instead of a diagonal flat mirror, and it would reflect the optical rays back down through the center of the main mirror, where it would be viewed from behind. This would also require that I, somehow, bore a 1-3/8-inch-diameter hole through the center of Pyrex primary mirror. The Cassegranian would have some other good features. It would be short, yet it would have the properties of a much longer telescope, meaning it would be high-powered and especially good for the moon and the planets.

The primary mirror would have to be ground almost twice as deep for the short focal length it required, but the most difficult part would be to figure the smaller convex secondary mirror (because there were no simple tests to determine when it was right). I found it was nice living in city big enough to have its own telescope-making store (Ashdown Brothers), where I could wander through and drool over all the larger mirror kits on display.

Rough grinding to achieve the 3/16-inch depth at the center took nine hours. At this point, I set up a fixture to core the hole through its back, to within a 1/16-inch of the optical surface. This would allow fine grinding, polishing and figuring of the optical surface, unimpeded by the hole; then, when the polishing was finished, I could break through to complete the mirror.[68] Coring the hole was all done by hand and took nearly ten hours. Optical activity continued over a fairly intense five-month period and then I packed everything away and put it all on hold. There were new distractions.

The owner of the estate I was renting my carriage house from was a Mrs. House. She was a charming old lady, whose husband had passed away a few years before. I would sit to chat and have tea with her every month when I brought my rent check over. As I understood from our conversations, she was originally the nanny of the house and later married the widowed Mr. House. She was now getting along fairly well, but I could tell that she was tight on money. She was also renting out a few rooms in the main house to young women, a nurse, a teacher, and alike. While I visited several times, I never became serious with any of them, except I did like a friend of theirs

---

[68]   The boring was not an action of digging a hole in the glass, but rather one of using a thin wall brass tube to make a thin deep ring-cut, leaving a glass core intact, nearly to the front surface. This required jigging up a fixture to hold the boring tube, centered over the mirror. The standard procedure was really quite clever. The cutting edge of the brass tube would be notched to catch carborundum grit, which would be judiciously poured down the center of the tube, along with a sprinkling of water. The mirror blank would be taped, face down on to a turntable, and be turned with one hand while steadily feeding water and abrasive down the tube with the other. The water would flush the grit outward where it would be caught in the notches, abrading the glass around the tube wall. This would continue while a thin circular groove was being cut into the glass. The grit created its own clearance as it washed down the inside of the tube, past the cutting notches, and then flushed itself back up and out.

that came by at times, and I took them all out one time, to see the movie *One Eyed Jacks*.

The one I liked was named Susan. She came from a manufacturing family; her father, Don Connor, had been the president of Micromatic, a machine tool company. He was in early retirement, having recently survived a small plane crash. Her mother, Lucy, was a gregarious soul; and we all got along very well. Susan also had a brother, Tom, who was about my age and had graduated from Dartmouth. They all lived together in a nice house on Orchard Lake, some twenty miles northwest of Detroit. Needless to say, we steadily became more involved, and she accounted for more and more of my time outside of GM.

Meanwhile, back at Styling, I heard that GM had set up a new Defense Systems Division that would undertake the kind of work our team did in Indianapolis. They were located about a mile below the Tech Center, also on Mound Road. The key people in the new organization apparently left RCA to join GM. My first awareness of their presence was when I saw several scale models of rockets in the Styling Model shop. They were in the process of submitting a proposal, and they had Styling make some models for them. They were all a variety of mobile missile launchers, disguised as Allied moving vans and such. The idea was to keep the missiles moving on the highways where they could be safely hidden against Soviet detection and missile attack.

Organizationally the division was set up with three groups: Land, Sea, and Space Operations. Land Operations at the time was the most developed and was headed by Don Friedman, supported closely by Sam Romano. While their charter was to provide off-road mobility expertise for military and commerce, this, technically, would also include lunar vehicles for lunar exploration. Sea and Space Operations were somewhat behind in their manning, and apparently Detroit was only a temporary home for the division as they had plans to eventually move to California.

A few months later, McLean called me to his office to introduce me to some people. They were Dr. Greg Bekker and his protégé, Ferenc Pavlics, both new hires for the division. They had recently been employed at the Chrysler Tank Arsenal, which coincidentally was just across the tracks from my old apartment in Centerline. They apparently were the best in the field of off-road mobility and already had some ideas for lunar vehicles—Bob thought I would be interested in meeting them. We had some pleasant conversations, exchanging ideas on lunar vehicles and lunar exploration. Coincidentally, we had some similar thoughts on six-wheeled vehicle concepts, mine being of the "gut feel" type and theirs, based on sound technical foundations. After parting, we would meet again.

I next heard that they were going to submit an unsolicited proposal to NASA for a Lunar Sample Return mission. The plan was to transport the system to the moon on the Surveyor soft-lander spacecraft and after landing, take some pictures, scoop up some soil, load the film and the samples into a basketball-sized package, and rocket it back to earth, where it would reenter the atmosphere and parachute down for a standard sea recovery.

They asked if I could support them with some artwork that they would need for their presentation in Washington. I made a colored tempera illustration, which showed the Surveyor firing the return module back to earth. It turned out to be a very enjoyable task. I never heard whatever came of the proposal. Then, less than a year later, the entire group moved to Santa Barbara, California, and I thought, "Well that's the end of that."

That summer, they threw a birthday party for Susan's brother Tom, at their lakeside home. For entertainment, one of Tom's friends loaned them a water novelty that they placed in the lake near their small boat dock. It was a ship's "crow's nest," mounted on top of a short mast, which itself was mounted atop a three foot diameter fiberglass sphere. In the water, the sphere provided flotation, and a mass of concrete cast inside would ballast the mast upright. It was balanced so that someone could climb up the mast to get into the nest and remain stable, standing on the small platform while comfortably holding on to the surrounding rail.

From the normal upright position, one could swing back and forth on the inverted pendulum and get it to swinging so that they could actually "kiss" the water on opposite sides, at the end of each swing. It was really a lot of fun and very smooth in its motion. I went back to it several times that day and then again, that evening. It was then, when I looked up at the stars, that I was aware of how smoothly I was moving. A thought came to mind, "Gee, this would make a good telescope mount." Then the party was over and it was back to work on Monday.

———————————

That October in '61, the Defense Systems Division formally asked for my support on a more detailed proposal that was being prepared for the same Lunar Sample Return concept. McLean told me I would be loaned to them for about five months, and that I would be on a *per diem* to cover expenses. I was expected to drive my car to California and rent an apartment during my stay. I was excited about the opportunity to go, but was concerned about separating from Susan, since we were starting to get serious about each other. I broke the news to her that evening and while she was disappointed, it was okay. I then found out that, by pure coincidence, her folks were planning a trip to Santa Barbara over the holidays, when they would visit Susan's uncle, who was also the chairman of board at Micromatic, living in Hope Ranch, a very plush suburb. They would drive out towing their Airstream trailer. Susan and Tom would be traveling with them, so it would be only a few months before I would see her again.

I packed the few things I needed and piled them into my Corvette, preparing myself mentally for the long haul. The drive turned out to be quite a revelation, since I had only known it as fly-over country before. Once I passed through the flat lands and entered into New Mexico, it really started to get exciting. At the pace I was going, it would take me about three and a half days, the Interstates being only about 10 percent complete at the time. I arrived in Tucumcari, very late one night and, feeling fatigued, decided to stop there. I found I had a choice between two motels, so I picked the one that had the new vibrator beds. After checking in, I found the beds were coin operated and cost 25 cents for fifteen minutes. After a moment's pause I thought, "What the Hell . . . I'm on expense account" so I put in 75 cents and went right to sleep. I woke up at one point and the bed was still vibrating. I hadn't realized how tired I was since I felt as though I had been asleep for hours, and then I went right back to sleep. I had set the alarm for 6:30 AM, because I still had a full day's drive ahead of me. When the alarm woke me, I realized the vibrator was still going. As I got out of bed, I was literally shaking, as if I had been driving a thousand miles. After breakfast, I felt okay and I resumed my journey on Route 66.

Approaching Los Angeles, I put my top down and was really enjoying California. It was Sunday and I was listening to a Rams game, thinking it was a good way to kill a block of time, and distract me from the ache of wanting to get the drive over with. Passing through LA, I was now on State Route 101, drying out from the sun and the wind and still sixty miles out of Santa Barbara. I stopped for gas and a bite to eat at Moore Park, which was only a four-corner "gas and eats" intersection at the time. After gassing up, I went into DuPar's Restaurant near noontime, and it was busy, filled up—even at the counter—and the hostess asked me to sit in the waiting area out front until a seat was available. I thanked her and mentioned how dry and parched my throat was. I sat for a short period when I looked up and realized she had brought me a glass of ice water. Few things in my life have impressed me more than that kind gesture. I thought, "Californians are really nice people."

Arriving in Santa Barbara, I pulled out McLean's directions. He recommended that I stop at the Lemon Tree Motel on upper State Street. I found it easily. It was quite modern in its architecture and interiors, which was why McLean recommended it. It was the kind of place that designers always look for to patronize and promote good design. I went to bed early, fatigued from the long drive and wanting to be reasonably fresh for the next morning.

Monday, October 16. After breakfast, I got back into my Corvette and continued on State Street, as the road started turning west,[69] going for a few more miles before changing its name to Hollister Avenue. Soon I was in Goleta and continued past the airport to find the GM Defense Systems Division, a short distance ahead on my left. I turned into the parking lot and walked into the lobby, asking for Don Friedman. I was taken to his office on the second floor, where I sat and we talked for a while. As I did, I noticed the color rendering I had made for Lunar Sample Return presentation was framed and hanging on one of the walls.

---

[69] Santa Barbara's location in California places it between the Pacific coast to the South and the foothills of the Santa Ynez Mountains to the North.

I would be working almost exclusively on the same concept as before, but we would be taking it into more technical detail. The task, like McLean said, would run for about five months. Don then introduced me to Dr. Lloyd Brown, who was heading the project. He appeared to be in his fifties, wore glasses, and seemed very professorial. Dr. Brown then introduced me to Charlie Harper, whom I would be working under and who also perfectly fit the image of an aerospace engineer. They set me up to work in a vacant office nearby.

I was also given a tour of the facility, which turned out to be more like a campus than an industrial plant. Immediately behind the front two-story office building was the main high-ceiling manufacturing building. It was a few hundred feet long and almost as wide, with miscellaneous machining tools along the long east side. What struck me was a thick ten-foot high wall barrier running almost the full length of the long west side. Behind this barrier, one could see a hypervelocity gun that was used to fire small projectiles, accelerating them through most of its gun barrel length and then having them burst into a vacuum chamber where they could be photographed with high-speed cameras, as they hit test specimens. About once or twice a day, we would hear three short blasts of a klaxon horn, a pause, then a loud *blam* that shook the entire building, followed by a long "all clear" horn blast. This was all operated under the Space Operations Department. Some of the work they did, however, was in support of the lunar exploration studies, for example, the simulation of meteor impacts into soil concoctions, trying to figure what the composition of the lunar surface might be like.

At the south end of the building, there was an IBM mainframe computer and a soil mechanics laboratory run by Ferenc Pavlics whom I had met in Detroit. They had a long open trough where they would pour and mix all combinations of soils, trying to create whatever lunar surface concoction they could conceive of. Straddling the trough was a huge mechanical blender that could ride on tracks, the length of the bin, to mix the soil to any consistency. On these tracks, they could also pull test equipment to measure drag or traction of test vehicle hardware. They had already been testing self-propelled wheeled, tracked and screw devices. On this day, they had absolutely no knowledge as to what the lunar surface was like; they were only guessing, but they were working as hard as they could, to be ready for whatever it might turn out to be.

I was shown copies of correspondence between Harold Urey of University of California at San Diego (UCSD), and Tom Gold of Cornell, where Gold was predicting we would find fairy castle like dust structures that would take on strange gigantic shapes, clinging together by static electrical charge only. If a spacecraft tried to land, Gold suggested, it would sink some forty feet![70] The general consensus at DSD, however, was that the soil would most likely be

---

[70]   The scientific community referred to this theory as "Gold Dust."

volcanic in nature. NASA apparently concurred with this assessment, based on the large amount of testing that was being performed in Arizona on the Sunset Crater outflows.

The last building, on the south side was connected by way of an open sidewalk with an overhead cover (as were all the buildings), as if the sun and rain were the worst things they had to fear. This building was also a two-story housing: Engineering, with two man offices around the perimeter, a drafting room upstairs, and an electronics lab in the center core, downstairs. There were also a few offices for Sea Operations people who did marine research, but most of their work was actually done off-site in the field. I heard that some of their divers had just recovered a sensitive piece of military hardware that was lost offshore.

Outside the west gate was one of two parking lots and the company cafeteria. Immediately east of the property was the Santa Barbara airport, with our engineering building looking right down the main runway. Planes taking-off would fly right over us. To the north, past Hollister Avenue, was Highway 101 and beyond that were the foothills of the Santa Ynez mountains. To an eastern eye, it looked like it would be a pretty nice place to work.

After my first day of work, I drove around and found a nice large Spanish style apartment on Catalpa, near downtown Santa Barbara, which I could rent with a short lease. I would be able to hop right onto 101 and drive West twelve miles, past Goleta, and get off right at the plant.

Getting down to work, Charlie Harper brought me up to speed on the Lunar Sample Return project. It was pretty much the same as when I last saw it, except this time the actual return vehicle was better defined. The heart of the system was a spherical solid rocket motor coupled to the basketball-sized payload return module. The two spheres would be connected in flight by a short cylinder housing the flight trajectory and communications electronics. The completed vehicle would look very much like a snowman. The payload sphere, once separated, would be the only part to survive earth reentry. Because it was spherical, it didn't need an attitude control system and its whole surface would be ablative to protect the contents from the heat of reentry.

The mission itself would pass through several phases. In its descent from lunar approach, cameras would take pictures of the landing zone (to identify the site). An immediate problem would be to design a mechanism to safely transport the film cassette to the payload module before its return launch because the camera would likely be several feet away from the payload module. Upon landing, additional site photos would be taken, and then a drill would core out some lunar soil samples, which would also have to be transported to the payload module.

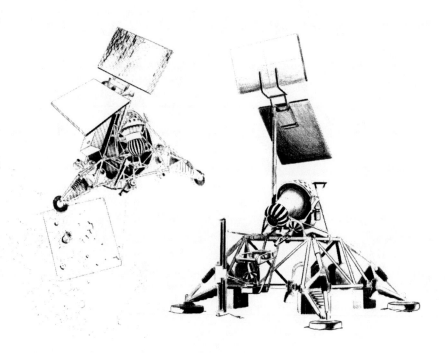

The Lunar Sample Return system is shown piggybacked onto the Surveyor soft-lander. It is shown photographing the landing site on approach (left) and drilling for a soil sample (right). *Images courtesy of GM Media Archives*

With everything loaded, a cover would close and secure the materials in the return module. The snowman, mounted within a gimbaled basket, would then be aligned into its launch attitude, spun up for spin stabilization, and the rocket ignited for its return to earth. The return trajectory would place reentry over the Pacific Ocean. Upon reentry, drag from Earth's atmosphere would convert velocity into heat; the surface of the tumbling sphere would burn and char. Embers would then break free, taking away excess heat before it could migrate inward. The rocket motor and electronics modules, having separated, would be consumed in the upper atmosphere. At a set altitude, a small para-balloon (parachute/balloon) would deploy to reduce the impact velocity as it hit the water. It would then discharge a yellow dye marker and transmit a homing signal to help the recovery team find it

The montage continues with the sample transferred to the return module, which is then aimed and launched toward Earth for reentry over the Pacific, paraballooning to a water landing and signaling for recovery. *Images courtesy of GM Media Archives*

The major amount of work this time would be to design the Surveyor mounted equipment, the gimbaled mount, the scientific payload, and the transport mechanisms to accomplish the mission. My task would be to work directly with Charlie Harper, designing hardware and creating technical illustrations for the proposal. On Surveyor, the snowman return vehicle and its launch platform would be stacked on top of the soft-lander's triangular truss architecture. There had been some debate whether the snowman and gimbals should lie horizontal, which would simplify the transfer of film cassettes and soil samples or whether it should stack vertical to reduce asymmetrical landing loads and shocks on the system. The photo cameras and soil collection mechanisms would be dispersed about the Surveyor truss structure, depending on where best they could do their jobs. Now we had to figure that part out.

On the first weekend, I decided to take a short drive to see more of California. I continued west on 101 to where the highway made its sharp turn northward. It was mostly rolling hills up to that point when I then entered a long inland valley. Still to my left were more barren hills and Vandenberg Air Force Base along the coast. Vandenberg was the U.S. Military's primary rocket-launching facility. Almost all the spy satellites launched from there were directed southward, into polar orbits so that the satellites would (almost) pass over every spot on Earth twice a day. On this day, I continued only a few more miles to a road junction with an Anderson's Split Pea Soup restaurant where I stopped for lunch. Afterward, turning east, I followed another valley road inland to Solvang, which was another Swedish theme community—good for another stop. The weather was clear and beautiful, and I was enjoying it all, top down in my Corvette. I stayed on the Santa Ynez valley road, which brought me back to Santa Barbara, returning by way of the back door, through San Marcos pass, then on down the steep mountain road into Santa Barbara.

The drive back up through that same pass would become one of my favorite rides, as I would either continue on to Lake Cachuma at night to see clear black star-filled skies or on weekends to take a day trip along the mountain ridge overlooking Santa Barbara. The latter was on an unimproved ridge road, which required full attention for rock falls and possible traffic around blind hairpin turns. The most spectacular sensation was looking out at the Pacific horizon line. From a height of probably only three thousand feet, I would swear that I could actually see the curvature of the earth! I loved it. The downhill portion was always very dicey, as the brakes would become hot and soft about half way down, before finally leading me into the foothills of Montecito, and from there, back to my apartment.

––––––––––––

At work, the first thing I noticed was that the stock room had no real graphics supplies, at least not as I was used to at Styling. Anything unusual that I needed had to be purchased from the art supply store in town. Vellum pads were handy, however, and I found that black ballpoint pens worked out rather nicely for technical publications, as these would only require black on white line art—nothing in color. There was one thing they had that did come in handy. The print shop was near by, in the center building, and they could take my pencil or ballpoint pen drawings, and using a manual xerography process, make a print plate and run immediate prints for my review. I was surprised at how thin faint pencil lines could be converted into crisp-black details in prints. Another surprise was that the drawings could be reduced in size giving them a sharpness I had never experienced before.[71]

I spent several weeks developing mechanical motion concepts for transporting the lunar sample and film canisters to the return module. Our goal was to reduce risk and improve the reliability of the systems. Concepts would be judged almost entirely by these guidelines.[72] There was one concept that I particularly liked, coming from a creative background, but it only raised everyone else's eyebrows. It was to transport the film canister from the remote camera to the return module by a simple ballistic transfer, i.e., fire it by an explosive (low caliber) charge, to be received, stopped (and the energy dissipated) in the module, with no connecting hardware. My rationale was that since the Surveyor was in free fall, gravity would be zero, and there would be no other forces present to disrupt a pretested and verified bore-aimed device. Some of my other ideas were better received, one being a tricky double rotation motion of the film/soil canister from low on the Surveyor framework to the reclining snowman above.

We had breaks during these inventive periods when I was able to relax with my coworkers. I learned that Dr. Brown was married but that his wife still lived in New Jersey. He remained socially active with the local crowd, mostly promoting parties with the younger married and single employees, and invited us to join him and others to beer parties at the local taverns. He had developed a rapport with this younger group, and was a fixture of the GM social society. After learning more about me, mostly about the telescope making, he said there was another young man that worked in the optical group that I should meet "because you both have a lot in common." I usually don't respond well to these types of introductions, but I was to find a rare individual that was very modest but knowledgeable and informative on things in a way that was not offensive. His name was John Siebert.

John would explain optical concepts and describe some of the optical devices they were developing, like a remote alignment device for an ICBM

---

[71] Reductions in print size are common in almost all copiers today, yet in the early days of xerography, stand-alone copiers were all 1:1. The print shop could scale up or down as a necessity of the publication business, but it took a cumbersome manual process to make the print plates.

[72] The cost of an item was never a real issue because if something cheap failed, the loss would be measured as the cost of the entire lost mission.

gyro navigation system. They were designing optical configurations that I could understand and could offer suggestions on. He showed me how they could optimize optical systems by running FOCUS, a ray trace program on the mainframe. The program would continuously change lens and mirror radii and separations until the image was optimized for quality. We tediously keypunch data onto IBM cards (ourselves) and then left them overnight, hopefully to be processed by the next day. John performed an interesting demonstration of inventing a Maksutov type telescope by starting with a spherical mirror and adding a flat window in front of it. By running the program, it then optimized everything and came up with the classic optical design of a spherical mirror and concave meniscus lens invented by the Russian D. D. Maksutov in 1941 and currently a backbone of advanced commercial amateur telescopes.

As a frame of reference, standard engineering offices were running desk-type Frieden calculating machines made up of about thirty pounds of small gears, electric motors, and relays. These machines had a giant keyboard with ten keys below each answer digit. Each command to add, subtract, multiply, divide, square, or root would be followed by a "galloping of horses" (as John called it) until the final calculation brought it to a crashing stop. The answers appeared as rolling (old automotive odometer type) drums, indexed with each digit behind its own little window. A favorite demonstration was to request a solution for the square root of a negative number. The machine would sit there and gallop all day until someone stopped it.[73] Later, we were to receive one of the first Frieden electronic calculators—a sign of things to come. It had a small four-inch CRT screen and displayed four lines of data in what Hewlett-Packard would later make famous as "Reverse Polish Notation," where the data is processed in a stack according to protocol.

At one point, Lunar Sample Return entered a technical and cost-estimating phase and I was loaned to Dr. Bekker's group to help support a RFP for large lunar-roving vehicles. It was an opportunity to do a whole series of loose sketches to represent our thinking on large vehicles for lunar exploration. It was a very enjoyable exercise.

---

[73] There is no solution, as this condition cannot exist; yet the calculator would continue in earnest, looking for the answer.

Sketch rendering of a tracked lunar-roving vehicle traversing a craggy terrain. *Image courtesy of GM Media Archives*

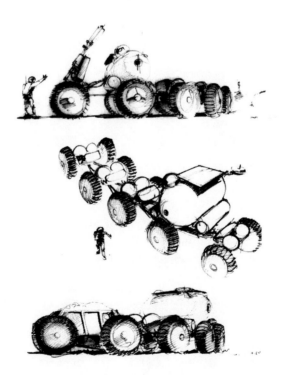

A montage of very early lunar exploration and base-building vehicle concepts. *Images courtesy of GM Media Archives*

Additional early lunar vehicle concepts based upon using large Saturn-class landers. *Lower left*, A study to maximize the size of the vehicle to be effectively much larger than the rocket stage that carried it. *Images courtesy of GM Media Archives*

At the Thanksgiving holiday break, I drove to Los Angeles to see the famous Watts Towers and meet former Styling associates, Dagmar Arnold and Gere Kavanaugh. I had known Dagmar from my original Pratt class. She was brilliant and very talented. She had joined GM to work in their Exhibition/Frigidair group but was now working for IBM in Palo Alto and was in town visiting Gere who was now an interior designer in Los Angeles. We had a nice Thanksgiving dinner together and discussed old times.

In another break, on a Saturday, John Siebert and I drove to the Mount Wilson Observatory. It was located north of Los Angeles, overlooking Pasadena. The final trek up the mountain was by way of a narrow winding road. It was the first time I had been above 5,000 feet and I was surprised at how quite it was and especially in noticing a shortness of breath, being exhausted after only walking the short distances between the observatories. I enjoyed seeing the hundred-inch Hooker Telescope, the solar tower telescopes and all the other instruments that I had read about in the *Glass Giant of Palomar*. George Ellery Hale was one of my idols, and he had built all of this and the Palomar observatory. Palomar, I would see on another weekend, driving alone, almost to San Diego, before turning east to another winding mountain road, on the way to my personal Mecca.

One afternoon, after stopping at the bank in Goleta, I was headed back to work when I saw a contrail and was startled that the airplane appeared be on fire. Then I realized it was a rocket, launched from Vandenberg, some fifty-five miles West. It was a spectacular sight, adding one more thing to the list of things, I liked about California. The nicest thing of all, however, was an experience as we were nearing Christmas. The weather was nice and they had doors open at both ends of the cafeteria. Inside was a Christmas tree, all decorated out, and the tinsel was blowing in the pleasant breeze; a sight I had never seen before and I think it was here that the hook was set.

With the approach of the holidays, I knew that Susan, her mom, dad, and brother would all be arriving shortly. As they had their trailer, they would be staying at a trailer park when they arrived. Susan, I understood, would be staying at her uncle's estate in Hope Ranch. When they finally arrived we got together and it was just like old times. They planned to stay a few days and then drive up the coast to San Jose for Christmas, visiting with another uncle on her mother's side. Susan and I followed a day later, in my Corvette. We spent Christmas Eve and Day with them, exchanging gifts and talking politics. While in the area, we made a quick run into San Francisco, Tom and I sharing a motel room overnight. I remember waking up that morning to the strange sound, of snow chains banging automobile fenders. I looked outside and had a rare view of snow falling in San Francisco. It cleared up in short order, and by midmorning, we were able to do the tourist spots, capping off our visit. Susan returned to Santa Barbara with her folks, and I drove back by myself, adding a side trip to Mount Hamilton to see the Lick Observatory. This would complete my trifecta, and I drove back to Santa Barbara, quite content.

We had a few more days together in Santa Barbara before they had to leave for Detroit, and, as I guess everyone expected, Susan and I returned to the trailer park with a bottle of Mumm's, to announce we would be getting married, after asking her father for her hand, of course. I still had at least another month of work at DSD before I could return, so we guessed that the wedding would take place some time in June. Everyone, at least, could start making plans.

After they left, with my attention divided, I went back to work, finishing details on the LSR project. The various mechanical systems were sorted out to give us our best prospects, and drawings were prepared for the proposal, which was now almost ready for publication. With my part of the work almost finished, I started planning for my return to Detroit.

An event that was about to be visible nearby was an annular solar eclipse[74] on February 5. The path the moon's shadow would take traveling eastward across the Pacific would bring it to just off the California coast, where it would end at sunset. Because of this, the best we could hope for would be a partial eclipse, crescent like, but with perhaps as much as 90 percent of the solar disk covered. Seibert and I decided to try for it. When the day came, it was overcast that afternoon, and we figured our best chance for seeing it would be to drive up the coast a short way and then up to one of the Santa Ynez mountain ridges. This would get us above the clouds where, hopefully, it would be clear. We set off, allowing ourselves a few hours to find a good spot. We picked a trail and took it to its highest point, where we found a ridge overlooking the ocean. We arrived in plenty of time but were disappointed because we were still below the cloud layer. It was a solid cover overhead, however, when we looked to the horizon, we could see a shimmer of light far out, perhaps a hundred miles or so, to where the cloud cover appeared to break and the bright light turned out to be sunlight on the ocean.

I set up my 16mm Bolex, and looking through the zoom finder, I could see a clean but narrow slit of clear sky. The eclipse by now had already started, but nothing was visible because the sun was still up in the clouds. I was confident we would see some stage of the eclipse, however, as the sun had to pass through the slit to set.

Soon we saw the crescent image of the sun descend into the opening—my camera was running. Within the next few minutes, the sun passed completely through the opening, setting below the Pacific horizon but never fully visible at any one time. It turned out to be an exciting film clip and was a nice way to end my California experience. I would start my drive back to Detroit the following week on Monday.

That last week, I completed my assignment[75] and made my rounds of the plant saying my goodbyes, stopping last to see Don Friedman and to thank him

---

[74] It would not be a total eclipse because the moon was relatively farther away from earth and would appear smaller in front of the sun, leaving an annular ring of the sun still visible outside the moon.

[75] The proposal was submitted to NASA, but nothing came of it. Surprisingly, the Russians were to successfully accomplish a similar mission after they failed to land a man on the moon.

for the opportunity of participating on the proposal. He in turn thanked me for my effort and mentioned in passing that, "You know, one GM division can't steal an employee from another division, but if you ever found your way back here, we could certainly find work for you." The invitation was clear, and the ball was in my court.

By week's end, I had finished all my business and my Corvette was packed and ready to go, the first thing Monday morning. I timed my start so as to miss the LA rush hour traffic as I passed through. The problem was that a large storm front was gathering, and it was on the same schedule. I left Santa Barbara just as it was peaking in its fury. It would turn out to be an interesting companion throughout the remainder of the trip. The rains were heavy but only proved to be a nuisance as it was just starting to clear as I was leaving Los Angeles, heading east on one of the early interstates. Passing San Bernardino, I broke out of the storm and into beautiful weather. I would continue easily and enjoy the scenery while reliving my last few months. It started getting late, but I was making good time, so I decided to continue on to Flagstaff, another town with an astronomical history. There I found a Ramada Inn and pulled in for the night.

The next morning I woke up, showered, shaved, and looked outside. The storm had caught up with me, and light snows were just starting to fall. There was not much on the ground yet, but I was sure the roads would be clear if I left right after breakfast. Sure enough, even though we were at a high altitude, the main roads had been salted, and were in good shape as I started descending the long eastern slope of the wide Arizona highway. These were the prettiest surroundings I had seen on my drive out, yet now they were all colorless, from the overcast and in the light snows. Not too much further, the snowfall stopped, and again, a little further, the grounds were free of snow. I was now ahead of the storm again and in the clear for the rest of the day; I could expect good roads all the way to Oklahoma. The drive was easy and I made my evening's stop in Oklahoma City.

Sure enough, the next morning I departed in a light snowfall with mixed rain, but this time I had a good start and I felt I could leave the storm behind, expecting fast level roads from the turnpike here and on. I could count on covering a lot of miles. That was all fine while I was headed east, but by midafternoon, the roads were turning northward, and I was contemplating the storm flanking me from my left, as I lost the favorable angle. I also knew that by going north, I could expect the rains to start turning back into snow again. I figured that I had better try to make as much time and cover as many miles as I could this day. As evening fell, the snows greeted me again. They were light at first but after a time, they started accumulating, and I started counting the number of spinouts I passed. I was being cautious driving, not fast, but steady. Even though it was getting late and I was pushing near a thousand miles that day, I decided to continue as I approached Chicago. The snows had stopped and the roads were clear. Passing through the Chicago freeways after midnight, I saw salt and sand trucks parked in the medians, just waiting for the storm to arrive. I decided to keep going, while things were still clear.

Having achieved my first (and last) one thousand mile day, things were still going well and while approaching West Bend in Indiana, at around 3:00 AM, I starting to feel a bit fatigued so I pulled into a motel to get a few hours of sleep. Sure enough, I woke up at 5:30, saw it was starting to snow and decided, "Well, I may as well be driving." So I got up, found some breakfast and got back on the road. This time, I knew my next stop would be Detroit, so I allowed my mind to start thinking about all the things that had to be done. The storm never reached full strength before I reached Detroit, but it still looked like Detroit when I got there—a sharp contrast from my last five months.

The next months were a blur, between getting back into the flow of things at Styling and getting wedding rings, making wedding and honeymoon plans and so forth. We set the date for June 9. The wedding would be on a Friday night in the *Kirk of the Hills* Presbyterian Church. A travel agent friend of Susan's family planned a three-week European honeymoon for us, we picking up the actual costs. Before we knew it, that Friday arrived. My family and several of our relatives, including a few that lived in Detroit, attended. My brother Pete was the Best Man and Sevil Kolonkia, Susan's close friend who lived with the Connors as an exchange student from Turkey, was the Maid of Honor.

The family gathers in Detroit for Norm and Susan's wedding. *Above left*: Herb, Basil, and Case Tech. student Pete; *right*, Constance and Basil.

The wedding went well and was quite dramatic in the ornate church, as we exchanged vows, with bolts of lightning and crashing thunder claps reverberating outside the beautiful stained glass windows. I should have realized that God was angry, even though everyone said it was a sign of future wealth. The rains that accompanied it were strong, but brief and clearing, everyone then making their way to the Connor residence for the reception that followed. All had a good time, and Susan and I split around ten o'clock to stay in a motel, half way to the airport, before our flight out on Sunday.

Our plane departed, and our first stop was in London. We were greeted by an agent, handing us all the tickets we would need for that stop. We traveled by ourselves, rather than as part of a tour group, and each stop was customized for us. This repeated itself in Stockholm, Oslo, Copenhagen, Amsterdam, Paris and Rome, we staying two or three days at each stop, and four days on our last. At the end of three weeks, we flew back, and I was ready to find out what it would be like, as a working married man.

Returning to work, there was a new sense of urgency in the country for mass transportation with the activity peaking in San Francisco with their Bay Area Rapid Transit system to be known as BART. Surprisingly, BART was being designed by Sundberg-Ferar, that (once-small) industrial design firm in Detroit. It had been growing slowly over the years and had been grabbing up frustrated automobile designers, including my old roommate, Vince McPherson. They just seemed to be getting bigger and bigger and moving into larger quarters all the time.

Under our Research Studio charter, we thought we should take a look at mass transportation but from an overall integrated community standpoint. One thing we explored was the linking of personal cars, forming trains, along the median center strips of new freeways. We had taken the first steps with the Firebird III, which had a working drive-by-wire steering system, where the wire would be buried in the roadway. What we would look at now would be to develop a system that would allow individual vehicles to enter into and depart from these medians as trains of cars.

As the concepts developed to a coherent level, a decision was made to document the concept in a 16mm movie presentation. GM Photographic would handle the production, and our studio would build and run the model set, including all the special effects we would need. Mike Lathers, who headed one of McLean's groups, took the lead in building the set, and we were all pulled in to support him. He had already run some model tests, and we would now increase the size of the set so that it would almost fill our (original) Research Studio.

We would build a table high set with scale model traffic running three lanes in each direction, using a standard model car scale, so we could easily populate the set with cars. The lanes were individual strips of Masonite, with each strip/lane being pulled along by cables on pulleys, simulating the slow to fast lanes. A wide median strip separated the lanes, and we landscaped the set with model railroad props. Our AutoLine concept was then animated to demonstrate the system for the cameras. The lanes floated on shuffleboard wax (actually glass beads) and used pipe-threading machines at each end to turn the pulleys. Attached cables actually pulled the lanes at the three speeds. We introduced some special effects by routering slots beneath the lanes to work like cams so that selected model cars, sitting over slots in the lanes, would ride a pin into the groove below, causing them to weave left and right, adding realism to the motion.

The actual filming turned out to be quite exciting. We would design the props and have our shops build them, after which we would supervise their installation into the set. It was fast paced, since we were alternately filming or rebuilding sets, literally working around the clock in randomly defined shifts, trying to stay out of each other's way. It still ranks as one of my best memories from Styling.

The AutoLine led to another vehicle study. With all the cars running in train fashion, we looked at placing them within a trough-like roadway and having the cars rotate all four wheels out and upward into a flat pattern so they would be constrained by the sides of the trough and the cars would now all be supported on a bubble of air by ground effects. We experimented along this line for a while and built another full-scale mockup for such a car. At the time, there was a possibility it could develop to become the Firebird IV and shown at the 1964 World's Fair in Flushing Meadows, New York. This did not materialize, however, most likely because there just wasn't enough time.

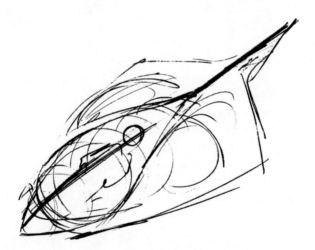

Vehicle concept sketch for an advanced high-speed automated highway system. This configuration was considered for a while as a possible Firebird IV, but the project was dropped. *Image courtesy of GM Media Archives*

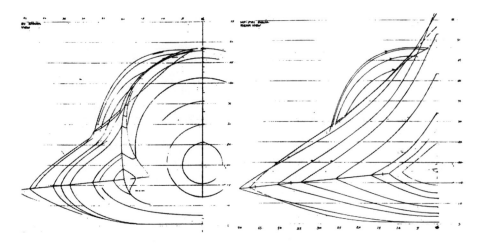

Full-size drawing section cuts were developed for front and rear views on five-inch grid vellum. *Images courtesy of GM Media Archives*

XP721 mockup. In the photo: the author, R. F. McLean, and Chuck Torner. *Photo courtesy of GM Media Archives*

We were also asked to try to come up with some original themes for the fair. We could even look for spectacular themes for the GM Pavilion itself. One line I was exploring was to place the entire pavilion in Flushing Lake, floating it on a shallow pre-stressed concrete dish. The idea was that the dish would be a spherical segment that would barely rise above the water line (freeboard), so that from shore, it would look like an illuminated hole in the water. The exhibit building would have been suspended above on a spindle, and the whole thing would have rotated slowly, for dramatic effect.

While drawing variations on the theme, my mind wandered to the time I was riding the floating crows nest, on Tom's birthday, and I started thinking, in the same scale, that I might be able to mount a giant radio telescope in the same way. It would be built like a geodesic dome, with the cross members being hollow tubes (providing the flotation). The major part of the sphere elements would be submerged in the lake, but the radio dish itself, would be suspended in the air above. The concept then slowly evolved into a simpler smaller spherical shell, where an optical telescope could be mounted, working through a single small opening on top. I left it there, making a mental note that this might really work, but then of course, somebody would have already thought of it.

While Susan and I were settling down to married life, her Mom and Dad sold their home on Orchard Lake and moved to Santa Barbara. Her brother Tom, who was in middle management at Micromatic, decided to make his own career change and went with them. Rather than returning to Turkey, Sevil, Susan's maid of honor, also decided to go to Santa Barbara, to study at UCSB. Susan and I were left behind to hold the fort.

I never forgot that Don Friedman had given me a back door invitation to join them in Santa Barbara. It was after an especially hard drive to Jamestown, during a Christmas snowstorm, that I decide to see McLean and request a transfer. When I talked to him, he was open to the suggestion, and tried to be even-handed. He did not try to discourage, me but he did warn me that I would risk becoming a small fish in a big ocean, asking again if I was sure that, that was what I wanted. When I answered yes, he accepted it and said he would put things in motion.

A few weeks later, while having lunch in the cafeteria, someone came up to me and told me that he heard my transfer had been approved. Bob and his wife Gladys hosted a very nice going away party in his home for Susan and me; it was perhaps fitting that we had a light snowfall on that late April evening.

7 Santa Barbara

Even though I had requested the transfer, GM still picked up the moving and travel expenses, sending a moving crew to box our housewares and pack our furniture. We didn't have a shipping address yet, so they would just hold it for us in Santa Barbara. The packing went quickly, and they departed, leaving us to sleep in the empty apartment overnight. The next day, I packed my cameras and valuables into my Corvette and headed west. Susan still had some unfinished business to attend to in Detroit and would depart a week later in her '57 Thunderbird.

The cross-country drive this time was relatively uneventful as my thoughts were of the West Coast and having made a major career change, really starting a new life. Once I arrived in Santa Barbara, I checked into a motel on upper State Street, this time much closer to GM and next to a Pancake House, which may have been the tiebreaker. I would stay there, at least a few weeks, until Susan arrived.

Once unpacked, I called the Connors and asked for directions to their house. It was small but beautifully situated on Alameda Padre Sierra (APS) Highway, running along the foothills, with a grand view overlooking the Santa Barbara Riviera, only a short distance from the beaches. They had a *dichondra* front lawn, which made me wonder how such fragile vegetation could thrive so well. Lucy met me with a glass of campaign, which was her signature greeting. Tom and Sevil were there also. Tom was working in a real estate office in *Isla Vista*, which was a rapidly growing area off the new UCSB campus, and Sevil had been accepted to start in the next semester. We then talked about Susan and our plans. I then returned to my motel to be ready for work the next day.

May 1, 1963. When I showed up for work, everything looked pretty much the same as it did before, except that there had been an organization change and they had lost their division status, becoming the GM Defense Research

Laboratories. Most of the day was taken up with the formalities of new employee indoctrination and reporting for physical and eye examinations. I would still be under Don Friedman in Land Operations but assigned to the Mechanisms Group headed by Sam Romano. I heard that Lloyd Brown had left GM to join North American Aerospace in Los Angeles. John Siebert and the optical group were still there and intact. I would see them later. Dr. Bekker and Ferenc Pavlics were still in the Mobility Group doing serious soil mechanics research and testing. After a tour of the facilities, I was taken back to the south building, set up at a drafting table, and given some reports to look at. I paused for a moment and felt a let-down from what I had left behind at Styling. Well, anyway, I had made my decision and I would make it work

The first week went by quickly, and Susan arrived as expected. After some time with her family, we started looking around for a place to live. There were several nice homes on the market that were readily available, and we almost made an offer on one of them when we ran across a new development off Patterson Avenue that had some really attractive model homes. The model we liked was almost 2,000 square feet, had four bedrooms, two baths, and a den, but the most notable feature was an open courtyard[76] in the center. There was also a single car-garage and a carport under the same roof. We fell in love with it and bought it. Being a new home, construction would start in August, and we could expect to move in sometime in December. That part being settled, we now had to find a temporary apartment to live in until then. We found a nice one just east of downtown on Anapamu. It was in a four-story building and had a large heated community swimming pool. Contacting the moving company, we were able to pick out the few things we needed and left the rest in storage. There were several other young tenants in the building that we would befriend and mix with. It would do very nicely while we waited, and I could now focus on work.

I was pleased, one day, when they found a small office for me on the first floor. I would share it with John Calandro, another engineer in Land Operations. We would be teamed together on several projects over the next few years. John Siebert and the rest of the optical group were also just down the hall, in similar offices. The arrangement was campus like, with small offices running the length of the building on both sides. We could sit at our desks and watch the gardener manicuring the lawns just a few feet away. The manufacturing and test building was just across the way but close enough to get a good shake every time the hypervelocity gun went off.

---

76   It was not advertised as such, but I would find later that it was based on or was a good copy of an Eichler model home that would win national architectural awards and later be identified as a classic design.

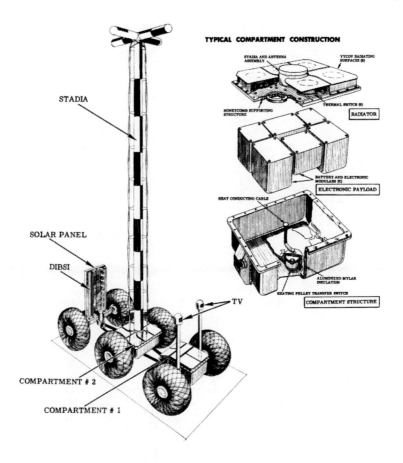

Images courtesy of GM Media Archives

Our assignment was to do engineering design for the Surveyor Lunar Roving Vehicle (SLRV) proposal. The SLRV would be an unmanned vehicle that would land on the moon, piggybacked on the Surveyor soft-lander. Once on the moon, it would deploy to the surface and after performing soil measurement tests, would certify whether the site would, or would not, be suitable for an Apollo landing: clear of obstructions and, more importantly, assuring there were no soft spots they could sink into. The SLRV was six feet long and had six wheels on three axles, all connected by a flexible leaf spring/frame, which was also its suspension. The end axles would articulate in unison to turn the vehicle.

It would be controlled from Earth by way of telemetry through the Surveyors stronger transmitters. Operators could observe the vehicle's progress through a camera mounted on the vehicle and through Surveyors own cameras. The SLRV would have thermally insulated compartments on the first two axles, for the video and communication electronics. The last axle would carry solar panels, and the soil mechanics instruments, which would deploy to the surface to measure the soil's bearing strength. Because of the time delay between sending vehicle commands and then seeing the results of those commands, all moves would be broken down into discrete steps, to move forward or backward six feet, turn left or right so many degrees or follow other instructions.

To test all of this, a Lunarium had been constructed to simulate a lunar surface, and we would conduct actual missions, proving our concepts. It was located immediately south of the engineering building in a dirt field, measuring some one hundred by one hundred fifty feet. It was graded into small hills and mounds, and was then strewn with rocks and boulders. There was a remote controlled video camera on top of the engineering building that would play the role of Surveyor. Our SLRV prototype would be placed in the Lunarium and be observed by the high camera, while its own video camera was transmitting its views from the field directly to the control room, buried within the bowels of the building. In this way, we could have an operations team conduct a simulated mission to validate feasibility.

Photos courtesy of GM Media Archives

I was slowly beginning to realize that we were designing to a new standard. The mission was deemed to be more critical than the hardware and it would require a higher-level design effort than I had ever experienced before.

Reliability would be most important, and hardware would always be assessed to see if something simpler might be able to do the same job. "The part that's left off never breaks," was an often-repeated phrase. Then another mission variation was introduced. If something does fail, what can we still salvage from the mission? This would bring us into failure mode analysis, doing our best to avoid failures but also positioning ourselves to have a plan if failure did occur.

We worked in a team environment but it was competitive in the sense that if anyone found a simpler or more reliable way of doing something, it would be accepted, until something better came along. In the meantime, the mobility group had already specified and sized the general arrangement of the vehicle. Our group would now have to define the hardware to implement it. The selected configuration was to have the highest mobility possible, because the terrain was still almost completely unknown and considered to be hostile.

/06

Schematic showing the mobility stages of a 6x6 vehicle climbing a step obstacle 1-1/2 times higher than its wheel diameter.

With the payload compartments defined, the flexible frame was engineered so that it would alternately transfer loads between the axles in the process of climbing over a wall, which could be up to 1-½ times higher than its wheel diameter, i.e., a twenty-seven-inch step for our eighteen-inch wheels.[77] The mechanics were quite novel, but it had been demonstrated that a six-wheeled

---

[77] All wheels would provide traction to drive the vehicle forward, into the wall. The front wheels would then be loaded sufficiently so as to walk up that wall, the frame bending enough to maintain full contact at all wheels. Upon reaching the top of the wall, the frame would be bent to where the middle set of wheels would start to lift off, but by this time the top set of wheels will have gotten a sufficient bite for the first and last wheel sets to carry the entire load, still driving forward. The middle set of wheels would now be walking up the wall, until they crested; they would then take a bite and the vehicle would lift the rear set of wheels, as it begins to walk down the other side in a mirror motion.

(6x6)[78] flexible-framed vehicle offered the maximum mobility possible for a given size wheel. This would become GM's preferred approach for all of our lunar vehicle proposals.

There were a few mechanical details that would torment us until we were able to develop and test enough hardware to resolve them. The main problem was that the lunar surface could range anywhere from between +200 to -300 degrees Fahrenheit, depending on whether it was in the sun or in shadow. Lunar night would last about two weeks, but we never expected to operate at that time, at least not for any missions we had anticipated. Conventional rubber tires were out of the question for thermal reasons. The risk was that they wouldn't be able to maintain pressure and would go flat.

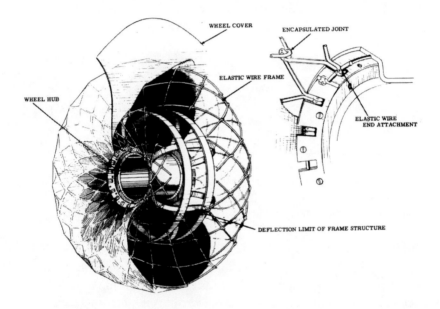

Construction of an 18-inch diameter wheel for the Surveyor Lunar Roving Vehicle (SLRV). The mesh skin provides a bearing surface to protect against sinking into the lunar soil or dust. The inner deflection limiter prevents over-flexure of the wires should they be driven into a rigid obstacle. *Image courtesy of GM Media Archives*

---

[78] The first number represents the number of wheels, the second, the number of those wheels that are driven. It is always preferred that all wheels be driven for maximum mobility. Additional axles could always be added, and it would still work, such as 8x8, 10x10, etc.

The near total vacuum on the moon introduced other problems. For this environment, the mobility group had conceived and developed a system of metal tires comprised of interwoven doughnut-shaped wire baskets. The intersecting wires would be chain-linked and shaped to attach to the wheel hubs very much like conventional tires. The total vehicle weight would be carried by the spring deflection of the wires at ground contact. To improve the load distribution across the wires, it was envisioned that the baskets would be skinned with a fine stainless steel mesh. This metal wheel would satisfy all the concerns previously noted.

We were confident that it would work, but issues remained regarding its operation in a vacuum. There was a school of thought that said that in a near perfect vacuum, wires in contact with each other would be subjected to what was called vacuum welding that the metal molecules of wires in contact, without separating air molecules, might form a molecular bond and fuse together. Such a condition would rigidize the wheel into a brittle state that could then break. This problem and its solution would be typical of our entire engineering process, i.e., concerns would be identified and tests devised to verify that such and such a concern would or would not be a problem. Our verification for this example was to build a small section of the wheel rim, the wire basket and a ground plate, so that it could be placed in a vacuum chamber and flexed through a number of cycles, until the concern was resolved. If proven to remain a problem, some process, such as the application of a Moly coat or other lubricant, would be tested to see if that would solve the problem.

The vacuum of outer space posed another problem, at least, if we had to have parts that rotated, like wheels. It meant we could not physically seal those parts since they would always have relative motion between them. Exposed to a hard vacuum, lubricating fluids eventually boil off into space[79]. For a lunar wheel bearing, the solution is usually to reduce the size of the gap so as to minimize the leakage, or by the creation of a labyrinth, through which the molecules can be confused as to which way to go and in so doing inhibit their escape.

---

[79] Just as high pressure in a pressure cooker will raise the boiling point (temperature) in the mountains (conversely), in the low pressure of a pure vacuum, all fluids will boil off, even at the lowest temperatures.

SLRV mock-up in its final configuration. *Photo courtesy of GM Media Archives*

This was what we were working on in November of '63, a month when other events took precedence. The week following Kennedy's assassination, Herb called to tell me that our father had had a heart attack and the prognosis was very bad—he was not expected to last more than a few days. I took an emergency leave from work, and Susan and I flew to Erie, Pennsylvania, where Herb picked us up and we continued on to Jamestown. My father was still alive when I got there, and he even lasted another week before he passed away from another attack. We stayed a few more days for the services and to help our mom with other arrangements. Returning to Santa Barbara in early December, we heard that our new house would be ready for occupancy the week before Christmas. While it had been a difficult month, it was good to be busy, which helped ease the pain.

Because of my strong sense of three-dimensional space, I was drawn into the task of integrating the SLRV within the Surveyor envelope, exploring different places and ways to stow and deploy it. Our proposal was completed in April of '64 and submitted to NASA. We received no word, at least down to our level, on how it was accepted. Time was to pass, without any feedback and reason indicated that the delay was due to basic slippages in the Surveyor program itself.[80]

Our efforts then shifted to the more adventurous post-Apollo period—supporting manned exploration of the moon, just as Chesley Bonestell and Willy Ley had been dreaming about, in the past decades, except that this time it would be for real, and we at GMDRL were in at the ground floor!

Our basic problem had not changed. We still did not know whether or not vehicles would sink deep into the surface. Because of this, we had to developed concepts for all contingencies—things that might be like screw worms, to tunnel through fairy-castle dust, or tractor treaded, to crawl over boulder strewn lave outflows, or to roll over soft planar surfaces, on large tires.

The first opportunity to improve our knowledge of the lunar surface came from the Ranger program. Ranger was the first of JPL's lunar exploration programs and consisted of a series of spacecraft that would be launched on a collision course with the moon. They would continuously take and transmit photographs in their final minutes, before crashing into the moon. They were called Hard Landers, for obvious reasons, and they would not survive. Surveyor, with which we had prepared all of our previous proposals, was to be the second phase of lunar exploration, as a Soft Lander. Its speed would be reduced during final approach so as to land safely and perform useful scientific functions from its landing site.

With Ranger, we would get closer pictures of the lunar surface and be able to assess the actual sizes of the rocks, debris crevices and craters, so we would know better what to expect. With this knowledge, we could at least start sizing our wheels and chassis. So far, the smallest lunar features, distinguishable from ground based telescopes, were at least one thousand feet across. No matter how bad the Ranger pictures might be, they would still be a major improvement in our knowledge.

We kept following the progress of the Ranger program, and waited in anticipation for Ranger III, the first craft that would actually target the moon. One problem remained, however. The scientific community was concerned that if any biological life existed on the moon, bacteria from Earth could have catastrophic consequences to the Moon's biosystem. The solution appeared simple. After manufacture, each of the Rangers would be heat sterilized, before being staged atop their Atlas-Agena rockets.

Ranger III missed the moon altogether, Ranger IV crashed as planned but transmitted nothing, V also missed the moon and was tumbling out of control as it passed.

---

[80] By the time Surveyor did fly, it was too late for any SLRV mission to have supported Apollo.

William H. Pickering was the Director of the Jet Propulsion Laboratories at the time and his job, as well as his reputation, was at stake, as Rangers VI and VII were in final preparation. The scientific community had finally relented, accepting the fact that the risk of contaminating the moon was really quite small and, therefore, sterilization would no longer be required. Proper approvals were received and Ranger VI was launched. The decision was the charm. It flew flawlessly. This mission would be broadcast via live network television. What was exciting was that we, the public, would be seeing the pictures at the same time as they would be seen by the technical team that put the whole thing together. It flew perfectly, right on through to impact, but for some reason, the cameras did not power up in time to send any pictures.

Ranger VII was launched with some confidence, in spite of Ranger VI's failure because they now felt they understood the problems. The launch was clean, and the trans-lunar trajectory looked good, impact predictions were nominal. I was watching from my TV set at home. On schedule, the pictures began coming in at regular intervals. You could clearly observe the slight change in each frame, as the Ranger got closer to the moon. Even in black and white, they were absolutely spectacular, as the same picture kept repeating itself, except each time it was a little bigger and a little better than the last, and more and more of the surrounding background kept dropping off. The mind was being numbed by the constantly improving detail, knowing that the next and the next would be even better yet. There was awareness that this was truly a historic moment. The last few pictures seemed to be even more hectic, as the scale and rate of enlargement was dramatically increasing with each shot, until inevitably, the last picture froze-incomplete. It was spectacular and the moment lingered, as it was true; it really had happened.[81] At last, we would have something to work with, as we knew NASA would further reduce the data and analyze the pictures. From the first impressions, it appeared as though the moon would be pretty close to what we had been expecting. We could stop looking at all the variations.

These are live pictures taken from broadcast television of the Ranger IX on its final approach into Alphonsus crater.

---

[81] Launched on the Atlas-Agena B rocket, Rangers VIII and IX also were successful, with Ranger IX transmitting even more spectacular pictures as it crashed into the *Alphonsus* crater.

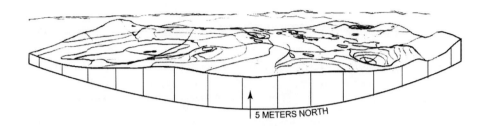

5 METERS NORTH

The author's curved panorama drawing of the Ranger IX impact site, as developed from a NASA topographical map. *Image courtesy of GM Media Archives*

Just as we had been following the failures and successes of Ranger, we also kept an eye on the technical and schedule slippage problems of Surveyor. Progress was slow. While potentially superior in the quality and quantity of imagery data we could expect, its launch date kept slipping month by month. When the first Surveyor was finally launched on its Atlas-Centaur, it had only a few scientific instruments on board because it was primarily an engineering vehicle and its only task was to smoke out the difficult soft landing procedure. There was still high public interest in the mission, so there was radio coverage of the final approach. Because there were no approach cameras on the mission, there was no network television coverage as there had been with Ranger. Even for audio though, there was good technical coverage, starting fifty-two miles out, with the firing of the ten-thousand-pound thrust main retro-rocket and three vernier (landing) rockets to reduce the closing speed. The data was being read off as velocity, in miles per hour, and altitude, in thousands of feet. Mission control kept calling out the numbers, all slowly getting smaller and smaller. We were all waiting for the inevitable failure. We just didn't know what it would be.

The main retro-rocket shut down on schedule, and the vernier rockets continued, maintaining stabilization and further decelerating the spacecraft. We kept waiting. The numbers kept getting smaller, velocity in feet per second and altitude in hundreds of feet. At some point, everyone, each at his or her own threshold, started thinking, "This thing might just make it!" The numbers were now really in the low digits; finally, we all knew there was no way it couldn't make the last few feet and then it was down and everyone went crazy.

Voices in the background: "Where's the data? Is it still working? Is it okay? Will it be able to send pictures? When can we see the pictures?" It did have video cameras, so it should have been able to take panoramic views once they were activated. There were other instruments, a drill and a few soil analysis devices, but they would all be turned on later. Yes, there would be something available to see "in a few hours;" and maybe, if we're lucky, there will be a tomorrow.

There was no telling how long the telemetry would survive as the lunar surface would soon be pouring more heat into the electronics compartments.[82]

We apparently were lucky. Pictures started coming in, and we even saw the drill bore a hole into the soil and collect samples that would be analyzed. The Surveyor lasted more than just the next day; in fact, it even ran into the next week, as everyone congratulated themselves on the more-than-successful mission and trying to think of tributes to pay themselves as Surveyor I was only days away from entering lunar night (the sunset line of shadow, as it crept over the landing site). The novelty was lost as its solar panel fell into darkness, and Surveyor I was turned off. We would have two weeks of night at -300F that would surely kill it. There would be satisfaction, however, with even such a loss because absolutely nothing had been expected of it in the first place.

When lunar morning finally arrived for Surveyor I, mission control tested to see if they could awaken it. It was faint at first, but sure enough, it was still alive and as the sun rose higher and it was able to recharge its batteries, it was fully functional again, waiting for more instructions. "OK, what do you want me to do now."

The next two weeks of daylight saw most of the same tests and pictures repeated, all with the same success. It had performed all the tests they had planned and all the others they could think of. Finally, they sent a request to the scientific community, professors and even science teachers, to ask if anyone could think of something else to try. Once again, it entered lunar night. This time, when the sun finally rose and they tested it—just like a bad horror movie—it was still alive.

Surveyor was a great success[83], but it did not resurrect our SLRV hopes. It was too late to support Apollo. Not only did they learn all they needed from Surveyor to safely land Apollo, but we also learned what more we needed to design lunar vehicles.

Program-wise, we had already begun teaming arrangements with Boeing on NASA contracts. Our six-wheeled-design concepts were maturing. Now we were incorporating a much larger pressurized crew compartment spanning two axles (in front) and then having a two-wheeled cart, trailing from a flexible

---

[82] The Surveyor was designed for these temperatures, if everything worked right. In transit it could radiate excess heat to anything colder, i.e., the "heat sink" of cold space at -450F. On the moon, from the horizon on down, instead of cold space, everything would appear to be at 200 degrees Fahrenheit.

[83] Surveyor II crashed on its mission, as did IV, but III, V, VI and VII all landed successfully and improved our knowledge of the moon.

frame. In other variations, we would add more trailing carts, all powered and improving mobility in their train configurations. These carts would carry the extra power supply and auxiliaries that would be required for extended missions. The power systems were envisioned to be fuel cells, converting liquid hydrogen and oxygen to electricity. All the modules would be topped with large radiator plates to shadow the hardware below against the sun and to radiate excess heat into cold space.

A lunar exploration mission is drawn with complex intersecting perspective planes to help create an illusion of depth. *Image courtesy of GM Media Archives*

Our studies where based on using the Saturn V and a 20 foot diameter upper stage, as the size limitation of our payload envelope. We studied a whole series of vehicles as we would need to construct a lunar base and Sam Romano presented a paper on the study at an SAE conference in Los Angeles. Evolving from this study, we converged to a six-wheeled configuration, with five-foot-diameter tires. We subsequently received a NASA contract to build a full-scale test vehicle to prove the concept. The vehicle would be a mobile laboratory—project name—MOLAB. Boeing, as the prime contractor, would develop the mission, but we would have the fun part of building and testing a full-scale vehicle, i.e., the mobility system.

Left, MOLAB lunar exploration vehicle. *Right*, The Mobility Test Article (MTA) with Ferenc Pavlics driving the full mass chassis on earth with a Firebird III-type joystick controller. *Image and photo courtesy of GM Media Archives*

What proved interesting was that we had to demonstrate the vehicle on earth, but on the moon, it would weigh only one-sixth as much because of the reduced lunar gravity. Normally, we would have had to make critical adjustments in our hardware—springs and metal gages—in order to get an equivalent stiffness. But in our case, we determined our chassis and running gear alone would weigh one-sixth as much as the full vehicle, so all we had to do was leave off the manned compartment and scientific gear in front, and the power supply in back, trailing an umbilical cord from there instead! This way, we could build the chassis exactly to the design specifications, and yet test it on earth.[84]

The MOLAB front chassis module had conventional upper and lower arm suspensions for both the first and second sets of wheels, with the lower arms sprung on torsion bars, running along each side of the center box frame. The trailer was attached at the end of a short flexible frame, by way of a steering mechanism, which turned the rear axle.

Our wheels, by now, had also been simplified; instead of being twist linked together, they were fashioned into an array of interwoven piano wires, sprung from one wheel rim, diagonally across to the other rim. With the wire ends firmly constrained, the interwoven main field was free to pantograph, seeking its least energy (deflected) condition against the ground.

---

[84]   We could even take movies at 6X speed and play them back at normal speed to get the same slow motion effect as it would really appear under lunar gravity, just like the Apollo astronaut's kangaroo hop.

Since I had experience in Human Factors, I was assigned to develop the driver's station. In keeping with the weight limits imposed, it ended up being a minimal roll cage construction. Working with the electronics people, I suggested using the same joystick controller that we used on the Firebird III. I contacted the Research Staff people in Detroit and we bought a similar unit. I then built a mockup of the driver's station and incorporated the small control panel to the operator's right. We had the entire roll cage painted white, and I was particularly proud of the matt-black antiglare panels I had painted on the inside of the one and a quarter-inch tube roll structure that fell within the driver's view.

The MTA weighing the exact same weight as the complete MOLAB vehicle on the moon. *Photo courtesy of GM Media Archives*

The completed MOLAB Test Article (MTA), was driven to our Lunarium, and successfully put through its acceptance tests. We had accepted some performance trade-offs with the MOLAB, when we went to the rigid 4x4 forward platform and the 2x2 trailer because it could carry a larger payload, even though we knew it would not be as mobile as a fully flexible 6x6. We consistently ran across this trade-off when proposing against Bendix in Ann Arbor, who was our only competitor for lunar vehicles. As a philosophy, they always advocated simple 4x4 vehicles. We were confident our systems were better, but we did take note of the benefits of simplicity. We delivered our test vehicle to NASA and then awaited the next call.

When Susan and I moved into our new house, one of the first things I did was set up one of the bedrooms as a hobby room so I would be able to resume my optical work for telescope making. Initially, I did very little because most of my time was spent fencing in the backyard, landscaping, and building a patio barbeque center in back. It wasn't until August of '64 that I was able to resume the optical work. I had purchased two small fused quartz mirror blanks for my Cassegranian secondary mirrors, and I now began grinding and polishing them. I had proceeded far enough with them that I next had to unpack the ten-inch primary mirror and resume work on it in order to test the secondaries.[85]

Early in 1965, while reading through an engineering journal, I noticed an advertisement by Structural Fibers in Ohio where they were selling a line of spherical fiberglass pressure vessels. It reminded me of the idea I had in Detroit for floating a telescope. The largest size they offered was only fourteen inches in diameter, but after doing a few calculations, I figured it was large enough to hold my small four-and-a quarter-inch RFT telescope. I guessed at the weights, and it looked like I could do it within the eleven pounds[86] I would be limited to, so I wrote a check and placed an order for the sphere.

A few weeks later, the sphere arrived. It was heavier than I had expected, but it looked like most of the weight was in the thick wall around the threaded flange. Most of this would be cut away for my telescope tube so that would reduce the weight somewhat. The sphere looked a little lumpy, so I decided I would have to clean it up some. I would also need a supporting basin to hold the water; I would have to make this. I figured I could lay one up in fiberglass, casting it against the sphere, using it as a tool. Then I could grind the two against each other, with Carborundum grit, just like making telescope mirrors to make them both perfectly spherical—a good ball and socket fit. I purchased the polyester resin and glass fabric from a local boatyard and the lay-up came along easily.

---

[85] I had determined I would test them with real stars, and I would need to finish the primary mirror to do so. The 2.8-inch diameter secondary would amplify the focal length 4X and the 1.8" diameter secondary would amplify it 6X. I never completed the 6X secondary.

[86] This was calculated by assuming the tube would be horizontal and that would tell me how high the basin could rise under the tube. That would give me an immersed depth of about 4-1/4 inches. The weight of the displaced water (and the telescope) would be: Weight=.1134 $h^2(r-h/3)$, where h= depth of immersion and r = the radius of the sphere.

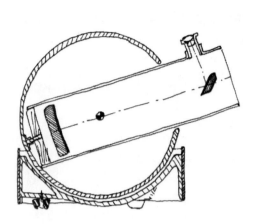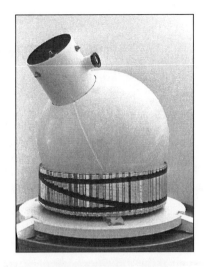

The Spheremount prototype: a 4 1/4 inch RFT telescope mounted in a 14-inch diameter fiberglass sphere. The buoyant weight is 11 pounds.

I found I had to modify my small telescope slightly to get some weight out of it, and I added a fastener at the bottom of the tube, so I could secure it into the bottom of the sphere. The upper part of the tube would center itself in the hole cut out. There would still be four inches of tube sticking out of the sphere from which the viewing eyepiece would protrude.

I eagerly waited for the first clear night sky to test it. Its flotation checked out okay during the day. The basin, at four inches of depth, required only a shot glass of water to float the eleven-pound telescope and sphere. It was not balanced yet, but it could be moved freely in any direction. That first clear evening came in July of '65. I waited for it to start getting dark, watching for the first stars to appear. I brought out my "Spheremount" as I decided to call it and set it up on my backyard barbeque pit. I added water until it was light and free. I then started looking for stars, holding it lightly with my fingers because it wasn't balanced. I thought I found some stars, but it wasn't dark enough to focus them, until . . . yes . . . there they were . . . and now they were in focus. I could see them clearly, then my subconscious started kicking in . . . something was different. My fingers were trembling; at least to the extent that what I was looking at was magnified sixteen times . . . and the stars were moving. Moving because my fingers were not steady and they were responding to those finger tremors; then they would instantaneously stop—in between those motions! This was astounding; I had never seen such rapid damping of star images in my life! This system can really work!

I had to take a deep breath. I thought to myself, what do I do next? Well, my four and a quarter-inch RFT was only magnifying at sixteen power, and that would convince no one. Then I thought about the ten-inch Cassegranian that I had just resumed polishing on a few months earlier. It would be capable of very high powers, and if I spheremounted it, it would make a good demonstrator. That was it. That would be my new priority. There was no need to balance or do any more work on the small RFT. I would now focus on completing the Cassegranian optics and start figuring out how to make a larger sphere, as I knew I could not buy one accurate enough in the marketplace.

By December, I had decided how I would make the sphere. I would first make a master plaster model of a twenty four-inch diameter sphere, using the same techniques we used at Pratt, but on a significantly larger scale. I would turn the sphere upside down, so it could be attached to the turntable on the flat end of the truncated sphere (where it would be cut out for the tube). I would then take a matched set of plaster casts off of the sphere, just as they did at Styling, and use those casts as tooling to lay up the fiberglass shell.

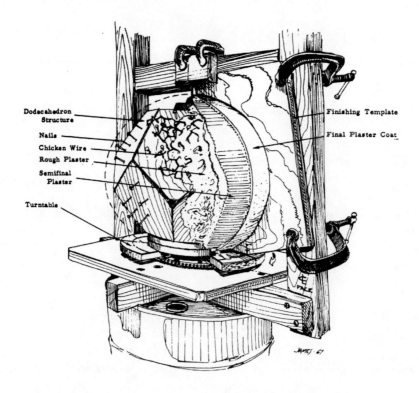

The turntable is setup to turn a 24-inch diameter plaster sphere.

I started the actual fabrication of the armature at the end of '65 and proceeded through most of 1966, going through the plaster stages and getting into the fiberglass in November and December, making both the sphere and the tube. Midway through the year, I returned to polishing the ten-inch mirror, working everything concurrently.

Because the primary mirror had a very short focal length, it would be much more difficult to figure the parabola. The Foucault tests I had used before were no longer sensitive enough to show the shape of the deeper curvature, so I had to take zone readings and convert them to graphic data, seen as deviations from the ideal, per Jean Texereau's classic book, *How to Make a Telescope*. Using this method, I was able to see where the errors were, and then applied polishing techniques to move glass from one zone to another.[87] Choosing from a variety of strokes and tools, a typical corrective process would involve only about ten to fifteen minutes of polishing to go after a targeted high zone. The mirror would then be washed, dried, cooled to room temperature, then placed on the test stand for new measurements,[88] and a new corrective plan would be made.

This routine was repeated seventy-eight times until, on January 5 1967, it was well within tolerances at $1/17\lambda$. I then set up the mirror to carefully punch

---

[87] I could choose between three polishing tools to rework the shape. The full-size tool that first brought the mirror to a full polish, a half-size tool that allowed me to push material outward from the center (to deepen the shape) and a two-inch diameter tool that allowed me to concentrate the polishing on any particular high zone to push material out of it. The smaller tools were always used with the mirror facing upward. The large tool could either be used with the mirror or the tool on top, and depending on the particular strokes employed, would generally be used to blend several zones together. The process of executing the planned strokes uniformly and applying them while walking around the barrel invariably, would result in the creation of target-like zones. For this reason, all strokes were constantly varied to be a little longer or a little shorter. This would result in both fewer zones and a smoother blending. The full-size tool was best for blending, when only a few zones remained, but it would also tend to lose any depth achieved at the center.

[88] The data collected would represent the actual radius of the surface (R), as compared to the radius of that zone (r). A correct parabolic surface would conform to the formula of r^2/R (adjusted for the test setup). A comparison against the actual data readings for those same zones would yield the amount of error in each surface zone. A corrective plan would be made and the required tool heated and hot pressed against the mirror to get full contact, allowed to cool to room temperature and then the next corrective actions would be applied.

out the center core, which was already bored 95 percent through. I was able to have the mirror aluminized in the optical lab at work, as it was convenient, and I could immediately start using it to test and figure the secondary mirror, which was next on my agenda.

I had made a wise decision when I bought the fused quartz secondary blanks—wise because fused quartz (glass) virtually does not expand when it is heated, and this allowed me to perform figuring operations on the secondary and immediately rinse, dry, and install it in the telescope for star testing.[89] The star tests were similar to the Foucault tests, except the razorblade at the eyepiece would cut the star image in half and any errors would be directly apparent, as hills or valleys on the surface. The ideal surface would look flat. In general, I would look for any zone that looked high and try to reduce it. This worked out surprisingly well, in spite of the presence of high altitude air turbulence. On April 5, I determined I had a good secondary. After ten figuring steps, my notes recorded "image of Mars showed persistent detail although fuzzy, even in slight turbulent higher altitude air . . . Knife edge test did not show obvious zones."

I concluded it was okay to aluminize the secondary. The optical work was finished.

———————————

There came a time at work when we realized that we were looking too far into the future where, perhaps, we should be looking closer to directly support the Apollo program. By providing a small vehicle to safely take the astronauts farther from their LEM Lander, it would increase the probability of finding more fruitful lunar sample sites. NASA was also arriving at these same conclusions, and we began receiving inquiries for proposals along those lines. There was no direction, however, whether those missions would be for one or two man vehicles. They were trying to assess whether it would be better to risk losing only one astronaut, if he got into trouble, or to risk losing them both by having one available to assist the other. They were really concerned that if one fell, he might not be able to get up—like a bug on its back.

Hamilton Standards was the leader in developing space suits for extravehicular exploration. Their suits would require separate personal life support systems (PLSS), which were quite sizeable and had to be carried as backpacks. These systems provided the essential oxygen for breathing and a thermal control system to maintain temperatures within the suit at acceptable levels. The space suit configuration itself went through several iterations. One

---

[89]   Otherwise, the surface would still be distorted from the heat of polishing.

of the biggest problems was that if it was just a rubber suit, like a deep sea diver's suit of Old, pressurizing it from the inside would just blow it up, like a big gingerbread man, and it would have about the same amount of flexibility. An astronaut bending an elbow would reduce the volume within the suit and thus increase the pressure. He would have to expend a great amount of energy even just to move. The way they solved it was to design the joints of the space suit such that when they flexed, they did not change the volume inside the suit. That would be required of every joint, and this would be a monumental task. Early on, solutions incorporated hard rather than flexible suits; at one time, the suit torsos were entirely hard, almost like a turtle. Thermal protection also varied from having hard suits with built-in insulation to simpler pressure suits with thermal insulating overgarments.

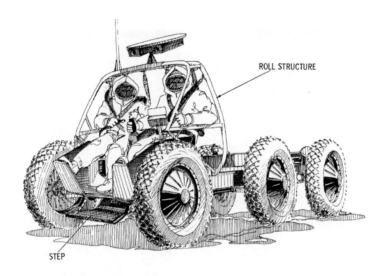

Image courtesy of GM Media Archives

As these variations were under development, we had to keep up with our designs to accommodate the suit of the day. There was another major requirement: we had to design our vehicle so that it could be stowed on the lunar lander module. As I was the 3-D space guy, I was assigned to investigate and find what the largest 6X6 vehicle could be and how it would be stowed. We had drawings of the Grumman Lunar Excursion Module (LEM) and its own stowage envelope within the Saturn V upper stage shroud. We had to make sure our 6X6 fit within both these limitations, as well as to assure that no part of it fell within the exhaust plumes of the LEM attitude control thrusters (not only to protect our vehicle but also, so as not to impede the LEM landing).

I had another related assignment: to determine the largest 4X4 vehicle that could be stowed under the same rules. This would be to determine what the best vehicle our competition (Bendix) could offer, so we could include comparative engineering analysis. I sized our 6X6 (with standard proportions) to have thirty-six-inch diameter tires, but widened the wheel track slightly so as to span a LEM compartment element. The 4X4 would have slightly larger wheels but it would be stowed in a similar manner.[90]

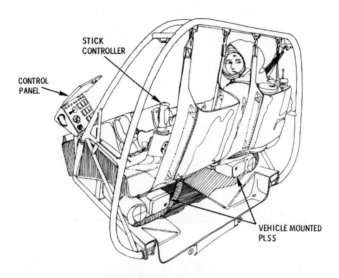

STICK
CONTROLLER

CONTROL
PANEL

VEHICLE MOUNTED
PLSS

Image courtesy of GM Media Archives

The Request for Proposal came from NASA shortly afterward. It was for the Local Site Survey Module (LSSM) and we would submit our design, hopefully to finally knock Bendix out of the competition. We submitted our proposal but NASA did not make an award, rather, they appeared to put everything on hold, in search of other directions. By this time, we felt we had a good handle on the wheel and tire size, so we continued to refine that hardware. Ferenc Pavlics had some promising improvements on the tire, which was similar to what we did with MOLAB, but we were not comfortable with the stainless steel mesh casing. Removing the mesh would degrade our capability to cross soft ground, so we felt we had to investigate some kind of tread-*appliqué* to give us flotation

---

[90]   I was to find, some months later, that the Bendix proposal was almost exactly as I had predicted.

on soft soil. John Calandro and I were working this problem with Ferenc, trying to find some means of interweaving a tread pattern within the wires. We were still concerned about materials, because of potential vacuum welding so we were exploring Vespel (polyimide) plastics that had good low friction/high temperature properties and would facilitate relative motions against the wires. Ferenc came up with a good solution of segmenting the treads and riveting them between openings in the basket weave. This allowed the smaller tread segments to pantograph easily within the wire array.

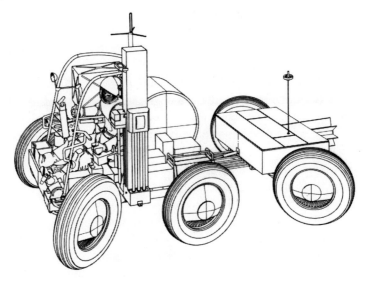

Final LSSM—drawn using the *Frieze* method. *Image courtesy of GM Media Archives*

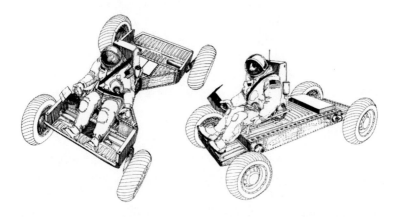

While we felt that 6x6 vehicles offered the highest mobility, we did explore variations of 4x4 vehicles. *Images courtesy of GM Media Archives*

NASA once again put out an RFP. We went through the same exercises but this time we felt we had a much better design. In addition to the higher mobility of the 6X6, we were also proposing slip frequency alternating current electric drives for each wheel. Our wheel would also incorporated a Harmonic Drive system that really simplified the way we sealed against the vacuum of space while also gearing down the power output. The only bearings now exposed to vacuum would be the final two that supported each wheel. Those bearings would be fitted with labyrinth—type seals.

Bendix proposed some kind of bellows seal with an offset crank, driving a wobble plate coupled to their wheels. Their tires were far simpler, using sheet metal loops and a single band around the circumference to bear against the lunar surface. Metal clips attached to the band would dig in to provide traction. The competition between GM and Bendix was simple. GM was betting on the best performance to overcome unexpected circumstances on the moon; Bendix was betting on expecting no problems and solving everything as simply as possible, at the lowest cost.

It would have been a classic battle, but it wasn't. NASA decided that it needed yet another interim test program to evaluate the wheel and drive systems of both concepts. They wanted to have a good technical basis for their final selection. They issued another RFP to both GM and Bendix to respond to—to conduct a test program assessing both hardware systems. The strange part was that the winning contractor would have the opportunity to build and evaluate their competitor's designs.[91] As it turned out, GM won that contract and Bob Peterson became the lead engineer for that program.

The GM test fixture was a glorified aluminum squirrel cage with a five-foot (inside diameter) drum surfaced in diamond plate, all supported from one side on six arms and a central hub. Within the hub was a dynamometer that could measure the amount of torque the squirrel (wheel and drive) was delivering. The hub was mounted on to a base structure, which also held the test wheel and its drive and suspension system (from the open side of the drum). There was also an array of quartz lamps surrounding the drum so that it could be

---

[91] While this might seem unfair, the test conductor's credibility would be at risk if they were not able to substantiate their analysis with hard data. Being the winner of this test program also did not mean they would win the final vehicle contract. The winning contractor could as easily be directed to engineer and build their competitor's design because NASA owned all the engineering anyway.

heated to lunar daytime temperatures. The whole fixture was sized to fit inside the AC Electronics Division vacuum chamber in Milwaukee, where the tests would be conducted.

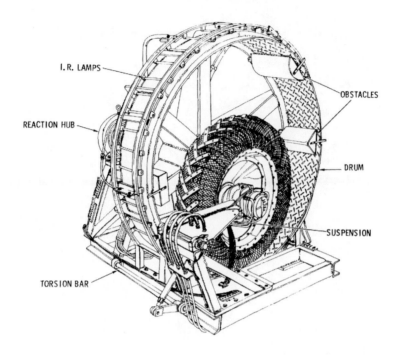

The lunar wheel and drive test fixture. *Image courtesy of GM Media Archives*

The competing wheel and drive systems would be subjected to the same test profiles. They would be brought to a lunar heat and (vacuum) pressure environment, then run for a length of time to calibrate normal performance. Next, with the wheel driving the drum, from a position above the wheel, three obstacles would be tripped and sprung into the drum, creating bumps on the tread way. The operation would then be filmed, and performance data collected for later evaluation. At the conclusion, technicians would access the facility to retract the obstacles, the chamber brought back to its operating environment and the wheel and drive rerun, to assess the amount of degradation from its pretest performance. Both wheel and drive systems would be tested, the data reduced and a final report submitted to NASA.

The completed fixture as installed in the vacuum chamber.
Photo courtesy of GM Media Archives

Walt Thiele was the designer of the fixture, and I was assigned to support its manufacture, functioning as a process engineer, to get parts bought or made. I was impressed by the work Bob Peterson did as the lead engineer on the project. On one occasion, he analyzed the Bendix design and predicted that they would get a performance spike (beneficial to them) at a particular RPM because their offset crank would come into a favorable reinforcement phase. Bendix had not been aware of it and did not predict it in their data. Subsequent testing verified the spike was there. On another occasion, Bob had just finished assembling our Harmonic drive test hardware, after making an adjustment (a tedious two-hour job because all the mechanisms were behind vacuum seals), then when he tested it, he found it had to be readjusted. This was late in the afternoon before a long holiday-weekend break; Bob then casually started disassembling it, as I and everyone else was leaving for the weekend.

Near this point in the program, we had a management change. Don Friedman was transferred to Detroit for a special assignment, and Sam

Romano was promoted to replace Don as the Land Operations Department head. There were no material changes that would affect us otherwise. Something that did affect me was that Susan entered into an early midlife crisis and felt she needed a break and wanted to seek some kind of employment in Los Angeles. We entered into what would be considered a trial separation. She quickly found a job in a medical office, which turned out to be very exciting for her. We still stayed in contact, and I would hear of all the interesting aspects of her work. I, of course, was disappointed that it was working out for her, so I transferred a good deal of my home energy into telescope making.

The telescope was a good healer, occupying most of my spare time. All the while I was building the telescope, it was in the back of my mind that ultimately I would take it to the Stellafane convention, in Vermont. I had started a work log on the system and even had a patent attorney do a preliminary search on the concept. While there were some other similar devices, there were no telescopes, as such. I also submitted a disclosure through GM, since they could have had legal claims, but they gave me a release on it. I was also aware that I had a one-year period, after its first public showing, to submit a patent application, if I was to do so. I would now focus all of my attention (outside of work) on completing the telescope—it would be my highest priority, and it would all be conducted in the secrecy of my garage. I was still apprehensive every month, as I opened my newest issue of *Sky and Telescope*, dreading to see that someone had beaten me to it. The nearest shock I had, surprisingly, turned out to be very close to home, but first, some additional background would be in order.

I had become active with the local astronomy club, *the Santa Barbara Star Cluster*, and even had remounted my old eight-inch telescope on to a conventional German Mounting, in order to participate in local activities. One activity was to go on grazing occultation expeditions. These were scientific excursions, in support of a Texas university doctorate student, David W. Dunham. Using the university's mainframe computer, he was able to calculate and print out predictions of where on earth, light from any given star would cast the moon's shadow on earth (if it could be seen) and he would list the earth latitude and longitude coordinates, as a plot, on where the Northern and Southern extremities of the shadow would pass (on earth), i.e., the graze lines. Working with several amateur astronomy groups, he would provide predictions for nearby grazes. The amateurs in turn, would collect timing and position data, and return it to him. In this way, Dunham would (for his thesis) be able to use the data to correct or refine astronomical records, as to the positions of the stars, the orbital mechanics of the moon, and/or the cataloged heights of the mountains on the moon.

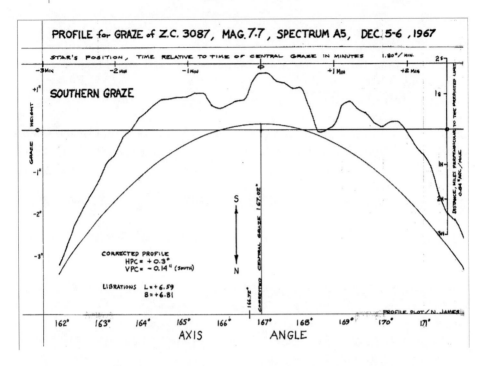

This is a typical lunar profile prediction prepared for a grazing occultation team.

Armed with Dunham's predictions, the local group would plot out the graze path onto U.S. Geological Survey maps, using longitude and latitude coordinates. They would then look for rural roads that crossed these paths at near-right angles, and then they would scout out and verify a suitable site. On graze day, the group would collect and set out telescopes, a few hundred feet apart, North and South of the predicted graze line.[92] In our team's operation, we would then string out a bell wire, connecting all the stations with hand phones. Also on the same line would be a tape recorder and a short-wave radio, picking up exact one-second time signals from WWV in Boulder, Colorado. Our team leader was Russ McNeil, who was the anchor of our group, running the recorders and reducing the data when it was collected. Each observer had a push-button frequency generator, which could place a beep tone on the tape. The tone frequency would correspond to their station's position on the line. We could all hear conversations and WWV signals from our headphones, but talk was kept to a minimum as in most cases we were listening for stations starting to see disappearances and reappearances.

---

[92]   The graze line assumes that the moon is billiard ball smooth, with no mountains or valleys.

When a given observer saw a star disappear[93], the observer would signal with a single beep, and when he saw the star reappear, as the moon passed by, he would signal with two beeps. This would place two-time hacks on the tape, indexed to the background WWV time code. Simply, an observer higher up on the lunar profile would see the disappearance a little later and the reappearance a little sooner, and so forth, for the rest of the observers. If one were to plot these marks on a graph, left to right for time and up and down for the (corrected) vertical separation of the observers, one would get a smooth curve for the edge of the moon. Where this became interesting was that the edge of the moon is mountainous, and the timings would be irregular. In fact, an observer would miss a disappearance altogether if they were above that peak's shadow line, or they would not see a reappearance if they were below a valley. What we would get, in effect, would be a scan of the lunar profile in that region. Considering that at the distance of the moon a star may appear to be about fifty feet in diameter and the moon is either there or it is not, it offered an unheard of positioning accuracy.

After a graze, the team leader would reduce the data collected and return it to Dunham. For amateur astronomers, it offered an exciting opportunity to enjoy their avocation in a dynamic state, as almost all other things in astronomy appear to be static.

There was one graze expedition that turned out to be quite memorable. We selected a site about a hundred miles up Highway 101, west of Santa Barbara and inland, away from populated areas. We had scouted the location the previous weekend and then caravanned to the site the prior evening to be ready for a 5:30 a.m. graze. We had plenty of time to set up as we arrived at the site two hours early. Our only concern was that there was a heavy overcast and the question was, "Would it clear in time for the graze?" We had prided ourselves with a true scientific spirit that we must be ready as there would be no excuse if it did clear. We set up our lines of communication, checking our WWV reception and tested beeping time hacks as they recorded on the tape recorder. Everything checked out and was ready, but it was still overcast some forty-five minutes before time zero.

We were all concerned as it was still overcast, and the minutes were passing away. We began to see traces of early dawn as the eastern sky started to lighten. We kept checking our systems, praying for the skies to clear, as we were now

---

[93] The limb of the moon would invariably be in shadow just beyond the brightly lit mountains near the edge; otherwise, it would be almost impossible to see stars against the bright edge. A star could normally be measured to disappear or reappear with an accuracy of within a fraction of a second.

only minutes away, but we were ready. Then, almost as if it were a message, with two minutes left to go—it started to rain. It was a profound experience, and surprisingly, we were proud of ourselves as we were laughing in surprise while restowing our equipment.

Returning to my original concern of finding someone else with my design, when I was first invited to participate in a grazing occultation, I was picked up by club member Fred Straubach in his Dodge passenger van. As he opened his side door, I saw an 8" f7 Newtonian telescope mounted in about an 18-inch diameter aluminum ball. It quite startled me. The upper end was comprised of small diameter tubing, made up into a truss structure. As we drove to the graze site a few miles away, I studied it very closely, noting that it was not using a flotation system, which I felt was the heart of my design. This made me feel a little better. There had already been several ball-type telescopes most recently: Bert Willard's bowling ball telescope that appeared in *Sky and Telescope* the year before and of course Russell W. Porter's garden telescope in the original *Amateur Telescope Making* bible. Fred's telescope turned out to be a fine instrument in itself, yielding crisp sharp images, better than I had seen in my own telescopes. The graze turned out to be successful and quite exciting for me as my first experience.

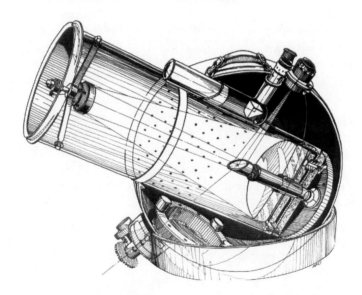

Cut-away drawing of the completed 10" Cassegranian telescope.

In anticipation of going public soon, I drove to Los Angeles to attend a Los Angeles Astronomical Society (LAAS) meeting and joined their membership. They held meetings on the first Monday of each month, at the Griffith Park Observatory, when it was closed (off-season) to the general public. It was open daily in the summers, but this worked out fine because the society usually hosted monthly star parties on Table Mountain or Mount Pinos on weekends with a dark moon. Both sites had large asphalt parking lots near their summits, so it was easy to park and set up telescopes nearby. At altitudes over 5,000 feet, viewing was above most of the atmosphere (air, moisture, and dust) so there would be very little turbulence to distort images. Seeing, as this condition was called, would be clear and steady, and the background skies would be ink black, revealing many more stars than would otherwise be visible. I was eager to try my telescope at one of these star parties.

On July 3, 1967, I completed the telescope and took it to a Santa Barbara club meeting. Afterward, I showed it to a few of the club members in the parking lot. There were a few thin clouds but I was able to pick out some stars, and while viewing at high power, was able to clearly resolve an Airy Disk,[94] with its surrounding diffraction rings.

Two days later, I took it for its first public showing, to a LAAS star party on Mount Pinos, some sixty miles north of LA. Driving north on Interstate 5, I turned off toward Frazier Park, then taking two lane and dirt roads through the pine forest, I reached a clearing and the paved parking lot, a few miles short of the summit. It was used primarily by hunters, during the hunting season. The skies were a beautiful deep blue at this eight thousand-foot altitude. The thin air made it a little difficult to breath, but it also brought a pleasant, peaceful quiet, even with the constant sound of the wind whistling through the high pine trees.

I knew no one there, as I was only a face in the back of the planetarium to most, but I started gathering attention as soon as I began to set up my telescope. Everyone was friendly and after darkness set in, were helpful in finding things to see in the heavens. It was my first chance to really try it out and it performed well.

---

[94] Stars are actually too far away to have any size as an image. What is really seen is an artifact of the optical system: an Airy Disk (which is a function of the diameter of the primary mirror and its focal length), surrounded by a series of, progressively fainter, target like rings. Surprisingly, the larger the primary mirror is, the smaller the Airy Disk will be (and the higher its resolving power).

The first public showing of the Spheremount on Mt. Pinos, July 1967.

One thing about the telescope, however, did bother me. That was that when I got the aluminizing job at work—the quartz over coating on the mirror had a slight brownish cast that appeared darker at the center and lighter at the edge. It was as if it had a wedge-shaped filter over the aluminum coating. I decided I would remove the mirrors and have them commercially recoated after I got back and before I left for the convention. There would just be enough time to do it. When I got home, I removed the mirrors and drove them to Pancro Mirrors, in Los Angeles, getting a commitment that they would be ready by the next Friday.

While I was planning my trip east, something else came up that I would add to my schedule. Our group had planned a grazing occultation for Friday, July 28, the night before I planned to leave so I incorporated it, and would use that event for my departure. I still had to reinstall the mirrors, collimate them, pack for the trip and close up the house. The collimation did not go well, but I thought it was good enough for the graze. I would just have to find some time later to finish the job. Since the graze site was near Palmdale, just northeast of Los Angeles, I figured I would do the graze, then separate from the group and keep heading east.

We caravanned to the site early, so we would have enough light to set up our telescopes. A few members of the LAAS and David Dunham himself joined us and took stations for the graze. The skies cleared, and the graze was successful;

Russ getting good data on his tape recorder. As the rest of the group was packing, I bid farewell and received many wishes for good luck. It was 10:30 PM and I figured I could get in about a hundred miles of driving—to get out of the L.A. area—and then find a place to pull over for some sleep in the back of my VW camper van.

The drive east was easy, as I could pit stop for essentials and pull over for a catnap any time I felt tired, even getting up after an hour or so to pick up a few more miles. When I arrived at Herb's house in Cleveland, I knew I would be able to relax for a few days, but also that I had to allocate some time to recollimate my optics. I found it was easy making adjustments in the daylight, but I really needed a dark sky and stars to test the final collimation and focus. Those skies never came, and soon it was time to leave.

I still had a few more planned stops. The first was in Chardin, Ohio, just east of Cleveland, at the Structural Fibers plant. I had bought the original fourteen-inch sphere from them, for my first mounting and I wanted to show them my telescopes, as well as inquire about additional sizes, they might be able to make. Their spheres were designed as pressure vessels, and their specialty was to make them out of chopped fiberglass, using a resin transfer mold (RTM) process. They appreciated my stop and gave me a tour of the plant. They also gave me a rejected seventeen-inch diameter sphere, which I could use for another telescope. Leaving Chardin, I continued on to Jamestown, where I would stay overnight with my mother.

Leaving Jamestown, I headed north to the Nagle plant, east of Buffalo, where they rotationally molded plastic globes—used for lighting in large mall parking lots. I talked to them about their thirty and thirty-six-inch globes, what materials they were made of, pricing, and shipping. My hope was that there would be something good enough to use as is. Leaving the Nagle plant, I headed east on the New York State toll road.[95] I continued as far as Troy before breaking away onto smaller roads, taking me to Vermont and then finally across the state to Springfield on the eastern side. I arrived there late on Friday night amidst light rain showers. In town, I saw a sheriff's car, and when I inquired about directions, he kindly escorted me to the top of Breezy Hill, where I was able to camp overnight. The next day would be the official start of the convention.

By the time I woke up, the rains had stopped. I cleaned up then walked up the road from the camping area to the observing site. On top of the hill, I saw

---

[95] In planning my stops, I had also sent a letter of inquiry to Edmund Scientific to see if they had any interest in my "new mounting." They responded, saying they would have a representative at Stellafane and that he would get in touch with me.

the Porter-designed clubhouse and his turret telescope, both made famous in *Amateur Telescope Making*. Several amateurs were already milling about, and a few telescopes were assembled, some still under their weather tarps. There was a very impressive 16" Newtonian telescope mounted in a modified Porter Ring mount made by the Montclair New Jersey club.

I went into the clubhouse, where I registered and advised them that I had a telescope to enter into the competition. They gave me forms to fill out and told me what to do. I returned to the camping area to get my van and brought it up the hill to unload. I found a good spot next to the Montclair telescope, stopped, and began unloading. Several people helped me drop off my disassembled telescope, and I left a thoroughly confused group of people, trying to figure what the various pieces were, while I returned my van to the camping area. A small group had gathered and patiently waited for what I'm sure they thought was another variation of Bert Willard's bowling ball telescope from the year before. There was a calm prevalent, until I picked up the water jug and began pouring water into the basin. As I was dropping my telescope in place, I noticed someone filming with an 8mm movie camera, and I decided to give him a show. In a practiced manner, I gently pushed down on the sphere, causing excess water to spill over the sides, eased off, and then gave the tube a sharp slap on the side, causing it to spin sharply in circles. Then I slapped the top of the sphere with both hands, letting go immediately, and the telescope was standing stationary, perfectly still and stable.

Photographs of the telescope in Santa Barbara (left) and at Stellafane (right). *Photo courtesy of Dr. H. Paul.*

From then on, I had a steady stream of people stopping by and basically asking the same questions, such as, "How do you intend to drive it" and "What do you do when it freezes?" In the early afternoon, they began their talks in a large open-air tent, with displays and handouts, but I missed most of them because I had to stand by my telescope to be ready to answer any questions the judges might have. I did have a chance to talk at length afterward with two of the judges, Mr. Allan Mackintosh[96], who published the *Maksutov Club Bulletin* and with Mr. Walter Scott Houston of *Sky and Telescope*. At around 5:00 p.m., one of the judges appeared and stapled a blue ribbon, "First Prize for Mechanical Ingenuity" on to my telescope.

Soon afterward, the "talks" were over and the crowd began to disappear into the camping area for their suppers. I tried to use the opportunity to complete the collimation of my telescope, as I knew I would finally have the stars I waited for. Toward sunset, the groups began to gather for the "Twilight Talks," but I stayed to collimate, waiting for the first stars. When they started appearing, I picked a bright one and aimed my telescope at it, using the finder scope. I was horrified to find I could not bring my main wide-angle eyepiece into focus. Cassegrainian telescopes are very sensitive in this, and my earlier adjustments must have shifted the final focus outside of the 3/8-inch range that my eyepiece could accommodate. It was necessary to advance my secondary a few threads on its screw to bring it into focus, but in so doing I had to start collimation all over again and now I was working in the dark. I ended up worse than when I had started. The talks were just finishing, and hundreds of enthusiasts began descending from the "talks" to look through the telescopes. They would form lines at the various telescopes, with the 16-inch Montclair[97] being very popular because of its large size (for 1967). A line formed for my telescope also, and while I was not able to get my main wide-field eyepiece to focus, I was able to focus at my high-power station, but I still had some residual astigmatism from the bad collimation. This caused the stars to have a slight flare in one direction. I was quite satisfied, however, that the images were stable enough to demonstrate the properties of my new mounting. A standard test for telescope

---

[96] Mr. Mackintosh requested that I submit an article on my telescope for his publication, which I subsequently did.

[97] As noted previously, telescopes are measured by the diameter of their primary mirrors. As a rule, the larger the mirror, the more light that can be collected from a star and, logically, more (in number) and far fainter stars will be visible in the bigger telescopes.

stability is to give the tube a sharp rap with the knuckle while looking at a star under high power. A good telescope will damp out the vibration in one to two seconds. Mine was damping out in a fraction of a second.[98]

As my telescope was not clock driven, I had to aim it at an object in the sky and then allow the next person in line to follow it through the eyepiece, as it drifted across the field of view (because of the earth's rotation). It would usually be in view for about forty seconds, after which I would reset it for the next person. When there were only a few people waiting, I would invite them to move the telescope through a star field, since it took only ounces of force to move it.[99] While the general public viewing was going on, the judges were making their rounds, judging for optical performance. They would take immediate priority over any general viewing and request of the owner that they point their telescope at the double-double, (stars) in Epsilon Lyra, or whatever, and they would perform their tests. I knew I was dead, as far as optical quality was concerned because of the collimation, but I was glad they were able to get a sense of the inherent stability of the mounting. Viewing continued on the hilltop, much like happens at regular star-parties, then at around 10:30 PM the sky started hazing up and the "seeing" started to deteriorate. By midnight it was a solid overcast and only a few optimists remained. The awards for "Optical Excellence" were announced over the loudspeaker, but by then the field was almost empty. A few of us gathered at the clubhouse and talked optics until about 2:00AM, at which time, I brought my car up from the field to load the telescopes. I then drove back down to the camping area to sleep—very tired, very happy and very wide-awake.

I got up early Sunday morning to get a good start. I decided to make an easy drive of it and bypass New York City, going directly to Uncle Roland's apartment, in New Jersey. I also thought that because Edmund Scientific was nearby, I would drop by cold turkey, on Monday. Their man never identified himself to me at Stellafane, so I didn't know how I would be received.

---

[98] Damping is usually achieved by having a mounting with a high mass. Another entrant for the event also had a 10" cassegrainian telescope, which he proudly demonstrated its mass by unloading it off its trailer by dropping it several feet to the ground, with a big bang. It must have weighed 300 pounds. In contrast, my entire telescope, weighed 65 pounds.

[99] The final balancing of the telescope was actually achieved when I put one too many ¼-20 nuts on the end of the secondary, causing it to move. To balance it, I put a little extra water in the basin, to make it super-sensitive in balance. Once it was nearly balanced, I would then drop the water level, transferring more weight to the annular foam band, which would then hold it in position.

When I got there and inquired, I was referred to Mr. Corry, who was head of their New Products group, and he was available to see me. I setup my Cassegranian, and the 4-1/4-inch telescope in the original small sphere. Mr. Corry collected a few others from his staff to see them also. It was daylight so I couldn't show him anything astronomical, but I was able to demonstrate the flotation system of the new mounting. I'm sure, having just won 1st Prize Mechanical at Stellafane, helped get his attention. They seemed very interested and asked what my manufacturing plans were, and how much I would be selling them for. I had to confess that I had no business plans as yet, and that I was just an inventor. All the while, Mr. Corry kept eyeing the smaller telescope in the fourteen-inch sphere, and he finally commented that, "There might be a good market for that small telescope."[100] Since I was not able to offer a business plan, we left it at that, and I packed up and headed for Jamestown.

I spent a few days in Jamestown and then continued on to Cleveland, where I would stay a few more days. Herb had some free time and offered go back with me, to share the driving, making the trip easier. We left together and the trip was uneventful, except that Herb picked up a stray white kitten that he found along the way and appropriately named him Needles. After arriving in Santa Barbara and staying a bit, Herb arranged to fly back to Cleveland with Needles.

I resumed my contacts with the local astronomy group and at work; enjoying telling local boy does good stories, while relating my mission to Mecca. A week later, I took the telescopes to Long Beach, California, to a convention of Western Amateur Astronomer and gave an impromptu talk. It felt good, after the years of secrecy, to be talking freely about the system, and apparently being well received. It was time now to return to the real world.

Susan was glad to hear about my fortunes and she told me she was doing well. She enjoyed working for William Jennings Bryant III, and was meeting a lot of

---

[100]   While I subsequently obtained a mechanical patent (U.S. Pat. No. 3,603,664) for the Telescope Mounting System, I learned from Sky and Telescope reporters in 1976, that Edmund Scientific was going to advertise a small ball mounted telescope in their next issue and that Edmunds' lawyers had advised them that their Astroscan did not infringe on my patent. They were correct, in that my patent was for a flotation system and theirs was a conventional three-point ball mounting. The irony was that if I had filed for a design patent (in addition), it might have been covered. The Astroscan turned out to be a very successful product in its lifetime and was copied by other manufacturers when Edmund's patents expired.

famous people. Bryant had been successful in several professions and currently was providing medical assistance to people through the use of hypnosis. Most notably, however, he was providing a service for prominent defense attorney, Francis Lee Bailey. Bryant's service amounted to assessing jury pools, and helping to select jurors that would be favorable to his clients. The jury pool would be observed during devoir questioning, and assessments would be made on the basis of their responses, behaviors, and body language.

Susan was trained to make these observations and to discreetly note them. The high point for her was when she was sent to New Jersey to observe the jury pool in the famous Capalino murder trial. She sent me a clipping from the local paper, with an attractive photo close-up of her, known only as "the mystery lady . . . who sat quietly in the back of the courtroom . . . for unknown reasons." I felt happy for her, but realized I was up against some high-powered competition.

At work, things were at a lull. With my home situation, I was concerned about not having had a merit pay increase in several years. It was becoming increasingly obvious that the "center of gravity" of General Motors was in Detroit. While they still appreciated me in Santa Barbara, I thought I had to explore other career opportunities—one possibility was to return to Detroit. I felt I had burned my bridges at Styling, at least for promotions, but I learned of a group at Research Staff (also at the Tech Center) that was apparently staffing up to focus on mass transportation. With my department's blessing, I arranged a trip back, to interview for an opening.

When I arrived at the Tech Center and entered the main gate, it felt strange turning left instead of right, after all those years at Styling. I would now head to the other end of the lake. I met with the manager of the new group, and the interview ran about a half-hour. He explained what the new group would be doing, and how I would fit in. The work looked interesting, and they seemed receptive, but my heart was not really in it. My silent decision against taking the job was cinched when he advised me of the same old line, "of course, we can't steal someone from another division," and they would only be able to offer me a $15 a month increase (to leave Santa Barbara and return to Detroit!). I left saying I would let him know. That evening, I took advantage of an opportunity to visit my old GMDRL boss, Don Friedman and his wife, who had just moved into their new home outside of Detroit. He related some of his experiences in his move back from Santa Barbara, and how he was adapting to the life, higher in the corporate structure. This visit reinforced my earlier decision.

I returned to work, resolved that I would knuckle down and ride out the adversities—just focusing on the task at hand. As with everyone else, I would wait for NASA to put out the next RFP, and hopefully award the contract to either Bendix or us—just get it over with. After a few weeks, I was finally getting comfortable with my mental adjustments when I happened to be up-front in the administration building, and Sam Romano's secretary, Mary McNamara hailed me, to tell me I had a phone call, and that they would transfer it to me on another line.

When I answered the phone, the voice on the other end introduced himself as Carl Sundberg, who I knew to be the main partner of Sundberg-Ferar, in Detroit. He said they would be opening an office in Burbank, California, to service their contract with Lockheed on the new L-1011 program. Lockheed was reentering the commercial airline business after an absence of several years, following the Lockheed Electra turbo-prop, and Sundberg-Ferar had negotiated a consulting contract for their aircraft interiors. Carl went on to say they would need an on-site representative in Burbank and he would like to interview me for that position, it would be as an Account Executive. I was flabbergasted, but immediately agreed to the interview. I requested a few days vacation from GM and made arrangements to fly back to Detroit. I tried to call Susan, but she was not home and I was not able to leave a message.

On arrival at the airport, I was picked up by their man, and taken to the Sundberg-Ferar offices in Southfield, Michigan, just Northwest of Detroit. When I arrived, I was sent to Sundberg's office and I found out what had happened. Apparently, when I turned down the mass transportation job at Research Staff, they then tried to fill the position with one of my former associates at Styling. In the conversation that followed, he advised them that he could not accept the job either because he had just given his two-week notice, and was going to join Sundberg-Ferar to work on the L-1011. When he arrived at Sundberg-Ferar and found they were looking for someone for a Burbank office, he said, "Hey, I know someone that must be available because he just interviewed at Research Staff and he already lives in California."

After more conversations with Sundberg, I was given a tour of their facilities; they appeared to be well organized, servicing a wide variety of clients. They had a good shop and were already doing some work on the L-1011. There was no resemblance to that small office—I remembered seeing in 1954, when I first started work in Detroit.

Returning to Carl's office, he made a decent job offer for the position and asked if I could let him know within a few days. I paused for a moment, then, told him I had all the information I needed, and accepted the job right there. I would go back to GM to give them my two-week notice, and be available to start on November 1.

Upon returning to Santa Barbara, I finally reached Susan and told her of the last few days. We decided to put our house up for sale, listing it with her brother's old firm, and to move some of the furniture to her Los Angeles apartment. We would have movers pick up and deliver the heavier stuff. She would take the cats, since I expected to meet Carl Sundberg at the Hollywood Burbank airport, to go with him and be introduced to the Lockheed people. Carl would go on to Rohr, in San Diego, where the BART cars were being built, and I would fly on to Detroit, to work for about a month—I to become familiar with Sundberg-Ferar and they with me. When I returned to Los Angeles, I would make my own living arrangements and Susan and I would remain separated.

At GMDRL, they were disappointed to see me go, but were happy for my opportunity, and were very supportive. They arranged for a going away party, on my last day at the *Timbers,* a nice restaurant, famous not for its food, but for having been shelled by a Japanese submarine, early in World War II. Sam Romano went beyond his call of duty in expressing appreciation for my work at General Motors and I was very moved by it. I received a pen and pencil set, engraved:

~ Norm James ~
General Motors Corporation
Styling Staff 1954-1963
Defense Research Labs 1963-1967
From your DRL friends
Oct. 27, 1967

It was then that I realized that the odyssey had ended.

Epilogue

After leaving General Motors, I worked for Sundberg-Ferar in their Burbank office for seven years. During that period, I became active with the Los Angeles Astronomical Society, serving on its board of directors and as its president in 1969. I filed for, and received, a patent on my telescope mounting, but allowed it to expire without having marketing it. I made several other telescopes, all Spheremounted, including a 12-½" f/5 RFT which, received four First Place Awards at the Riverside Telescope Makers Conference and, First Place-Mechanical and Second Place-Optical awards at Stellafane, all in 1972.

Susan and I divorced in 1971 and I remarried, to my present wife, Ginna (Froelich), who was born and raised on a ranch near Willcox, Arizona, sixty miles east of Tucson.

As a side note, I have concluded that Ginna was in fact, living within the far horizon view, I contemplated that day from the lookout ridge on the Apache Trail.

A graduate of the University of Arizona, she moved to Los Angeles where I met and married her. Two years later, Lockheed completed the design phase of the L-1011 and terminated their contract with Sundberg-Ferar. Rather than returning to Detroit, I left Sundberg-Ferar and accepted an Industrial Design position at Rohr Industries where they had just finished building the Sundberg-Ferar designed BART cars.

I was hired to work on a rapid transit city bus, which would be manufactured as the [correctly spelled] Flxible 870. By 1977, under financial pressures, Rohr exited mass transportation altogether and returned to their bread-and-butter aerospace business. They sold the Flxible Company to Grumman and dissolved the transportation division.

Rohr also had a navy contract to design, and build a three-thousand ton (air cushion) surface effects ship, the 3KSES. The ship would have been similar to a hovercraft, except it would have had hard sidewalls that cut into the water plane (like a catamaran), and fans to pump a bubble of air beneath, contained between seals fore and aft. This would raise the hull out of the water sufficiently so as to reduce drag in forward motion, and with four waterjet propulsers, would have been capable of 90-knot speeds. Rohr, an aerospace company, was awarded this contract because the program was weight critical and Rohr had experience with lightweight aluminum structures and gas turbine engine systems.

I was transferred to the marine division and assigned as a process engineer for the development of passive fire protection systems for its aluminum structures. A short time later, under the new Carter administration, the program was cancelled and our division was reduced from nine hundred to about two hundred fifty people. At that point, three of the division officers purchased the company, and its employees were given the option of joining the new company (taking their seniority with them) or remaining with Rohr. I elected to go with the new company.

Now known as RMI Inc., the company did some good and exciting work, but ultimately cash flow forced it into bankruptcy. I ended up returning to Rohr, starting all over as a new employee, in the now lean engine nacelle and pylon manufacturing business. I was placed in Design-To-Cost (which is similar to Value Engineering), and promoted to Group Engineer a few months later.

In August of '94, Rohr teamed as a partner with Lockheed-Martin, and others, in their bid to win the NASA Reusable-Launch-Vehicle (RLV) contract, the first phase being to design and build the unmanned X-33 proof-of-concept launch vehicle.[101] Rohr would be responsible for the entire outer skin—its Thermal Protection System (TPS). The full size RLV, of course, would ultimately be the replacement for the Space Shuttle. While the bulk of the work would be performed at the Lockheed-Martin Skunk Works in Palmdale, Rohr did all of

---

[101] Because the X-33 would be a test vehicle, it would only be required to fly fifteen sub-orbital flights. Launched from Edwards AFB it would fly downrange some four hundred fifty to nine hundred miles to landing sites in Utah and Montana, where it would land safely, all under automatic flight control. The plan was to qualify all systems in wind tunnels or test labs, wherever it was possible. Those things that could only be qualified in a reentry environment would be validated on the X-33 flights. It would not be necessary for the X-33 to go into orbit in order to achieve the maximum heating and dynamic loads of launch and reentry. At half the scale of the RLV, sub orbital X-33 flights, could satisfactorily validate the hardware and operating systems of the RLV vehicle at considerable cost savings.

its work in Chula Vista, as in practice we could jump into a car, and drive to their facility in three hours, any time we were needed. My task was to coordinate Risk Management for Rohr.

This turned out to be one of the most exciting programs I had ever worked on. Lockheed-Martin, won the contract in 1996 with its lifting-body proposal, and began the design and build phase. I put off retirement because of the peaking X-33 program activity, hoping to see it on through to launch, which was scheduled for July of 1999. I had another silly reason; since I'm often obsessed with symbolism, I thought I could bookend my career with similar events. When I started at GM Styling, the first program I really worked on was the Firebird II and its body was made of titanium. After its public release, Bob McLean and Stefan Habsburg gave an SAE paper on it entitled *Titanium Feathers for the Firebird*. Here now, at the end of my career, I was working on the thermal protection system for the X-33, with Carbon-Carbon panels on the critical leading edges but, at the next thermal protection level, there were individual body panels of titanium sandwich construction—clearly—protective feathers for the next generation Firebird.

Midway in the program, Rohr entered into a merger with BFGoodrich, which subsequently reorganized and renamed itself as Goodrich, to reflect that it was no longer in the (sold-off) tire business. Our division became the Goodrich Aerostructures Group.

The highest risk items of our thermal protection systems were the Carbon-Carbon panels and the seals between our metallic panels. Prophetically, the highest program risk for Lockheed-Martin was the aggressive schedule that demanded all systems be ready for the July 1999 launch—failure to meet that date was not an option. So it was that when the composite construction liquid-hydrogen fuel tanks were pressure tested and found to have delaminations, the program fell into an unrecoverable slip. NASA found it was easier to withdraw from the program than to increase the funding to correct it. [102]

With the demise of the X-33, I formally retired but returned to continue working part-time in the Goodrich R&D group, on advanced engine nacelle and thrust reverser systems.

---

[102] As it turned out, they did slip the launch date one year, but the tank failure was the last straw. One understanding of the program was that the RLV was supposed to be so commercially viable that industry would pick up any extraordinary development costs. The contract terms allowed either party to walk away at any time, so when NASA withdrew further funding, Lockheed-Martin deemed it was no longer commercially viable and stopped work.

§

The Brothers

Herb remained in Cleveland, eventually running his own advertising art studio as Herb James Inc. Early on, seeking some form of physical recreation, he took up fencing through the Cleveland Parks and Recreation system, studying under a former Hungarian Olympic coach, Menyard Kadar. Kadar took Herb under his wing, as he appeared to be one of his better pupils, doing well in cross-country team competitions. Kadar was also the fencing coach at Case Tech & Western Reserve. When he retired, he recommended that Herb assume his position at Case. The board concurred and Herb was hired, serving with distinction until his retirement in 2004. Herb died in the spring of 2005.

Pete went on to graduate from Case Institute of Technology and took a job with Pratt & Whitney in West Palm Beach, working on rocket propulsion systems. Later he became active in the Foreign Technology Division, involving intelligence analysis, and in support of black activities. He prepared an internal analysis from resources at Wright Patterson Air Force Base, which concerned him so much that he assumed a whistle-blower role, trying to influence policy. This ostracized him from the industry and cost him his aerospace career. He published a book to alert the American public, *Soviet Conquest From Space* (Arlington House 1974), which was a cleansed version of his Foreign Technology report, sans the classified material. He followed this with another book the *Air Force Mafia* (Arlington House 1975), which was a hair-raising cloak and dagger account involving the story behind the original book. Peter is now writing a memoir, which is nearing publication.

Having burned all of his bridges, he went on the lecture circuit as *Peter James—Spy* and did quite well, giving students their money's worth. With the fall of the iron curtain, the bottom fell out of that market and Pete settled down to raise a family. He went into Florida real estate, specializing in Punta Gorda lot sites. He is now retired and living with his wife, Zayra, in Costa Rica.

Coming full circle, I found my old companion polio still had another trick up its sleeve. In the '90s I began hearing of something called PPS—Post Polio Syndrome. What it turned out to be was that, in all those years, the remaining muscles which had picked up the burden of life long ago were now randomly giving up, some thirty to forty years later. Muscles would start to die off, leading to a general weakening. Exercise cannot restore strength to these muscles and if taken to fatigue, will further destroy remaining muscle. So it has become a balance of exercise to maintain existing fitness levels without overworking the affected muscles. I am still able to walk, with a more noticeable limp, but I do notice a progressive weakening.

Fortunately, with the introduction of the PC, I can comfortably spend my time collecting my memories, scanning old slides and filmstrips, sorting through log books and putting it all together to make some sense. Now, as an old aerospace warhorse, I can reminisce of that young colt, frolicking through memory's pastures.

§

Closure

Early in 1992, I heard from Bill Porter (a former Styling associate and Pratt graduate) that all three Firebirds would be on display at the Pebble Beach concours d'elegance that summer. It had been almost thirty years since I had last seen them in life, and now with this opportunity, I arranged a one-day round trip flight to attend. I had seen the Firebird III once prior, on network TV, when a GM scientist was being interviewed at the Tech Center and it appeared in the background of the Research Staff lobby. I later learned that Bill Porter had been instrumental in moving it (on loan) to the Henry Ford Museum.

Apparently, GM was able to borrow the car from time to time for special events and this was one of those times. Bill said the plan was to show all three birds, but he was not sure it would actually happen. When I arrived at the Concours and was walking to the display areas, I was apprehensive that it would not be there, but resolved that at least I would see a very good auto show.

Almost as if it were following Harley Earl's script, I saw the spread of automobiles and the high tail fin of the Firebird III just jumped out to catch my attention, then, sure enough, there were the other two. Seeing it again was very uplifting. I had forgotten how well the forms had worked together, details were resolved, and how the interior contributed so much to the exterior forms. The most notable change was the body color, a metallic gray, sharply differing from the original metallic gold with pearlescent overcoat. The interior trim was now all black, and upon closer inspection appeared to have been (nicely) retrimmed in black leather, but it still retained the original forms. Another change was that it had two clear plastic canopies instead of its original reflective aluminized canopies. I concluded that these were the canopies that were made for that one Motorama film sequence. Another observation was that, somewhere in the last thirty years, someone had stolen the chrome medallion from the right hand front grillwork. It was a small chrome and painted detail threaded on to a ¼-20 stud, and was easily removed. All in all, it was a memorable day, and I returned to San Diego that evening to the news of Hurricane Andrew hitting Florida.

In 1994, I heard from my former Detroit roommate, Carl Olsen[103] who told me that there was a publisher interested in talking to me. They would all be attending a design conference at the Henry Ford Museum, and it would be an opportunity for me to see both, them and the Firebird III. I met the publisher at the conference and he expressed interest in receiving an account of its design and further requested any information on design training I may have had that would be relevant. While at the museum, I toured their fine exhibits and took extensive video of the Firebird III exhibit.

Also on display near the entrance was a Lunar Roving Vehicle, which brought back memories of Santa Barbara. I felt pleased to have worked on two independent items of note in the highly respected museum. I thought to myself that few (if any) people would have been aware of the linkage between the joystick controller in the Firebird III and the controller in the lunar rover, now in front of me.

Afterward, the Olsens, Dagmar Arnold, Bill and Pat Porter and I had a nice dinner at the Porter's where we reminisced of things Pratt and GM Styling, and later we would have a spirited milk-truck discussion. I flew back to San Diego and began collecting my thoughts on the design of the Firebird III.

In 1995, I received a letter from Bob Peterson, informing me that there would be a 25th anniversary reunion in Santa Barbara for the Lunar Roving Vehicle team, and that I was invited, even though I left the program before the final contract was awarded. Ginna and I drove up to attend and sat with Bob and Claire Peterson at the banquet. Sam Romano emceed the ceremonies and Ferenc Pavlics gave a presentation on the Mars Sojourner,[104] where he was serving as a consultant to JPL, on mobility systems. I saw John Calandro at one of the cocktail parties and was pleasantly surprised to learn that a patent had been issued on the lunar wheel-tread design, which Pavlics, Calandro and I shared as coinventors (U.S. Pat. No. 3,568,748).

---

[103] After several years in England, Carl and Sonia moved to Paris where he headed the Citroen design office from 1982 to 1987. He then returned to Detroit to chair the Transportation Design program at the College of Creative Studies.

[104] It landed and deployed successfully after first demonstrating the bouncing balloon technique and executing a perfect mission in 1997.

In 2003, I received an E-mail from Larry Faloon of Detroit, informing me that there would be a major auto show at the GM Technical Center in June: Eyes-On-Design, a benefit for the Detroit Institute of Ophthalmology. There would be three hundred vehicles on display, one hundred twenty-five of them being concept cars dating from the original Buick Y-job to present day. The Firebirds would all be on display. Larry then told me that he had worked with Stefan Habsburg and said he almost knew me through Stefan. Larry was also one of the key people at General Motors in the restoration of the Firebirds to running condition, most recently having completed the Firebird III.[105]

I immediately made arrangements to attend the events and advised Larry that I would be going. I intended to reserve the Saturday to visit friends, but when Larry asked if I would be available to attend a press conference that Saturday to answer media questions, I agreed to do so. That would leave me only that evening to visit with the Porters.

The Friday cocktail party was held in the Styling auditorium, where I ran into Carl and Sonia and meet several of the current Design Center people. It was nice to return to the building that held so many memories. I looked up at the center stage turntable where Harley Earl stood that day and said, "Put it back to the way it was . . . ." There were some very moving moments.

On Saturday, I drove to the Tech Center and was directed to where the gas turbine vehicles were on display. They were just starting to brief the GM staff workers on what to expect, and of the plan to offer rides to the media on selected cars. The world media would arrive first, then the national media, and finally the local media. Also on exhibit were the Firebird II and III show chassis', which had no bodywork on them and were marked with small labels identifying the various subsystems. The Firebird II represented was the fiberglass body-running version, rather than the non-running titanium Waldorf Astoria show car.

One thing that struck me was that the Firebird III had a strange black V shaped housing hanging below the front end. Larry Faloon explained that when they went to restore the vehicle they found that the gasoline four-cylinder APU power plant had been removed, and there was no record of what had happened to it. They found a Honda engine to replace it and had to add the doghouse to cover it. Considering what they had to do, they did a pretty good job of integrating it.

Before the media arrived, I was given a ride in the Firebird III, around a short course. It was the second time I had ridden it, the first being some forty-four years earlier. The media started arriving, and the day went quickly as I had the opportunity to talk to many people and give them background on the Firebirds.

---

[105] This surprised me as it had no direct steering linkages but was a fly by wire system, using 40-year old technology.

On Sunday, the 23rd, classic cars were spread all over the Tech Center grounds in what I would have to think was one of the grandest auto shows of all time (and likely of some time to come). I stayed near the Firebirds, answering questions from the public where I could. I did find a few opportunities to wander about and take in some of the show myself. Almost all the old Motorama show cars were present as were the special Corvettes and more recent concept cars. I found the LaSalle II roadster on display—striped to its gel coat, in its first stage of restoration. It was the sister car of the Motorama sedan that I was first assigned to in 1954. All in all, it was another memorable day.

§

Reflections

In the years following the Firebird III, I have been asked many questions and have had time to reflect on my answers. The most frequent questions were of Harley Earl and the role he played in its design. While it was my hand that was mostly involved in its definition and Larry Simi's in its execution, I have never doubted that it was Harley Earl's vision that made it happen. Earl was the film director that put it all together. That he was not personally involved—as was in his tradition—was really a measure that we were executing his thoughts to his satisfaction, and they needed little midcoarse correction.

In another sense, once he had bought off the space frame mockup, from which he approved—our going to clay—we ourselves were locked in to the design, and were merely executing that vision. We did not feel we had the authority to deviate from what he had approved. Our only flexibility was in how to resolve those surfaces and details that were in conflict, or fell somewhere in between.

This interpretation is reinforced, perhaps, by the incident that happened in the auditorium, when Earl returned from Europe to say to the design committee:

> "You know . . . when I came into the studio that day—for the first time—and saw the mockup . . . I actually saw the finished car at the show . . . and it was exactly as I had pictured it."

I continued having after thoughts, trying to understand how the design elements fell into place.[106] At the time, tail fins appeared to be reaching their limit and actually started disappearing from production cars shortly after the Firebird III. This could have been attributed to Earl's retirement and Bill

---

[106]   An artifact of the creative process is that an artist cannot be conscious of decision making while he is creating, since the mind must follow an uncontrolled free association path to its completion. The artist can only contemplate on how he arrived there afterward.

Mitchell's succession, or perhaps, it was that we took fins to the limit and there was no place further for them to go.

The original concept that Stefan and I attempted was a clean design without fins—this would have been considered to be in good taste by the elite (non-automotive) design community. After Earl's Motorama vision, we recognized we needed something exciting. I found an analogy that I thought was appropriate. It was of the downhill racer (in skiing). In competition, the winner of that event is never graceful or artistic in style but rather is always on the verge of disaster throughout the entire run. Sometimes it is even too difficult to watch, but there is no doubt that it is exciting. Flirting with nine, perhaps eleven fins (depending on how you parse them) may have placed us into that competition.

We were close several times to questioning the mix of tri-fin and quad-fin arrays. As already noted, my first reaction was "it's not right," but somehow it seemed to work. The design committee also came to that conclusion when they made us remove them. Trying to rationalize the arrangement that we ultimately stayed with, I found another analogy. For centuries, mariners around the world have claimed to have seen mermaids, half women and half fish. This should have fallen to exactly the same kinds of criticisms, however, for some reason, mankind has never objected.

The three-fin debate actually came down to execution. We needed the three fins for the mass distribution. By definition, we could not extend elements of the quad fins from their positions to the twelve, three and nine o' clock-root positions that would have been required. The dorsal fin was a natural because we could grow it out of the centerline widow's peak, which ran back between the blisters. The three and nine-o'clock tail fins actually emerged from the widest points of the body section at those fin stations, even though the accent of the curve had a slight downward (antidihedral) cant. A fin at the six o'clock position would have solved everything by making it a quad array; however, we actually had another graphic equivalent. The Firebird III also had aerodynamic speed brakes: alligator jaw like flaps that opened into the wind stream when the brakes were applied. These flaps were arrayed around the three tail fins—two straddling the main dorsal fin and one large flap full across the bottom at the 6 o'clock position. This array of three brake flaps was diametrically opposed to the array of three tail fins and effectively created a horizontal axis of symmetry, bringing the whole tail assembly into balance.

There was an incident on the occasion when I visited Bill Porter. Bill was one of the few friends I could get into deep philosophical design discussions with. On this occasion, he expressed his great admiration for the execution of the Firebird III but very practically followed that statement with, "but it's not the kind of vehicle you would drive to the corner grocery store to buy a quart of milk." I answered that the design was literally following Harley Earl's direction that the car be spectacular and look like the vehicle that would take the astronauts to their moon rocket. I had to finally confess that, as it turned out, what the astronauts ended up taking actually looked more like a milk-truck.

———————

There was a moment at Styling when I was alone in the studio and I was recollecting the teachings of Alexander Kostellow, considering now how they actually worked out in reality. I thought then, about another moment at Pratt, when I was sitting in Kostellow's class as he was lecturing and I was thinking, "I wish he would just focus on the important stuff." I paused for a moment, realizing what I had just thought, and then after another instant, I literally slammed my forehead with the palm of my hand, and exclaimed out loud to no one, "My God—Everything he said was important!"

———————

A final thought. I have already noted that while attending Pratt I always considered myself to be a renderer and was then surprised by the Art Center graduate when he complimented me on my sketching—I was actually shocked. I was neither aware that my sketching had improved at all, nor in fact that I had even made any conscious effort to try to improve it. It just happened, all by itself.

In my following professional years, there has been one related experience that has repeated itself many times. I have been fortunate to work with brilliant engineers, managers, and associates; and the one thing that grated me most was when these people wished to express an idea to me, by making a sketch, too often they would apologize in advance for their drawing ability. I would always be speechless, wishing them to get on with it and express the idea.

What I want to say now, in the strongest terms, is that the best thing one can do when trying to express an idea is to focus on the idea or the thought and just draw it, warts and all. Everyone has a natural drawing ability that has been repressed with education. The best way to recover this natural sense is through the subconscious, which can still distinguish what is good from what is better. By doing this—thinking only of the idea—in time, one will develop a style of their own and their sketching will become an effective communication tool—a tool that will serve them well.

The MOONMEN: Ferenc Pavlics, designer; Dr. Greg Bekker, project scientist; Sam Romano, project manager; and the Lunar Roving Vehicle. *Photo courtesy of GM Media Archives*

Bob Peterson (standing) and his son Chris, wife Claire on the left, Nan and Jake Andon (coworkers from both Detroit and Santa Barbara), and Norm and Ginna James at the 25th Lunar Roving Vehicle reunion held in Santa Barbara in 1994. *Photo courtesy of GM Media Archives*

Left, The author with his 8-inch f/7 Newtonian reflector, 1969; *right,* with his 12 1/2 inch f/5 RFT Newtonian telescope, 1972. A vacuum pump locks the sphere to a suction cup, rotating on a polar axis so that it can visually track the stars.

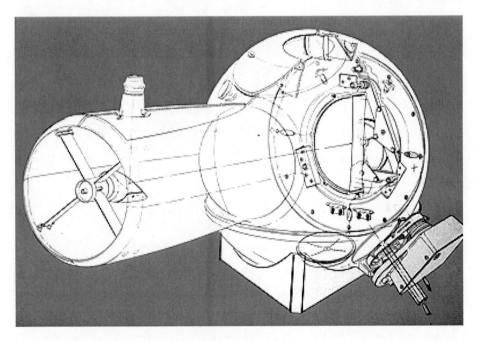

Cutaway drawing of the 12 1/2 inch RFT.

The James boys: Herb, Pete, and Norm at Niagara Falls, *circa* 1980.

Closure (1988). *An Interstate Runs Through It*. Paul Semo contemplates the remains of the family farm (inset).

Edwards Brothers Malloy
Thorofare, NJ USA
May 18, 2012